THE MACARTHUR NEW TESTAMENT COMMENTARY

GALATIANS

John MacArthur, Jr.

MOODY PRESS/CHICAGO

© 1987 by
THE MOODY BIBLE INSTITUTE
OF CHIGAGO

Unless noted otherwise, all Scripture quotations in this book are from *The New American Standard Bible,* © 1960, 1962, 1963, 1968, 1971, 1973, 1975, and 1977 by The Lockman Foundation, and are used by permission.

Library of Congress Cataloging in Publication Data

MacArthur, John F.
    Galatians.

    (The MacArthur New Testament commentary)
    1. Bible. N.T. Galatians—Commentaries. I. Title.
II. Series: MacArthur, John F. MacArthur New Testament
commentary.
BS2685.3.M3 1987   227'.4077   87-23969
ISBN 0-8024-0762-5

1 2 3 4 5 6 7 Printing/RR/Year 91 90 89 88 87

Printed in the United States of America

To Christopher Parkening,
a musician of unequalled skill,
who has ministered to me
with the beauty of his music
and has provided an example of excellence
born out of love for God's glory

Contents

Preface

It continues to be a rewarding, divine communion for me to preach expositionally through the New Testament. My goal is always to have deep fellowship with the Lord in the understanding of His Word and out of that experience to explain to His people what a passage means. In the words of Nehemiah 8:8, I strive "to give the sense" of it so they may truly hear God speak and, in so doing, may respond to Him.

Obviously, God's people need to understand Him, which demands knowing His Word of Truth (2 Tim. 2:15) and allowing that Word to dwell in them richly (Col.3:16). The dominant thrust of my ministry, therefore, is to help make God's living Word alive to His people. It is a refreshing adventure.

This New Testament commentary series reflects this objective of explaining and applying Scripture. Some commentaries are primarily linguistic, others are mostly theological, and some are mainly homiletical. This one is basically explanatory, or expository. It is not linguistically technical but deals with linguistics when that seems helpful to proper interpretation. It is not theologically expansive but focuses on the major doctrines in each text and on how they relate to the whole of Scripture. It is not primarily homiletical, although each unit of thought is generally treated as one chapter, with a clear outline and logical flow of thought. Most truths are illustrated and applied with other Scripture. After establishing the context of a passage, I have tried to follow closely the writer's development and reasoning.

My prayer is that each reader will fully understand what the Holy Spirit is saying through this part of His Word, so that His revelation may lodge in the minds of believers and bring greater obedience and faithfulness—to the glory of our great God.

Introduction

The book of Galatians has been conferred with such titles as the Magna Carta of spiritual liberty, the battle cry of the Reformation, and the Christian's declaration of independence. It is clearly the Holy Spirit's charter of spiritual freedom for those who have received Jesus Christ as Lord and Savior.

Many church historians maintain that the foundation of the Reformation was laid with the writing of Martin Luther's commentary on Galatians. The great German Reformer said, "The epistle to the Galatians is my epistle. To it I am, as it were, in wedlock. Galatians is my Katherine [the name of his wife]." It was out of his careful and submissive study of Scripture, especially the book of Galatians, that Luther discovered God's plan of salvation by grace working through faith, a plan unalterably contrary to the thousand-year-old Roman Catholic teaching of salvation by works.

Merrill C. Tenney wrote of Galatians: "Christianity might have been just one more Jewish sect, and the thought of the Western world might have been entirely pagan had it never been written. Galatians embodies the germinal teaching on Christian freedom which separated Christianity from Judaism, and which launched it upon a career of missionary conquest. It was the cornerstone of the Protestant Reformation, because its teaching of salvation by grace alone became the dominant theme of the preaching of the Reformers." (*Galatians* [Grand Rapids: Eerdmans, 1957], p. 15.)

The message of Galatians is the message of the Christian's spiritual freedom, his deliverance by Christ from the bondage of sin and religious legalism. Its message is particularly relevant in our own day, as personal freedom has become the dominant emphasis of countless philosophies both within and without Christendom.

Perhaps because Paul was so intensely concerned about the matter of gracious salvation in Christ and about the violent attacks on the gospel being made by the Judaizers, Galatians is the only one of his epistles that gives no word of commendation to its readers. After a brief salutation, the apostle immediately states the problem that prompted the letter: "I am amazed that you are so quickly deserting Him who called you by the grace of Christ, for a different gospel; which is really not another; only there are some who are disturbing you, and want to distort the gospel of Christ" (1:6-7). From that point until the closing benediction (6:18) the letter is a flashing sword wielded by a burning heart.

At first thought it seems strange that Paul would have words of commendation for the worldly, divisive, immoral, and immature Corinthian believers and yet have none for the saints of Galatia. To the Corinthians he wrote, "I thank my God always concerning you, for the grace of God which was given you in Christ Jesus, that in everything you were enriched in Him, in all speech and all knowledge, even as the testimony concerning Christ was confirmed in you, so that you are not lacking in any gift, awaiting eagerly the revelation of our Lord Jesus Christ" (1 Cor. 1:4-7). But for the churches of Galatia the apostle had no such praise.

The difference was that, as bad as the Corinthian situation was, the major problem there (with the notable exception regarding resurrection; see 1 Cor. 15) did not pertain so much to right doctrine as to right living. In the Galatian churches, on the other hand, the very heart of the gospel was being undermined by false teachers. The gospel of grace was being trampled, and in its place was being offered the gospel of works, which is no gospel at all but a distortion of God's truth (Gal. 1:6-7) that leads to damnation rather than salvation (Rom. 3:20).

Galatians is not a detached theological treatise but a deeply personal letter written from the grieving heart of a godly man for his spiritual children, whose faith and living were being undermined by false teachers. His heart cry to the Galatian believers was, "It was for freedom that Christ set us free; therefore keep standing firm and do not be subject again to a yoke of slavery" (Gal. 5:1).

DOCTRINAL EMPHASIS

Paul had special concern for the believers of Galatia and was gravely distressed about the doctrinal dangers that threatened them. The Jewish leaders who stoned Paul at Lystra no doubt continued to intimidate and persecute Jewish converts in Galatia. They were implacable enemies of the gospel and were used by Satan to sow confusion and discord in those and many other infant churches.

An even greater danger, however, were Jews who had made a superficial profession of Christ but turned back to Judaism and sought to make Christianity an extension of their traditional system of works righteousness. Like the false teachers about whom Paul warned the Ephesian elders, the Judaizers arose from within the church itself, "speaking perverse things" and trying "to draw away the disciples after them" (Acts 20:30).

The Judaizers were causing great confusion in the churches and were seriously distorting "the gospel of Christ" (Gal. 1:8). They taught that Gentiles must become Jews by circumcision before they could become Christians and that all Christians, Jewish and Gentile alike, were righteous before God only if they remained bound under the Mosaic laws, regulations, and ceremonies (see 2:3-5, 11-14; 3:3-5; 4:8-11, 21-31; 5:1-4; 6:12-13). This danger had probably threatened the churches even while Paul was in Galatia, and it doubtlessly intensified after he left. "As we have said before, so I say again now," the apostle reminded believers there, "if any man is preaching to you a gospel contrary to that which you received, let him be accursed" (Gal. 1:9; cf. vv. 6-8).

In addition to teaching the necessity of being circumcised and of keeping the Mosaic law, the false teachers also attacked Paul personally, seeking to undercut his authority and thereby his doctrine. Consequently, he was careful to reaffirm his apostolic credentials. He begins the letter by referring to himself as "an apostle (not sent from men, nor through the agency of man, but through Jesus Christ, and God the Father)" (1:1). Throughout the first two chapters he continues to affirm his divine authority as an apostle of Jesus Christ, equal in every way to the Twelve, including Peter (see 1:12, 15-17; 2:2, 7-9).

The theme of Galatians, and a central theme of the entire New Testament, is that true freedom comes only through Jesus Christ. In this letter Paul deals with spiritual freedom on two fronts. The first front (chaps. 3-4) is that of salvation, through which Christ sets a person free from bondage to sin and the law. As the apostle declares in the book of Romans, "The law of the Spirit of life in Christ Jesus has set you free from the law of sin and of death" (8:2). Paul's second front in Galatians (chaps. 5-6) is that of sanctification, the freedom God gives His children to live out lives of faithfulness and genuine righteousness, free from sin's control and legalistic bondage.

BACKGROUND AND DESTINATION

The name *Galatia* is derived from the barbaric Gauls, or Celts, who settled in Asia Minor after several centuries of plundering the Greek and Roman empires. Under Roman rule, the original region of Galatia was made part of a larger province by the same name in central Asia Minor (modern Turkey) that encompassed an area some 250 miles north to south and up to 175 miles from east to west.

In Paul's day the name Galatia was used for the original smaller region as well as the province. On the first missionary journey Paul and Barnabas established four churches in the southern part of the province, in the cities of Antioch, Iconium, Lystra, and Derbe (Acts 13:14–14:23), and those churches apparently came to form something of a regional body of believers. The Galatian epistle itself does not identify the specific local churches, but they were churches in which Paul had personally ministered (4:13-15). The fact that the book of Acts mentions the four churches established by Paul in south Galatia and mentions none in the rest of the province makes it probable that the epistle was addressed primarily to those southern churches.

Also in favor of that theory is the fact that in Galatians Paul makes no reference to the Jerusalem Council or its momentous decision regarding the Judaizing controversy, a decision that would have given great additional weight to his argument against Judaistic legalism. Such an omission strongly suggests that the letter was written before the Council convened, which was shortly after Paul's first journey (see Acts 14:24–15:6) and therefore before he had opportunity to travel in northern Galatia. According to that chronology, the letter would have been written around A.D. 50.

While in Galatia, Paul nearly lost his life, having been stoned and left for dead by antagonistic Jewish leaders who followed him from Antioch and Iconium to Lystra (Acts 14:19-20). After establishing a church in Derbe, Paul and Barnabas revisited the other three cities, "strengthening the souls of the disciples, encouraging them to continue in the faith" (14:22). On his second journey Paul visited the Galatian churches with Silas, "delivering the decrees, which had been decided upon by the apostles and elders who were in Jerusalem, for them to observe. So the churches were being strengthened in the faith, and were increasing in number daily" (Acts 16:1-5).

THE AUTHOR

Paul, whose original name was Saul, was a native of Tarsus, a city in southeast Asia Minor not far from southern Galatia. He was raised in a strict Jewish family and was steeped in traditional Jewish legalism. He had been educated under the famous rabbi Gamaliel and carefully trained in Jewish law (Acts 22:3). He was "circumcised the eighth day, of the nation of Israel, of the tribe of Benjamin, a Hebrew of Hebrews; as to the Law, a Pharisee; as to zeal, a persecutor of the church; as to the righteousness which is in the Law, found blameless" (Phil. 3:5-6). Before his conversion he "was advancing in Judaism beyond many of [his] contemporaries among [his] countrymen, being more extremely zealous for [his] ancestral traditions" (Gal. 1:14).

Despite his strong legalism and traditionalism, Saul does not appear to have been a religious hypocrite, as were so many other Pharisees. He was spiritually blind and was an enemy of God and His people; but he was not hypocritical. He sincerely believed and adhered to traditional Judaism as God's way of life for His chosen people. Like many other Jews of his day, Paul truly loved the traditional law and sincerely sought to keep every commandment, to observe every ceremony, and to offer every sacrifice that the covenant of Moses required. He was a legalist of the strictest kind, but he was honestly trying to please God by obeying what he thought was God's will and does not seem to have been trying to impress others with his religiousness.

Defending himself before the Sanhedrin, the apostle declared, "Brethren, I have lived my life with a perfectly good conscience before God up to this day" (Acts 23:1). Although by that time Paul had been a Christian for many years, the context suggests that his statement about having a good conscience before God included his life before conversion. When he persecuted Christians, causing many of them to be imprisoned and put to death (Acts 22:4-5; 26:10-11), he doubtlessly did so with the sincere conviction he was doing God's will (see Acts 22:3). Although he "was formerly a blasphemer and a persecutor and a violent aggressor," he nevertheless was "shown mercy, because [he] acted ignorantly in unbelief" (1 Tim. 1:13). Long before Saul of Tarsus became a zealous and dedicated legalist God "had set [him] apart even from [his] mother's womb, and called [him] through His grace" (Gal. 1:15).

The apostle spoke of legalism from firsthand experience, and he also spoke of grace from firsthand experience as well as from firsthand revelation. More than any other apostle he understood the bondage of the law and the freedom of grace.

OUTLINE

Personal: Paul's apostolic authority (1-2)
    Salutation and introduction (1:1-9)
    Apostolic credentials (1:10-24)
    Apostolic commendation (2:1-10)
    Apostolic confidence (2:11-21)
Doctrinal: Salvation only by grace through faith (3-4)
    Confirmed by experience (3:1-5)
    Affirmed by Scripture (3:6–4:31)
Practical: Living in Christian freedom (5-6)

The Salutation (1:1-5)

Paul, an apostle (not sent from men, nor through the agency of man, but through Jesus Christ, and God the Father, who raised Him from the dead), and all the brethren who are with me, to the churches of Galatia: Grace to you and peace from God our Father, and the Lord Jesus Christ, who gave Himself for our sins, that He might deliver us out of this present evil age, according to the will of our God and Father, to whom be the glory forevermore. Amen. (1:1-5)

One way to deny the truthfulness of a message is to deny the authority of the one who gives it. The Galatian church had received the true gospel of grace from Paul and had believed it until some false teachers came in after he was gone. They not only attacked the validity of the message but also that of the messenger. Apparently the Judaizers had convinced some of the Galatian church members that Paul was a self-appointed apostle with no divine commission. So at the outset of the letter Paul dispensed with the usual personal greetings and immediately began to establish the genuineness of his apostolic authority, which he later (1:11–2:21) expands on in detail.

In this brief salutation Paul summarizes his authority (his right to speak), his message (the truths he speaks), and his motive (his reason for speaking).

PAUL'S AUTHORITY

Paul, an apostle (not sent from men, nor through the agency of man, but through Jesus Christ, and God the Father, who raised Him from the dead), and all the brethren who are with me, to the churches of Galatia: (1:1-2)

Following the custom of his times, the apostle begins his letter by stating his name, **Paul.** He then establishes his authority as an apostle, first on the basis of his right to the title "apostle," second on the basis of the manner in which he was chosen for that office, and third on the basis of his relationship to fellow believers.

THE TITLE APOSTLE

an apostle (1:1a)

An **apostle** ("one who is sent with a commission") was an envoy, ambassador, or messenger who was chosen and trained by Jesus Christ as His special emissary for proclaiming His truth during the formative years of the church. In its primary and technical usage, the term applied to the original twelve who were chosen at the beginning of Jesus' earthly ministry (Mark 3:14; Luke 6:13) and were set aside to lay the foundation of the early church and to be the channels of God's completed revelation (Acts 2:42; Eph. 2:20). They were also given power to perform healings and to cast out demons as verifying signs of their divine authority (Acts 2:43; 2 Cor. 12:12; Heb. 2:3-4). It should be noted that, shortly before Pentecost, Judas was replaced by Matthias (Acts 1:26).

In a wider sense, the term apostle is also used of men like Barnabas (Acts 14:14), Silas and Timothy (1 Thess. 1:1; 2:6), and other outstanding leaders (Rom. 16:7). Such men are more specifically called messengers (*apostoloi*) of the churches (see 2 Cor. 8:23; Phil. 2:25), whereas the Twelve and Paul were "apostles of Jesus Christ." Neither group was perpetuated. Except for Judas, there is no New Testament record of an apostle in either the primary or secondary group being replaced after he died.

Because he was not among the original twelve, Paul needed to defend his apostleship in ways that they did not. Because one of the qualifications was witnessing the risen Christ (Acts 1:22), Paul explained to the Corinthian church that between His resurrection and ascension Jesus first "appeared to Cephas [Peter], then to the twelve. After that He appeared to more than five hundred brethren at one time; . . . then He appeared to James, then to all the apostles; and last of all, as it were to one untimely born, He appeared to me also" (1 Cor. 15:5-8). Paul witnessed the resurrected Christ in a unique way. As he was traveling to Damascus to arrest and imprison Christians there, "suddenly a light from heaven flashed around him; and he fell to the ground, and heard a voice saying to him, 'Saul, Saul, why are you persecuting Me?' And he said, 'Who art Thou, Lord?' And He said, 'I am Jesus whom you are persecuting'" (Acts 9:3-5). Through the godly Ananias of Damascus, the Lord declared this former enemy of the gospel to be "a chosen instrument of Mine, to bear My name before the Gentiles and kings and the sons of Israel" (v. 15). Just as the Lord "effectually worked for Peter in his apostleship to the circumcised [He] effectually worked for [Paul] also to the Gentiles" (Gal. 2:8).

Further personal appearances of the Lord to Paul are recorded in Acts 18:9; 22:17-21; 23:11; and 2 Corinthians 12:1-4 (cf. 1 Cor. 9:1).

THE MANNER IN WHICH HE WAS CHOSEN

(not sent from men, nor through the agency of man, but through Jesus Christ, and God the Father, who raised Him from the dead), (1:1b)

Because false teachers were accusing Paul of being a spurious, self-appointed apostle who had no authority to teach and to rule the churches, he emphatically stated that his was no human commission, that he was **not sent from men.** He had not appointed himself and had not even been divinely appointed **through the agency of men.** No human means of any sort was involved in his apostolic commissioning. No human source, no human ceremony, no laying on of hands by any group in Jerusalem, Antioch, or anywhere else was involved in his call to apostleship, though the elders at Antioch were a part of the sending process of his special mission tour to evangelize (Acts 13:1-3).

Paul's original call to apostleship was directly **through Jesus Christ, and God the Father, who raised Him from the dead.** Jesus called Paul and set him apart before he had contact with any of the other apostles. After several years of divine preparation (see Gal. 1:17-18), he was sent out to begin his work among the Gentiles directly by the Holy Spirit, whose divine appointment was acknowledged by the leaders of the church at Antioch (Acts 13:2-3). Paul's authority was not man-given or self-given but **God**-given, and his right to instruct the Galatians was grounded in that divine prerogative.

Paul never missed an opportunity to mention the resurrection, without which the gospel would be powerless. The God who appointed Paul an apostle was **God the Father, who raised** His Son **from the dead.**

Paul certainly had a vastly superior commissioning to any of the false-teaching, self-appointed Judaizers who were confusing the Galatians and trying to set themselves above his authority.

The apostle's frequent mention of **God** and **Father** in relation to **Jesus Christ** throughout the New Testament marks an emphasis that should not be missed. The intent is not for us to understand God as *our* Father (although that truth is mentioned in 1:4) but **the Father** in relation to the role He has in the Trinity, particularly His relation to the Son. The intent is to emphasize the significance of the relationship between the first and second members of the Trinity as to essential nature. The title is to express equality of deity between the two, a Father and Son who share the same nature (cf. Matt. 11:27; John 5:17-18, 22; 10:29-33; 14:9; 17:1-5; Rom. 15:6; 2 Cor. 1:3;

Eph. 1:3; 1 Pet. 1:3; 2 John 3). It asserts that **Jesus Christ** is the One who is of the nature of God and that the true God is the One who is **the Father** of **Jesus Christ**.

and all the brethren who are with me, to the churches of Galatia: (1:2)

A third basis of Paul's authority is implied by his referring to companions with him at the time of writing as **brethren,** in contrast to his own identification as apostle.

Liberal Bible scholars and theologians maintain that the apostles were no more significant or inspired than other human witnesses of Jesus Christ who happened to live at the same time He ministered on earth. What they taught and wrote was based on their own human insight and understanding and was not divinely authoritative or binding on other believers, either of their own day or of later ages. Every believer has his own experiences of what is often called "the Christ event."

Roman Catholic dogma maintains that the church wrote the Bible and is therefore a higher authority than the Bible. The church can therefore add to or modify Scripture as it sees fit, and its ecclesiastical pronouncements are held to have the same spiritual and moral authority as Scripture—even when they clearly contradict scriptural teaching.

Paul would have argued against both of those views with every breath in his body. If he and the other apostles of the New Testament were not divinely inspired in a unique and authoritative way, they were the most presumptuous of men, because they boldly and unequivocally claimed to speak and write in God's name. As apostles they spoke *to* the church, not on behalf of the church. The church derived its doctrine from the apostles, who received it directly from God (Eph. 3:5). They are never spoken of as apostles of the church but always as apostles of Jesus Christ.

Jesus told the Twelve, "Truly, truly, I say to you, he who receives whomever I send receives Me; and he who receives Me receives Him who sent Me" (John 13:20). A short while later He said to them, "These things I have spoken to you, while abiding with you. But the Helper, the Holy Spirit, whom the Father will send in My name, He will teach you all things, and bring to your remembrance all that I said to you" (14:25-26).

Because the apostles' teaching came directly from the Lord, the writings of Paul, Peter, John, and the others are every much as divinely inspired and authoritative as the words that Jesus spoke in person during His earthly ministry. It is for that reason that red letter Bibles may be misleading, because they suggest that the words Jesus spoke during His three-year earthly ministry are in some way more inspired and precious than other parts of Scripture. As Paul made clear to Timothy, however, "All Scripture is inspired by God" (2 Tim. 3:16), who is the Author of its every word, whether through the prophets, the Lord Jesus Christ, or the apostles.

Because the Bible is God's own Word, to be subject to God is to be subject to the Bible. It is not an amalgam of human opinion but the repository of divine truth.

As discussed in the Introduction, **the churches of** southern **Galatia** were in the central Asia Minor cities of Antioch of Pisidia, Iconium, Lystra, and Derbe, where Paul had ministered on both his first and second missionary journeys (Acts 13:14–14:23; 16:1-5). The fact that Paul founded those **churches** certainly gave him some authority in dealing with them (cf. 1 Cor. 4:14-21, where Paul expresses his right to reprimand the Corinthians because he was their spiritual father).

The mention of these **churches** is brief and impersonal, and there is an apparent lack of the amenities usually found in Paul's epistles. His resentment of their defection from the gospel of grace forced him to dispense with any commendation or personal remarks, and he simply gave a gospel greeting before he rebuked them.

PAUL'S MESSAGE

Grace to you and peace from God our Father, and the Lord Jesus Christ, who gave Himself for our sins, that He might deliver us out of this present evil age, according to the will of our God and Father, (1:3-4)

As Paul explains later in the epistle, the gospel he preached was "not according to man. For I neither received it from man, nor was I taught it, but I received it through a revelation of Jesus Christ" (Gal. 1.11-12). Two of the most precious words related to that God-given gospel are **grace** and **peace**. The first is the source of salvation and the second is the result. **Grace** is positional, **peace** is practical, and together they flow **from God our Father** through His Son and our Savior, **the Lord Jesus Christ.**

In the Greek culture of Paul's day the common greeting was *chara* ("joy"). But although joy is among the many blessings Christians receive from God and should reflect in their lives (Gal. 5:22), the distinctly Christian greeting of **grace . . . and peace** held special meaning and significance for Paul and for other believers in the early church.

Since it offered no grace and provided no peace, the law system being taught by the lying Judaizers is attacked even in this simple greeting. If being right with God and possessing salvation is by works, as those false teachers maintained, then it is not of grace (Rom. 4:4-5) and can bring no peace, since one never knows if he has enough good works to be eternally secure.

In verse 4 Paul gives a succinct summary of the true gospel of **grace** and **peace**, showing its nature, its object, and its source.

THE NATURE OF THE GOSPEL: CHRIST'S ATONING DEATH AND RESURRECTION

who gave Himself for our sins, (1:4a)

In turning from grace to a legalistic system of salvation by works, the Galatians had ignored the significance of the death of Christ.

The heart of the gospel is Christ's willing sacrifice of **Himself for our sins.** Salvation is not earned by one's efforts to eliminate sin, but by one's trust in God's promise to forgive sin through the work of Jesus Christ. His atoning death was the most essential part of the divine plan of redemption, without which all of His teachings and miraculous works would have been meaningless and a mockery. Apart from Christ's sacrificial death, His earthly ministry would have portrayed the power and truth of a great and wonderful God—but a God with whom men could never be reconciled, because they had no way out of their sin. Since no man can eliminate sin by works (Rom. 3:20), it must be forgiven. That is why it was absolutely necessary that "He Himself bore our sins in His body on the cross, that we might die to sin and live to righteousness" (1 Pet. 2:24). If Christ had not died on our behalf, He could not have been raised on our behalf; and if He had not been raised, Paul says, then preaching the gospel would be vain, trusting in the gospel would be worthless, and all men would still be in their sins (1 Cor. 15:14-17).

The statement **who gave Himself for our sins** affirms that the purpose of Christ's coming was to be a sin offering (cf. 3:13).

THE OBJECT OF THE GOSPEL: TO DELIVER FROM THE PRESENT AGE

that He might deliver us out of this present evil age, (1:4b)

The purpose of the gospel is to **deliver** (the Greek subjunctive expresses purpose) those who believe in Christ from **this present evil age.** Jesus' death was a rescue operation, the only possible means of saving men from the doomed world and from eternal death by providing for them eternal life.

Exaireō (**deliver**) carries the idea of rescuing from danger. The word was used by Stephen in his sermon before the Sanhedrin as he described the divine deliverance of Joseph and the children of Israel from Egyptian affliction (Acts 7:10, 34). Peter used the word to describe God's deliverance of him from prison (Acts 12:11), and the Roman commander Claudius Lysias used it of his rescue of Paul from the belligerent mob in Jerusalem (23:27; cf. v. 10). Galatians 1:4 contains the only metaphorical use of the term in the New Testament.

Age (*aiōn*) does not refer to a period of time but to a passing, transitory system, in this case the **evil**, satanic world system that has dominated the world since the Fall and will continue to dominate it until the Lord's return. Although they are not removed from the earth until they die or are raptured, believers are rescued **out of this present evil age** the moment they receive Jesus Christ as Lord and Savior. They are still in the world, but they are no longer of it (John 17:11, 14-18; Phil. 3:20-21; 1 John 5:5). The faithful Christian life is the heavenly life lived on earth.

THE SOURCE OF THE GOSPEL: THE WILL OF GOD

according to the will of our God and Father, (1:4c)

The source of the saving gospel of Jesus Christ is the sovereign, loving, compassionate, gracious **will of our God and Father,** who "so loved the world, that

He gave His only begotten Son, that whoever believes in Him should not perish, but have eternal life" (John 3:16).

Jesus prayed in the Garden, "Father, if Thou art willing, remove this cup from Me; yet not My will, but Thine be done" (Luke 22:42). It was *not* the Father's will for that cup to be removed, because otherwise the world could not be saved. It was the **will** of the **Father** for His precious Son to die in order that those who trust in Him might live. The Father sent the Son to die, and the Son willingly laid down His life.

Specifically, every rescued believer is delivered because of the sovereign, gracious will of God. "But as many as received Him, to them He gave the right to become children of God, even to those who believe in His name, who were born not of blood, nor of the will of the flesh, nor of the will of man, but of God" (John 1:12-13). Salvation is thus removed from the will of man and is buried deep in the sovereign decree of God.

PAUL'S MOTIVE

to whom be the glory forevermore. Amen. (1:5)

Paul concludes his introduction with a doxology fitting for such a saving God. His motive for writing to the Galatian churches was that he might acknowledge that God is worthy of **glory forevermore.** The apostle's supreme purpose was to glorify his Lord, and he calls all believers to do everything "to the glory of God" (1 Cor. 10:31).

In these five opening verses of Galatians Paul covers the four stages of man's salvation. The first stage was the sovereign decree of God to save, the second was the death of Christ for man's sins, the third was the appointment of apostles to testify to that divine provision, and the fourth was the gift of God's grace and peace to those who believe in Jesus Christ. In each of the stages the Father and the Son work together, because Their will and Their work are always one (John 5:30; 6:38; 10:30).

Paul and the other apostles were commissioned and sent out by the Father and the Son, and the grace that brings salvation and the peace that salvation brings are likewise both from the Father and the Son. Salvation is provided, preached, and granted by the common operation of God the Father and God the Son. Together They planned salvation, together They provide salvation, together They announce salvation, and together They grant salvation to every person who comes to Them in faith.

Amen expresses the affirmation fitting the worthiness of God to receive glory for such a wondrous provision of eternal, gracious salvation. Alan Cole writes of this word: "When the old-fashioned Cantonese-speaking Christian says at the end of a prayer *shing sam shoh uen* ("with all my heart this is what I wish") he approaches very nearly the original Hebrew meaning" (*The Epistle of Paul to the Galatians* [Grand Rapids: Eerdmans, 1970], p. 37).

Devoted to Destruction (1:6-9)

2

I am amazed that you are so quickly deserting Him who called you by the grace of Christ, for a different gospel; which is really not another; only there are some who are disturbing you, and want to distort the gospel of Christ. But even though we, or an angel from heaven, should preach to you a gospel contrary to that which we have preached to you, let him be accursed. As we have said before, so I say again now, if any man is preaching to you a gospel contrary to that which you received, let him be accursed. (1:6-9)

Throughout history God has devoted certain objects, individuals, and groups of people to destruction. Of ancient Jericho He declared, "And the city shall be under the ban, it and all that is in it belongs to the Lord; only Rahab the harlot and all who are with her in the house shall live. . . . But as for you, only keep yourselves from the things under the ban, lest you covet them and take some of the things under the ban, so you would make the camp of Israel accursed and bring trouble on it" (Josh. 6:17-18).

But "Achan, the son of Carmi, the son of Zabdi, the son of Zerah, from the tribe of Judah, took some of the things under the ban," and because of his disobedience, "the anger of the Lord burned against the sons of Israel" (7:1). Because he disobeyed and attempted to selfishly salvage something from what God had previously devoted to destruction, he brought tragedy on his fellow Israelites, and they could no longer "stand before their enemies" (v. 12). After Achan, his family, and all his possessions were destroyed, "the Lord turned from the fierceness of His anger. Therefore the name of that place has been called the valley of Achor to this day" (vv. 25-26). Achor means "trouble" and symbolizes the destiny of those who try to take advantage of that which God has condemned.

The New Testament speaks of two general categories of people whom God devotes to destruction. The first category is "anyone [who] does not love the Lord" (1 Cor. 16:22). The second is false teachers, who in Galatians 1:8-9 Paul twice calls accursed. Jesus warned His disciples that "false Christs and false prophets will arise and will show great signs and wonders, so as to mislead, if possible, even the elect" (Matt. 24:24). False teachers are children of their "father the devil, and . . . want to do the desires of [their] father," who "whenever he speaks a lie, he speaks from his own nature; for he is a liar, and the father of lies" (John 8:44). Paul reminded Timothy that such people in the leadership of the church at Ephesus he had "delivered over to Satan, so that they may be taught not to blaspheme" (1 Tim. 1:20).

In the early days of the church, Elymas the magician opposed the preaching of Paul and Barnabas and in particular tried to keep the Roman proconsul Sergius Paulus "away from the faith. But Saul, who was also known as Paul, filled with the Holy Spirit, fixed his gaze upon him, and said, 'You who are full of all deceit and fraud, you son of the devil, you enemy of all righteousness, will you not cease to make crooked the straight ways of the Lord?'" (Acts 13:7-10). In that rebuke Paul exposes four characteristics of false teachers: they are deceitful, children of the devil, enemies of righteousness, and perverters of the gospel.

Among the chief characteristics of Satan and his followers is deception. Paul warns that in the end times the Antichrist will come "in accord with the activity of Satan, with all power and signs and false wonders, and with all the deception of wickedness for those who perish, because they did not receive the love of the truth so as to be saved" (2 Thess. 2:9-10). John tells us of "the great dragon [who] was thrown down, the serpent of old who is called the devil and Satan, who deceives the whole world" (Rev. 12:9; cf. 13:14; 20:3, 10).

Satan and his demon emissaries do their deceptive work usually through human beings and most often through religious leaders. Among such religious leaders are those who pose as Christians, whom Paul describes as "false apostles, deceitful workers, disguising themselves as apostles of Christ" (2 Cor. 11:13). "And no wonder," Paul goes on to explain, "for even Satan disguises himself as an angel of light. Therefore it is not surprising if his servants also disguise themselves as servants of righteousness" (vv. 14-15). Paul acknowledged the human agents used by Satan when he spoke of the "deceitful spirits" who propagate "doctrines of demons, by means of the hypocrisy of liars" (1 Tim. 4:1-2).

Satan has effectively accomplished his most destructive deception through demon-energized false teachers who pose as God's spokesmen. It was when their own priests and prophets compromised God's truth that the Israelites were most prone to idolatry and other pagan practices. It was false teachers claiming to preach the gospel who were most successful in weakening the early church, epitomized by the legalistic Judaizers who wreaked spiritual havoc on the churches of Galatia. It was false teachers within the church of the late eighteenth and the nineteenth centuries who gradually turned biblical theology into the various forms of modernism and liberalism. Today even the tenets of Eastern mysticism and occultism are finding their way into the church, often under the guise of spiritually "neutral" philosophy, psychology, or self-image improvement.

In the life of the churches, Paul feared nothing so much as false doctrine, since it is the underlying source of ungodly behavior. His deep concern for the spiritual welfare of the Corinthian believers would be fully as apropos for the church today. "I am afraid," he wrote, "lest as the serpent deceived Eve by his craftiness, your minds should be led astray from the simplicity and purity of devotion to Christ" by one who "comes and preaches another Jesus whom we have not preached, or you receive a different spirit which you have not received, or a different gospel which you have not accepted" (2 Cor. 11:3-4).

To the Ephesian elders on the beach at Miletus, Paul said, "Be on guard for yourselves and for all the flock, among which the Holy Spirit has made you overseers, to shepherd the church of God which He purchased with His own blood. I know that after my departure savage wolves will come in among you, not sparing the flock; and from among your own selves men will arise, speaking perverse things" (Acts 20:28-30).

Satan's primary target for false teaching is the doctrine of salvation, because if people are confused about that they have no way of coming to God in the first place and thus remain under Satan's influence and control. He teaches lies about church organization, Christian living, the Lord's return, and many other things. But his first concern is to undermine the heart of the gospel, which is salvation by grace, made possible through the Person and work of the Lord Jesus Christ. Peter warned his readers, "There will also be false teachers among you, who will secretly introduce destructive heresies, even denying the Master who bought them, bringing swift destruction upon themselves. And many will follow their sensuality, and because of them the way of the truth will be maligned" (2 Pet. 2:1-2). The most destructive of all heresies is "denying the Master," the Lord God incarnate.

False prophets are also more interested in popularity than in truth. Their concern is not to serve the Lord and minister to His people but "to make a good showing in the flesh" (Gal. 6:12) and to gain a following for themselves (Acts 20:30). They are in their work for money; and "in their greed they will exploit you with false words," Peter says, because their hearts are "trained in greed" (2 Pet. 2:3, 14).

Since they have no true spiritual life and power to subdue the flesh, false prophets are sinful in private life, and sometimes even in public, "having eyes full of adultery and that never cease from sin, enticing unstable souls" (2 Pet. 2:14). As in Jeremiah's day, they commit adultery and "strengthen the hands of evildoers" (Jer. 23:14). Peter refers to them as "unreasoning animals, born as creatures of instinct to be captured and killed, reviling where they have no knowledge. . . . They count it a pleasure to revel in the daytime. They are stains and blemishes, reveling in their deceptions, . . . accursed children; forsaking the right way they have gone astray. . . . These are springs without water, and mists driven by a storm, for whom the black darkness has been reserved. For speaking out arrogant words of vanity they entice by fleshly desires, by sensuality, those who barely escape from the ones who live in error" (2 Pet. 2:12-15, 17-18). Religious ceremonialism, ritualism, and legalism cannot restrain the flesh, so people who rely on such outward props contain only evil in their lives, which eventually breaks any self-imposed restraints they try to use on themselves.

It was such accursed false teachers, specifically the Judaizers, who were plaguing the Galatian churches. The book of Galatians is Paul's only epistle in which he has no word of commendation for those to whom he writes. After his brief salutation he immediately launches into the reason for his writing: his extreme concern and perplexity about the false teachers who were undercutting the gospel of grace he had so carefully preached and expounded while he ministered in Galatia. He was deeply grieved that the truth of God's sovereign and gracious offer of redemption through the atoning sacrifice of Jesus Christ alone was being corrupted by the teachings of salvation by works, namely, that a Gentile had to become a Jew surgically and ceremonially before he could become a Christian and that all Christians had to obey and honor the Jewish law and traditions in order to obtain and maintain righteousness from the Lord.

In Galatians 1:6-9 the apostle gives three features involved in his strong opposition to that grave and damning heresy: his wonder, his wisdom, and his warning.

PAUL'S WONDER ABOUT THE GALATIANS' DEFECTION

I am amazed that you are so quickly deserting Him who called you by the grace of Christ, for a different gospel; (1:6)

Paul could hardly comprehend that the Galatian believers were already abandoning his apostolic teaching. He was **amazed** (*thaumazō,* a strong word, meaning to be astounded) and bewildered. He could not fathom why they were **so quickly deserting Him,** that is, God, **who called** them by means of **the grace of Christ.** He was not surprised by what the false teachers were doing but was shocked by the favorable response they received from Christians in Galatia.

The apostle was especially surprised that the defection had come **so quickly.** (For an excellent treatment of the time sequence of Paul's writings, see *Galatians: The Charter of Christian Liberty,* by Merrill C. Tenney.) *Tacheōs* **(quickly)** can mean either easily and readily or soon, and sometimes both, as was probably the case with the Galatians' **deserting** the true gospel. The believers apparently offered little and ineffective resistance to the false teachers and therefore were fickle in their allegiance to Paul and his teaching. They **quickly** and easily came under the influence of heretical doctrines.

The Galatians had been privileged to be taught by the greatest teacher the church has ever known apart from the Lord Himself; yet they readily rejected the truths of grace they had learned from him. There is still a great and urgent need for preaching and teaching that continually repeats the central truths of the gospel (see 2 Pet. 1:12-15). It is possible even for longtime believers to lose a firm grip on those truths and allow themselves to be weakened and perverted by ideas that purportedly improve on the pure and plain teachings of Scripture.

These Galatians were true believers who had come to salvation in the power of the Holy Spirit (3:3, 5; 4:6, 8-9). They were Christian brothers (1:2, 11; 3:15; 4:12, 31; 5:13) who had become seriously confused.

The Galatian Christians not only were being confused and weakened in their confidence to live by grace but were actually **deserting**. The term behind **deserting** (*metatithēmi*) was used of military desertion, which was punishable by death during time of war, much as in modern times. The Greek verb is reflexive, indicating that the act is voluntary. The believers were not passively *being* removed, as the King James translation suggests, but were in the process of removing themselves from the sphere of grace. The false teachers were accountable for their corruption of God's truth, but the Galatian Christians were also accountable for being so easily misled by it to pursue legalism.

To desert the gospel of grace that Paul had taught them was not simply to desert a doctrine but to desert **Him, the God who** had **called** them **to salvation**. **Called** is an aorist participle and could be translated, "who called you once and for all" (cf. 2 Thess. 2:13-14; 2 Tim. 1:8-9; 1 Pet. 1:15). The call spoken of in the New Testament epistles is always an effectual call to salvation (see Rom. 8:30).

The only gospel of God is the gospel of **grace**, which is the gospel of divine redemption totally apart from any work or merit of man. "For by grace you have been saved through faith," Paul declared to the Ephesians, "and that not of yourselves, it is the gift of God; not as a result of works, that no one should boast. For we are His workmanship" (Eph. 2:8-10). And it is continually that "grace in which we stand" (Rom. 5:2). We live in grace from the moment of salvation, and if grace ever stopped, we would lose our undeserved salvation and perish in sin. **The grace of Christ** is God's free and sovereign act of love and mercy in granting salvation through the death and resurrection of Jesus, apart from anything men are or can do, and of His sustaining that salvation to glorification. It is absurd to accept a gracious salvation and then endeavor to maintain righteousness through human efforts, ceremonies, and ritual.

The Judaizers who plagued the early church claimed to be Christians, and much of their doctrine was orthodox. They must have recognized Jesus as the promised Messiah and even acknowledged the value of His sacrificial death on the cross—otherwise they would never have gotten a hearing in the church. They claimed to believe all the truths that other Christians believed. They did not purport to overtly deny the gospel but to improve it by adding the requirements, ceremonies, and standards of the Old Covenant to the New. But anything added to grace destroys it just as surely as does anything taken from it. When law—even God's own law—is added to His grace, His grace ceases to be grace (cf. Rom. 11:6).

The most destructive dangers to the church have never been atheism, pagan religions, or cults that openly deny Scripture, but rather supposedly Christian movements that accept so much biblical truth that their unscriptural doctrines seem relatively insignificant and harmless. But a single drop of poison in a large container can make all the water lethal. And a single false idea that in any way undercuts God's grace poisons the whole system of belief.

Paul would not tolerate a single drop of legalism being intermixed with God's pure grace. To turn away from any part of **the grace of Christ** is to turn away from the power of God to that of human effort. Those who seek to sustain their justification in any degree by law have "fallen from grace" and "have been severed from Christ" (Gal. 5:4). Paul is not speaking of losing salvation that is already received but of polluting the pure stream of living grace by putting a barrier between oneself and Christ and therefore of being severed, or separated, from His power and from fellowship with Him. It is impossible to forsake grace without forsaking the Lord, so Paul called Timothy to "be strong in the grace that is in Christ Jesus" (2 Tim. 2:1) and testified to his own life in grace in 1 Corinthians 15:10.

The Judaizers were promoting **a different gospel**, a completely contrary and ineffective means of being right with God. Consequently, although they had "begun by the Spirit," some of the true believers in Galatia were trying to be "perfected by the flesh" (3:3). Although they had "come to know God, or rather to be known by God," they had turned "back again to the weak and worthless elemental things" (4:9); and although they had been "running well," they were now being "hindered . . . from obeying the truth" (5:7).

PAUL'S WISDOM REGARDING THE FALSE TEACHERS' DECEPTION

which is really not another; only there are some who are disturbing you, and want to distort the gospel of Christ. (1:7)

The distorted teachings of the Judaizers presumed to be a form of the gospel, but Paul declares that their "different gospel" (v. 6) was **really not another** gospel at all. There is only one message of good news, the gospel of salvation by God's sovereign grace working through man's faith. Any message that is either more or less than that is not the good news in any sense.

Another translates *allos,* which refers to something of the exact same kind. As already noted, much that the Judaizers taught corresponded to the true gospel. They no doubt affirmed that Jesus was the Son of God, the Messiah predicted by the Old Testament prophets, and a great miracle worker. They likely believed that He was crucified and resurrected and that salvation demanded belief in Him. But they also taught that to be right with God and to maintain that righteous salvation a person must conform to all the laws of the Old Covenant. In doing so, they undercut the power of the true gospel, God's sovereign, saving, and enabling grace. By adding works to salvation they had subtly but completely undermined the gospel of God's grace, of which there **is really not another**. This was bad news, since man cannot maintain his right relationship to God by self effort and good works. He will produce good works as a result of God's saving grace and power working in him (Eph. 2:10; James 2:14-26), but he does not do good works to earn or keep salvation.

Because of their deception, false teachers such as the Judaizers are even more dangerous than those who openly deny "that Jesus is the Christ" and thereby clearly participate in the work of the antichrist (1 John 2:22). False systems labeled as Christianity always distort the nature and work of Jesus Christ. Those who deny Christ altogether are easily seen as the unbelievers they are; but those who *claim* to teach and follow Christ while undermining the gospel of His grace are immeasurably more dangerous—because they give the appearance of leading people to Christ while they are actually erecting barriers to salvation by grace.

Are disturbing is from *tarassō,* which literally means to shake back and forth and therefore to agitate and stir up. Figuratively, it connotes deep emotional disturbance and refers to an unsettled mind. It is the word used of Herod when he heard about the birth of the King of the Jews (Matt. 2:3), of the disciples when they saw Jesus walking on the water (14:26), and of Zacharias when he saw the angel of the Lord (Luke 1:12). It was also used by Jesus in His command, "Let not your heart be troubled" (John 14:1).

Although they were oblivious to it, the churches of Galatia were being shaken to their very foundations by the false teaching of the unregenerate Judaizers, who were acquiescing to the basic truths of Jesus Christ but who were spiritually **disturbing** and subverting the believers by adding works to grace, which is to utterly **distort the gospel of Christ.** *Metastrephō* (to **distort**) carries the idea of turning something into its opposite, of reversing and thereby perverting it. The least bit of law that is added to the **gospel of Christ** reverses its character and turns it into that which is contrary to God's gracious provision of salvation and sanctification based entirely on the merits of His sinless, sin-bearing Son.

Law does not moderately pollute grace but reverses and destroys it. As a means of salvation, the two are diametrically opposite and cannot coexist. Grace can be destroyed, but it cannot be modified. It can be rejected, but it cannot be changed. As Paul declares later in the epistle, "If you receive circumcision, Christ will be of no benefit to you. And I testify again to every man who receives circumcision, that he is under obligation to keep the whole Law. You have been severed from Christ, you who are seeking to be justified by law" (Gal. 5:2-4).

Whenever the gospel is perverted the church is unsettled. To change the message of grace is to stifle and eventually asphyxiate the church. Paul wrote to Titus, "For there are many rebellious men, empty talkers and deceivers, especially those of the circumcision, who must be silenced because they are upsetting whole families, teaching things they should not teach" (Titus 1:10-11). The greatest enemies of the church are not those who openly contradict the Bible and denounce Christ but those children of hell who, proposing to speak in His name, subtly undermine and distort His true gospel with a system of works righteousness.

PAUL'S WARNING OF GOD'S DESTRUCTION

But even though we, or an angel from heaven, should preach to you a gospel contrary to that which we have preached to you, let him be accursed. As we have said before, so I say again now, if any man is preaching to you a gospel contrary to that which you received, let him be accursed. (1:8-9)

The Judaizers who were misleading the Galatian churches probably had impressive credentials and may have been among those who claimed to be from the Jerusalem church and to be authorized by James, the leader of that church (see Acts 15:24). In addition to proclaiming their modified form of the gospel, which Paul declared to be no gospel at all, they sought to undermine Paul's authority and teaching in every way they could.

Although the particular heresy of the Judaizers was legalism, Paul's warning applies equally to the opposite perversion of libertinism or antinomianism, which, under the guise of freedom in Christ, removes all standards of righteousness and morality. Of such false teachers Jude wrote, "For certain persons have crept in unnoticed, those who were long beforehand marked out for this condemnation, ungodly persons who turn the grace of our God into licentiousness and deny our only Master and Lord, Jesus Christ" (Jude 4). Whether as restrictive legalism, permissive liberalism, or cultic perversion, any teaching that adds to or takes away from God's revealed truth is a distortion of the gospel and perverts the nature and the work of Christ.

Against any and every distortion of the gospel of Christ, Paul declares, **But even though we, or an angel from heaven, should preach to you a gospel contrary to that which we have preached to you, let him be accursed.**

Even if Paul or any of his associates were to change their teaching, the Galatians should not listen to them but treat them like heretics, which they would then be. Even **an angel from heaven** should be rejected if he were to present a gospel different from the one originally taught by Paul. The Jews believed that the divine law came through angels (cf. Heb. 2:2), and the Judaizers may have made the point that this made the Old Covenant and its attendant ceremonies and traditions binding.

Paul was, of course, speaking hypothetically. He would never have changed his teaching, and **an angel** who was truly **from heaven** (and therefore set apart from the fallen angels identified with hell) *could not* teach anything contrary to God's revealed truth. But the apostle was reaching for the most fanciful possibilities imaginable to make his point that absolutely no messenger, no matter how seemingly godly and good, should be believed or followed if his teaching does not square with God-revealed apostolic doctrine. The truth outranks anyone's credentials, and every teacher or preacher must be evaluated on the basis of what he says, not who he is.

Many false systems are attractive because they emotionally appeal to love, brotherhood, unity, and harmony. Many false teachers are popular because they seem to be warm and pleasant and claim to have great love for God and for others. It is because distortions of the gospel by such deceptive personalities are so appealing that "Satan disguises himself as an angel of light" (2 Cor. 11:14).

William Hendricksen paraphrases Galatians 1:8 in this way: "Even if we or a holy angel must be the object of God's righteous curse, were any of us to preach a gospel contrary to the one we humans previously preached to you, then all the more divine wrath must be poured out on those self-appointed nobodies who are now making themselves guilty of this crime."

Paul turns from the hypothetical to the actual as he reiterates his concern. **As we have said before, so I say again now, if any man is preaching to you a gospel contrary to that which you received, let him be accursed.** The repetition reflects the passion of the apostle for gospel truth.

As we have said before refers to an earlier visit, not to the preceding clause in the text, since **now** (*arti*) is an adverb of time. The sense seems to be, "What I said at that time I am saying again now." From the start of his ministry among them, Paul had warned them of imminent gospel perversions. The gospel **which you received** refers to the once for all (aorist tense) preaching of the good news of grace in Christ which they had previously believed.

False teachers not only should not be believed or followed but should be left to God's judgment to **be accursed. Accursed** translates *anathema,* which refers to that which is devoted to destruction. The apostle John wrote, "For many deceivers have gone out into the world, those who do not acknowledge Jesus Christ as coming in the flesh. This is the deceiver and the antichrist. . . . If anyone comes to you and does not bring this teaching, do not receive him into your house, and do not give him a greeting; for the one who gives him a greeting participates in his evil deeds" (2 John 7, 10-11).

Christians are to have nothing to do with false teachers, no matter what their credentials. It is both naive and unscriptural to believe, for instance, that staying in a religious school or church that denies the Bible and distorts the gospel gives a believer the opportunity to be a positive influence for the Lord. Even a leader like Timothy, well trained in divine truth, was warned to stay away from error and to concentrate on the pure truth of God (1 Tim. 4:6-7, 13; 2 Tim. 2:15-17). To subject oneself to false teaching, no matter how orthodox one's own convictions may be, is to disobey God and to compromise and weaken one's testimony and to tolerate distortion of the grace of God in Christ.

Apostolic Credentials (1:10-24)

3

For am I now seeking the favor of men, or of God? Or am I striving to please men? If I were still trying to please men, I would not be a bond-servant of Christ.

For I would have you know, brethren, that the gospel which was preached by me is not according to man. For I neither received it from man, nor was I taught it, but I received it through a revelation of Jesus Christ. For you have heard of my former manner of life in Judaism, how I used to persecute the church of God beyond measure, and tried to destroy it; and I was advancing in Judaism beyond many of my contemporaries among my countrymen, being more extremely zealous for my ancestral traditions. But when He who had set me apart, even from my mother's womb, and called me through His grace, was pleased to reveal His Son in me, that I might preach Him among the Gentiles, I did not immediately consult with flesh and blood, nor did I go up to Jerusalem to those who were apostles before me; but I went away to Arabia, and returned once more to Damascus.

Then three years later I went up to Jerusalem to become acquainted with Cephas, and stayed with him fifteen days. But I did not see any other of the apostles except James, the Lord's brother. (Now in what I am writing to you, I assure you before God that I am not lying.) Then I went into the regions

of Syria and Cilicia. And I was still unknown by sight to the churches of Judea which were in Christ; but only, they kept hearing, "He who once persecuted us is now preaching the faith which he once tried to destroy." And they were glorifying God because of me. (1:10-24)

One of the primary objectives of the Judaizers who were stirring up so much controversy and confusion in the Galatian churches was to discredit Paul's apostolic authority. They knew they could not successfully undermine his teaching of God's gracious gospel until they undermined his divine authority in the eyes of the church members. In order to accomplish that end, they spread the idea that Paul was not a legitimate apostle but was self-appointed and that his motivation was to elevate himself and build up a personal following. They accused him of putting aside the Mosaic ceremonies, standards, and practices in order to make the gospel more appealing to Gentiles by removing its Jewish associations. He also made the gospel easier for Jews to accept, they argued, because he removed the demanding requirements of traditional Judaism to which all loyal Jews subscribed.

The strategy worked as the accusations of the Judaizers had caused many members of the Galatian churches to begin doubting Paul's apostolic legitimacy. Since he was not among the original apostles, whom Jesus personally called, taught, and commissioned, just where *did* he get his message and authority? Did he get them second hand from the other apostles, or did he simply make up his own brand of the gospel and arrogate apostolic authority to himself? What right, they asked, did Paul have to speak for God, as he persistently claimed to do?

There is no evidence that the early church ever doubted the apostleship of the Twelve (the original eleven and Matthias, who replaced Judas). The eleven were hand-picked and trained by Jesus; and under the Lord's direction they chose Matthias, who had been among the disciples who accompanied them "all the time that the Lord Jesus went in and out among us—beginning with the baptism of John, until the day that He was taken up from us . . . a witness with us of His resurrection" (Acts 1:21-26). The credentials of the Twelve were well known and well attested.

Jesus had promised them, "When they deliver you up, do not become anxious about how or what you will speak; for it shall be given you in that hour what you are to speak. For it is not you who speak, but it is the Spirit of your Father who speaks in you" (Matt. 10:19-20). Although many Christians like to claim it for themselves, that promise was given to the apostles alone. The Holy Spirit may bring things to our remembrance and give us clarity of mind when we are called to testify for Him under oppressive conditions. But Christ promised new revelation only to the apostles, who were the sole authoritative spokesmen of His Word before the New Testament was written. "These things I have spoken to you, while abiding with you," Jesus told them. "But the Helper, the Holy Spirit, whom the Father will send in My name, He will teach you all things, and bring to your remembrance all that I said to you" (John 14:25-26). The Holy Spirit not only enabled the apostles to remember accurately and completely what Jesus had taught them during His three-year earthly ministry but divinely revealed to them every additional truth He later declared through them.

After Pentecost believers "were continually devoting themselves to the apostles' teaching" (Acts 2:42), because they recognized that those men were divinely appointed to preach and minister in Christ's stead. Their apostolic authority was confirmed by "many wonders and signs [that] were taking place through the apostles" (v. 43). When they spoke for God, it was God Himself speaking through them.

But Paul was not even a believer, much less an apostle, when Jesus made those promises to the Twelve and when the early church in Jerusalem submitted to their instruction and leadership. He was not converted until several years later and, in fact, after he had been the most destructive enemy of the infant church.

It was not difficult, therefore, for the Judaizers to raise doubts about Paul in the minds of many believers. Now that he was no longer with them in person to teach and protect them, they became prey for false teachers. The fact that Paul declared himself to be "an apostle of Gentiles" (Rom. 11:13) may not have endeared him to some Jewish believers, who still harbored strong prejudice against Gentiles, thinking them to be utterly outside the sphere and privilege of God's concern and grace. And the fact that Paul frequently affirmed and defended his apostleship suggests that it was frequently questioned (see, e.g., Rom. 1:1; 1 Cor. 1:1; 9:1-2; 2 Cor. 1:1; 1 Tim. 1:1; 2:7). Although in humility he saw himself as "the least of the apostles" (1 Cor. 15:9), he knew that, as far as his calling and authority were concerned, he was "in no respect . . . inferior to the most eminent apostles, even though I am a nobody" (2 Cor. 12:11).

It must have wounded Paul deeply to learn that many believers in Galatia had been persuaded by those false teachers to question his motives and to doubt his authority and the truth of his gospel. But he did not make his defense on the reflex of feeling but on the basis of fact. He did not make an emotional appeal for renewed personal loyalty to himself but rather presented clear evidence that contradicted the accusations being made against him. His concern was not for his own popularity or personal success but God's truth. His defense of his apostleship was for the purpose of defending his authority and the integrity of the gospel he had faithfully proclaimed in the Galatian churches and everywhere else he went.

In Galatians 1:10-12 Paul presents some general credentials of his apostleship and message, and in verses 13-24 he unfolds autobiographical credentials that include preconversion, conversion, and postconversion proofs of his legitimacy.

Paul's General Credentials

For am I now seeking the favor of men, or of God? Or am I striving to please men? If I were still trying to please men, I would not be a bond-servant of Christ.

For I would have you know, brethren, that the gospel which was preached by me is not according to man. For I neither received it from man, nor was I taught it, but I received it through a revelation of Jesus Christ. (1:10-12)

The accusations against him involved the lie that he was purposely watering down the divine standard to make it easy, so that he would be popular and win the support of people weary of the hard, demanding way of legalistic Judaism. They purported that he was simply saying what men wanted to hear.

PAUL WAS NOT A PEOPLE PLEASER

For am I now seeking the favor of men, or of God? Or am I striving to please men? If I were still trying to please men, I would not be a bond-servant of Christ. (1:10)

Gar (**for**) has numerous meanings, which are largely determined by context. It can also be translated "because," "yes, indeed," "certainly," "what," and "why." It can also sometimes mean "there," which is a helpful rendering in this verse. **For** is not an incorrect translation, but "there" seems to follow better the flow of Paul's argument in this context. "There," he is saying, referring back to the strong anathemas of the previous two verses, "does that sound like I am a people pleaser? **Am I now seeking the favor of men, or of God? Or am I striving to please men?**" Obviously, Paul's pronouncing a curse on men (v. 9) does not fit with the accusations of the Judaizers against him. Rather, it unquestionably seeks to honor God, whose truth was being perverted.

If I were still trying to please men refers to the days when he did seek to please his fellow Jews by zealously persecuting Christians, assuming he was being faithful to God while concentrating his effort on favoring traditional Judaism. But in light of what he taught and the way he had lived since his conversion, the idea that he was **still trying to please men** was preposterous. If that were true, he **would not be a bond-servant of Christ.** He had surrendered his life entirely to the lordship of Jesus Christ, and that surrender had cost him dearly in human terms. At the end of this epistle Paul reminds his readers, "For I bear on my body the brand-marks of Jesus" (6:17). Some of those marks he had received in Galatia, where, in the city of Lystra, he was once left for dead after being stoned (Acts 14:19). Suffering at the hands of people who were not pleased with him was a common occurrence for him and was the price of honoring God.

By nature, people pleasers are not martyrs. The desire to escape ridicule and trouble is one of their hallmarks. Pleasing men does not bring the severe persecution Paul endured and is totally incompatible with being **a bond-servant of Christ.**

It was rather Paul's Jewish accusers who were men pleasers. It was "to make a good showing in the flesh" that they tried "to compel [Gentile believers] to be circumcised," for the very purpose of *not* being "persecuted for the cross of Christ" (Gal. 6:12). Paul's first purpose was "to be pleasing to Him" (2 Cor. 5:9). And pleasing the Lord Jesus Christ meant that he had every right to pronounce a curse on anyone who tried by a doctrine of works righteousness to detract from the gracious finished work of the Savior (cf. Gal. 2:21). His second purpose was to see men saved and that required strong denunciation of any false gospel that would damn them by its deceit.

For I would have you know, brethren, that the gospel which was preached by me is not according to man. (1:11)

I would have you know is from *gnōrizō,* a strong Greek verb that means to make known with certainty, to certify. It was often used, as here, to introduce an important and emphatic statement that immediately followed. In vernacular English the phrase could be rendered, "Let me make it perfectly clear." "The gospel I preach," he said, "is not human either in nature or in authority. I did not invent it or alter it, nor did any other **man.** Its message is completely divine in origin, without any mixture of human wisdom whatever." That is why Paul's gospel is the standard by which all false human theories of salvation are measured and condemned.

Had Paul proclaimed a **gospel** that was **according to man,** it would have been permeated by works righteousness, as is every humanly devised system of religion. Man's sinful pride is offended by the idea that only God's mercy and grace can save him from sin, and he therefore insists on having a part in his own salvation. The very fact that Paul **preached** a message of salvation in which works play absolutely no part was itself evidence that his message was from God and **not . . . man.**

For I neither received it from man, nor was I taught it, (1:12*a*)

That statement was particularly directed against the Judaizers, who received their religious instruction primarily from rabbinic tradition by means of rote memorization. Rather than studying the Scriptures directly, most Jews—religious leaders and laymen alike—looked to human interpretations of Scripture as their religious authority and guide. Their theology, moral standards, and ceremonies had roots in God's revealed Word of the Old Testament, but the biblical truths and standards had been so diluted and distorted by human interpretations that the Judaism of New Testament times was largely **received . . . from man** and **taught** according to man's interpretation. Although the Scriptures, especially the Torah, or law, were ritually given the highest honor, they were not honored by the people through direct study and sincere obedience. In the eyes of many Jews of that day— just as in the eyes of many professing Christians today—Scripture was a religious relic that deserved superficial reverence but not serious study or obedience. The religious ideas they took seriously and attempted to live by were the man-made traditions related to their unique community culture that had accumulated over the previous several hundred years. Many of the traditions not only were not taught in Scripture but contradicted Scripture. With few exceptions, Jews "invalidated the word of God for the sake of [their] tradition" (Matt. 15:6).

But Paul's teaching and preaching had no such human basis. **Neither** translates *oude*, which is here used emphatically, meaning "not even." The idea is, "Not even I who might so readily have been taught by men was so taught." Although he had been highly trained in rabbinic schools and was "a Pharisee according to the strictest sect of [Jewish] religion" (Acts 26:5; cf. 23:6), he had discarded every unscriptural notion he had learned in that man-made religious system. No Jew had more reason than Paul to boast in his accomplishments in Judaism; but everything he had accomplished in the flesh before receiving Christ he counted "as rubbish" (Phil. 3:4-8), and even the elements of the story of Christ that he knew prior to his conversion were shallow and empty because of his unbelief. What he now believed and preached he **neither received . . . from man, nor was . . . taught** by man. There was no human source for Paul's message. The gospel was not invented by men nor transmitted to him by any human being. This response no doubt reflects another of the Judaizers' accusations against Paul, namely, that he had been taught his doctrine by the apostles in Jerusalem, who had also abandoned Judaism.

PAUL'S MESSAGE WAS DIRECTLY FROM CHRIST

but I received it through a revelation of Jesus Christ. (1:12*b*)

The gospel Paul preached and taught was neither a human invention nor a human tradition, but was given to him directly by God **through a revelation of Jesus Christ. Revelation** is from *apokalupsis* and means an unveiling of something previously secret. **Jesus Christ** is best understood as the object of that very **revelation.** It was not that he had no previous knowledge of Jesus. It was for the very reason that he *did* know something of Him and His work that he had fiercely persecuted those who believed in Him. He obviously had known that Christians believed Jesus was the Son of God and the promised Messiah of the Old Testament, because it was for those claims that Jesus was most criticized and eventually crucified (Luke 23:2, 35; John 5:18; 10:30). Paul had known that Christians believed Jesus rose from the dead and ascended to heaven. He also knew that Jesus not only dispensed with the rabbinic traditions but even with the ceremonial laws of Moses. Before his conversion Paul could have accurately stated many of the central teachings of the gospel. But he did not believe those teachings were true and thus had no grasp of their spiritual meaning and significance.

It was only after he himself at Damascus (Acts 9:1-16) came personally to encounter and to know **Jesus Christ** as Lord and Savior that he **received** the supernatural truth of the gospel **through** divine **revelation.** As he explained to the Corinthian church, it is only when a person turns to the Lord that the veil of spiritual ignorance and separation from God is removed (2 Cor. 3:14-16), so that the truth received can be understood. And for Paul the details and distinctions of that gospel truth came by special revelation directly from God (cf. v. 16).

It is one thing to claim direct revelation from God but another to prove it. Throughout the history of the church many people have falsely claimed such revelation, as many do today. But Paul was not content merely to make the claim. Nor did he expect his readers to believe him simply on the basis of personal assertions. In the next 12 verses, therefore, the apostle proceeds to substantiate his claim by presenting irrefutable evidence of that divine revelation and of his apostolic credentials.

PAUL'S AUTOBIOGRAPHICAL CREDENTIALS

For you have heard of my former manner of life in Judaism, how I used to persecute the church of God beyond measure, and tried to destroy it; and I was advancing in Judaism beyond many of my contemporaries among my countrymen, being more extremely zealous for my ancestral traditions. But when He who had set me apart, even from my mother's womb, and called me through His grace, was pleased to reveal His Son in me, that I might preach Him among the Gentiles, I did not immediately consult with flesh and blood, nor did I go up to Jerusalem to those who were apostles before me; but I went away to Arabia, and returned once more to Damascus.

Then three years later I went up to Jerusalem to become acquainted with Cephas, and stayed with him fifteen days. But I did not see any other of the apostles except James, the Lord's brother. (Now in what I am writing to you, I assure you before God that I am not lying.) Then I went into the regions of Syria and Cilicia. And I was still unknown by sight to the churches of Judea which were in Christ; but only, they kept hearing, "He who once persecuted us is now preaching the faith which he once tried to destroy." And they were glorifying God because of me. (1:13-24)

From the three periods of his spiritual life—preconversion, conversion, and postconversion—Paul shows how certain events before he was saved, when he was saved, and after he was saved all prove his message was received from God.

PRECONVERSION PROOF

For you have heard of my former manner of life in Judaism, how I used to persecute the church of God beyond measure, and tried to destroy it; and I was advancing in Judaism beyond many of my contemporaries among my countrymen, being more extremely zealous for my ancestral traditions. (1:13-14)

Here Paul describes his **former** standing and activities while he was **in Judaism,** offering them as a kind of negative proof that his message of grace had no foundation in the beliefs, circumstances, or events of his former life. It becomes clear that nothing in his unconverted life provided the source of the truth he was now proclaiming. In fact, both his conversion and his message were built on divine intervention.

Paul had been a Jew of the first order, "circumcised the eighth day, of the nation of Israel, of the tribe of Benjamin, a Hebrew of Hebrews; as to the Law, a Pharisee; as to zeal, a persecutor of the church; as to the righteousness which is in the Law, found blameless" (Phil. 3:5-6). His preconversion life was centered totally in law and tradition. Grace was a foreign concept to the religion of Saul the Pharisee, despite the fact that grace was as much the basis of the Old Covenant as the New. God's redemptive work originated from His grace and has never had any other basis. But most Jews, indoctrinated by the religiously dominant scribes and Pharisees, had long since lost sight of God's grace and had instead come to trust in their own works and goodness to please God. Accordingly, everything in the apostle's **former manner of life in Judaism** had been diametrically opposed to the message of sovereign and saving grace of Jesus Christ he now proclaimed and defended.

The first aspect of Paul's **former . . . life** that proved he had no previous grounding for the gospel was that he **used to persecute the church of God beyond measure, and tried to destroy it.** His preconversion knowledge of the gospel, veiled and distorted as it was, made him realize that this radical way of salvation allowed no place for works righteousness and therefore completely undercut legalistic Judaism. Conversely, legalistic Judaism allowed no place for a gospel of grace and therefore sought to **destroy** those who believed and taught it.

The original language is vivid in describing Paul's hostility. The phrase **used to persecute** is in the imperfect tense and emphasizes a persistent and continual intent to harm. The word **destroy** was used of soldiers ravaging a city. It is also used here in the imperfect, thereby emphasizing the persistence of Paul's destructive effort. He was determined to utterly extinguish **the church.** Apparently he used the title **the church of God** to stress that this was not just a group belonging to Jesus, so that whoever opposed it, opposed only Jesus. Rather, whoever opposes **the church** opposes **God.**

Saul the Pharisee had had such passion for traditional Judaism that he could tolerate no contradiction or compromise of it by fellow Jews. Immediately after the martyrdom of Stephen, "Saul began ravaging the church, entering house after house; and dragging off men and women, he would put them in prison" (Acts 8:3). Perhaps a year later, "still breathing threats and murder against the disciples of the Lord, [he] went to the high priest, and asked for letters from him to the synagogues at Damascus, so that if he found any belonging to the Way, both men and women, he might bring them bound to Jerusalem" (9:1-2; cf. 22:4-5; 26:10-11). His single, overriding passion was **to destroy** the infant church. It was partly because of that activity that he always had a great sense of unworthiness when contemplating God's saving grace in his behalf (cf. 1 Cor. 15:9; 1 Tim. 1:12-14).

The second aspect of Paul's former life that proved he had no previous grounding in the gospel was his unequalled zeal for traditional Judaism. **I was advancing in Judaism beyond many of my countrymen,** he declared, **being**

more extremely zealous for my ancestral traditions.

Advancing is from *prokoptō,* which literally means to chop ahead, as in blazing a trail through a forest. Saul kept on blazing his trail **in Judaism,** which meant cutting down anything in his path such as Jewish Christians, who in his mind were arch traitors to their **ancestral traditions.** He was so **extremely zealous** that he continually punished Jewish believers "in all the synagogues, [and] tried to force them to blaspheme; and being furiously enraged at them, [he] kept pursuing them even to foreign cities" (Acts 26:11). In his extreme zeal, he exceeded **many** of his contemporaries. Few Jews matched his passion for his religion and his intolerance for the truth about Jesus Christ.

Ancestral traditions refers to the body of oral teachings about the Old Testament law that came to have equal authority with the law. Commonly known as the Halakah, this collection of Torah interpretations became a fence around God's revealed law and all but hid it from view. Over a period of several hundred years it had expanded into a mammoth accumulation of religious, moral, legal, practical, and ceremonial regulations that defied comprehension, much less total compliance. It contained such vast amounts of minutiae that even the most learned rabbinical scholars could not master it either by interpretation or in behavior. Yet the more complex and burdensome it became, the more zealously Jewish legalists revered and propagated it.

Living as a devout Pharisee, Paul was outdone by few. John R. W. Stott writes: "Now a man in that mental and emotional state is in no mood to change his mind, or even to have it changed for him by men. . . . Only God could reach him—and God did!" (*The Message of Galatians* [London: Inter-Varsity, 1968], p. 32).

Paul's point in reciting these two general features from his past life was that, prior to his encounter with Christ, there was not the slightest human preparation or source for his understanding, much less accepting and proclaiming, the gospel of salvation by God's grace working through faith completely apart from works. It was foreign to all his previous thinking.

CONVERSION PROOF

But when He who had set me apart, even from my mother's womb, and called me through His grace, was pleased to reveal His Son in me, that I might preach Him among the Gentiles, (1:15-16*a*)

Not until Christ sovereignly in resurrection glory confronted him on the road to Damascus did Paul respond to the great reality of the gospel: that Jesus, though put to death and buried, was now alive. He immediately realized that only a resurrected Jesus could proclaim from heaven, "I am Jesus whom you are persecuting" (Acts 9:5).

No human explanation or influence could account for the 180 degree turnaround in Saul's life. He had been like a runaway freight train that crushes everything in its path. He had lost control of his life and was without restraint. His legalistic zeal had put him on a headlong course of destruction from which no natural force short of death could have deterred him. His apostolic calling could only have been supernatural and sovereign, completely apart from human testimony or persuasion (though he may have heard much truth from the Christians he captured).

Men's coming to God has always been on the basis of His sovereign will and grace. As Moses explained to Israel in the wilderness, "The Lord did not set His love on you nor choose you because you were more in number than any of the peoples, for you were the fewest of all peoples, but because the Lord loved you and kept the oath which He swore to your forefathers" (Deut. 7:7-8). Samuel confronted the people with the same message: "The Lord will not abandon His people on account of His great name, because the Lord has been pleased to make you a people for Himself" (1 Sam. 12:22). God chose the Jews for no other reason than His own holy pleasure and purpose.

David knew he was chosen and anointed king by God's sovereign election. "The Lord, the God of Israel, chose me from all the house of my father to be king over Israel forever," he said. "For He has chosen Judah to be a leader; and in the house of Judah, my father's house, and among the sons of my father He took pleasure in me to make me king over all Israel. And of all my sons (for the Lord has given me many sons), He has chosen my son Solomon to sit on the throne of the kingdom of the Lord over Israel" (1 Chron. 28:4-5). From the choosing of the nation of Israel, the tribe of Judah, the family of Jesse, and of Jesse's son David and grandson Solomon, the process was entirely divine and sovereign. God's election is based on nothing but His own good pleasure.

Paul did not initiate the choice to be saved, much less the choice to be an apostle. He was "called as an apostle of Jesus Christ by the will of God" (1 Cor. 1:1). The phrase **when He who had set me apart** refers to the elective purpose of God before Paul was even able to consider a choice. No person is saved or called to leadership in the church except by such sovereign and predetermined divine will. "He predestined us to adoption as sons through Jesus Christ to Himself, according to the kind intention of His will, to the praise of the glory of His grace, which He freely bestowed on us in the Beloved" (Eph. 1:5-6; cf. v. 9).

The Lord **set apart** Paul to salvation and apostleship not because Paul developed great leadership ability and writing skill or was a determined and hard worker. He had been **set apart** and consecrated by God **even from** his **mother's womb,** long before he could have demonstrated the least potential for anything. Paul was chosen to be an apostle before he was born, just as Jacob was chosen over his twin brother Esau before their births (Rom. 9:11-13), as Isaiah and Jeremiah were called and consecrated to their prophetic work while still in their mothers' wombs (Isa. 49:1; Jer. 1:5), and as John the Baptist was called even before his conception to be the forerunner of the Messiah (Luke 1:13-17). Paul's Jewish readers knew immediately that he was comparing his call to apostleship to the calls of those great men of God. He was not trying to rank himself with them but to establish unequivocally that, like theirs, his call was entirely God's doing.

This purpose became historical fact on the Damascus Road and in the subsequent days, when, Paul says, God **called me through His grace.** By means of unmerited love and kindness God actually and efficaciously brought the already elect Saul to Himself in salvation.

God **was pleased to reveal His Son to** Saul in a direct and absolutely unique way. As "he was approaching Damascus, . . . suddenly a light from heaven flashed around him; and he fell to the ground, and heard a voice saying to him, 'Saul, Saul, why are you persecuting Me?' And he said, 'Who art Thou, Lord?' And He said, 'I am Jesus whom you are persecuting, but rise, and enter the city, and it shall be told you what you must do'" (Acts 9:3-6). In his testimony before King Agrippa, Paul gives further details of his first encounter with the risen Lord. After identifying Himself as "Jesus whom you are persecuting," the Lord said, "Arise, and stand on your feet; for this purpose I have appeared to you, to appoint you a minister and a witness not only to the things which you have seen, but also to the things in which I will appear to you; delivering you from the Jewish people and from the Gentiles, to whom I am sending you" (26:15-17). God's direct revelations of Christ and Scripture to Paul began that day and continued during the short time in Damascus and the years in Arabia, and then as God desired throughout the apostle's life.

The phrase **in me** does not force us to interpret the revelation as a purely internal, subjective feeling but can mean "to me" and carry the idea of objective experience.

The call to be saved was accompanied by the call to serve, to **preach Him among the Gentiles.** Although the experience of Paul was utterly unique, God does not call any person to salvation whom He does not also call to service. Every believer is "created in Christ Jesus for good works, which God prepared beforehand, that we should walk in them" (Eph. 2:10). Speaking to believers, Peter wrote, "You are a chosen race, a royal priesthood, a holy nation, a people for God's own possession, that you may proclaim the excellencies of Him who has called you out of darkness into His marvelous light" (1 Pet. 2:9). We are saved to be witnesses and servants of the Savior.

And the subject of his preaching was **Him,** Jesus Christ. To the Corinthians Paul wrote concerning "the testimony of God," that it called for him "to know nothing among you except Jesus Christ and Him crucified" (1 Cor. 2:1-2). The Judaizers needed to see that **the Gentiles** did not need to hear the law of Moses or the traditions of the Jewish elders—only the gospel of Jesus Christ.

So the choice of Paul, his transformation, the revelation and call to preach to the nations were all done by God, not men. Even after that, men played no part in his preparation to fulfill his calling.

POSTCONVERSION PROOF

I did not immediately consult with flesh and blood, nor did I go up to Jerusalem to those who were apostles before me; but I went away to Arabia, and returned once more to Damascus.

Then three years later I went up to Jerusalem to become acquainted with Cephas, and stayed with him fifteen days. But I did not see any other of

the apostles except James, the Lord's brother. (Now in what I am writing to you, I assure you before God that I am not lying.) Then I went into the regions of Syria and Cilicia. And I was still unknown by sight to the churches of Judea which were in Christ; but only, they kept hearing, "He who once persecuted us is now preaching the faith which he once tried to destroy." And they were glorifying God because of me. (1:16b-24)

John Brown commented that, beginning with the Damascus Road encounter, Christ took Paul under His own immediate tutoring. It was essential for the Lord to establish Paul's independence as an apostle. He was not taught by the other apostles but was fully equal to them. After spending several days "with the disciples who were at Damascus" and preaching briefly in the synagogues there (Acts 9:19-20), Paul **did not consult with flesh and blood.** He sought from Ananias or other Christians at Damascus no advice or understanding, no clarification of the revelation he had received. It is not that he would not have been helped by going to learn from other believers, but his being given the unique place of reaching Gentiles seemed to demand that he not be seen as being merely convinced by some Jewish converts to this doctrine. Gentiles might have been more reluctant to accept his message if they perceived of it as of Jewish origination. And the Judaizers needed to understand that the gospel was not at all a heresy advocated by a few Jews.

Paul **went away to** Nabatean **Arabia,** a region that stretched east from Damascus down to the Sinai peninsula. Although he does not identify the exact location, it seems likely that he stayed near Damascus. The place and purpose of his sojourn in Arabia are unknown, but that was surely the place of his preparation for ministry.

After his stay in Arabia, the apostle **returned once more to Damascus** and continued preaching there for a period of time. He almost immediately encountered persecution from the Jewish leaders, a group that doubtlessly included some of the men with whom he himself had once planned to conspire against the Christians (see Acts 9:2).

The fact that "in Damascus the ethnarch under Aretas the king [of Nabatean Arabia] was guarding the city of the Damascenes in order to seize [Paul]" (2 Cor. 11:32) suggests that the apostle also preached in **Arabia** and had aroused the displeasure of its king. In any case, the Gentile civil authorities of Damascus supported the efforts of the Jewish leaders to arrest and execute Paul (cf. Acts 9:23-24).

The two periods of preaching in Damascus and the in-between sojourn in Arabia alone with Lord Jesus—learning, meditating, and studying the Old Testament—totalled **three years.** After that, Paul **went up to Jerusalem** (not to be confused with a later famine relief trip there from Antioch, mentioned in Acts 11:30, or the trip to the council of Acts 15) **to become acquainted with Cephas,** that is, the apostle Peter. Paul makes a point of noting that he went solely for the purpose of becoming **acquainted with Cephas,** who was the personal companion of the Lord Jesus and the most powerful spokesman in the early years of the Jerusalem church, from Pentecost on (Acts 2:14-40; 3:11-26; 4:8-20; 5:3-32; 8:20-25). He only **stayed**

with him fifteen days, obviously far too short a time to have been fully transformed from all his Jewish theology and tradition and fully instructed in the gospel. Nor did he **see any other of the apostles except James, the Lord's brother.** Paul's visit to Jerusalem was not to learn more about the gospel message but to meet and get **acquainted with** (the verb means "to visit with the purpose of getting to know someone") these two men who had been so close to Jesus and perhaps to learn from them some of their intimate experiences with the incarnate Lord, whom he had come to love and serve, and with whom he had spent those three years getting acquainted.

It should noted that Acts 9:23-25 indicates that Paul's leaving Damascus was the result of a dramatic set of events. The Jews strongly resisted his preaching and had developed a plan to kill him when the opportunity arose. They patrolled the city gates 24 hours a day waiting to capture Paul, but when his disciples heard of the plot they helped him escape by lowering him over the city wall in a basket.

Apart from such a predicament that threatened his life, Paul may have stayed longer in Damascus. No time frame is given for his going to Jerusalem, but when he arrived there and tried to see the apostles, he was rebuffed because of fear that he was not a true believer (Acts 9:26). Without the help of Barnabas, Paul would not have been able visit even Peter and James. He met none of the other apostles at all, who may have been too afraid or may have been away from Jerusalem at the time. It could be surmised that, though the apostles did not scatter under Paul's persecution (Acts 8:1), they may have done so by now. When Herod moved against them (12:1), it seems that only Peter and James the brother of John were still in the city, and Peter soon fled to avoid the fate of James (12:17). The mention of Paul's being "brought to the apostles" (9:27) must refer only to Peter and James the Lord's brother, who was certainly attached to the apostles at that time. Because of his having seen the risen Christ (1 Cor. 15:7) and his having been intimately associated with the other apostles (much like Barnabas; see Acts 14:14), this James would easily have been considered by Paul to be an apostle in the wider sense.

To give his readers the greatest possible confidence in what he was **writing,** Paul made a common Jewish vow: **I assure you before God that I am not lying.** That statement, along with many others, contradicts the claims of liberal interpreters that Paul was a sincere and highly capable leader but that many of his teachings reflect only his personal ideas and preferences. If that were so, he would either have been terribly self-deluded or else a shameless liar. He was either an authoritative and completely reliable spokesman for God or he was a sham.

Paul's point in this part of the letter was to affirm that he had received his gospel directly from the Lord, not from the other apostles. He only visited two of them for two weeks, and only after three years had elapsed since his conversion. Any accusation that he was a second-hand apostle, receiving his message from the Jerusalem apostles, was false.

After Paul left Jerusalem he **went into the regions of Syria and Cilicia,** the latter of which included his home town of Tarsus (see Acts 9:11, 30). This move was precipitated by another group of hostile Jews who were "attempting to put him to death" (Acts 9:29). He was escorted out of Jerusalem to the port city of Caesarea, where he likely took a ship to his home town of Tarsus. He preached there until

Barnabas called for him to come to Antioch in Syria.

During a stay of several years in those **regions,** Paul preached (v. 23). The other apostles were still in Judea and Samaria and had no contact with or influence on him. When word of revival in Syrian Antioch "reached the ears of the church at Jerusalem, . . . they sent Barnabas off to Antioch," who ministered there for a while by himself and then "left for Tarsus to look for Saul," with whom he then "taught considerable numbers" in Antioch. It was here that "the disciples were first called Christians" (Acts 11:20-26). Paul stayed on as a teacher in the church at Antioch until the Holy Spirit sent him and Barnabas off on their first missionary journey (Acts 13:1-3), and after that they returned to Antioch, from where they were sent to the council in Jerusalem (14:26–15:4).

At this time Paul **was still unknown by sight to the churches of Judea which were in Christ. Churches** is a plural designation indicating local assemblies that are part of the one church. Paul's two visits to Jerusalem did not include visiting **the churches of Judea,** which region was usually thought of separately from its major city, Jerusalem (see Acts 1:8). All that those **churches** knew about this independent apostle was what **they kept hearing, "He who once persecuted us is now preaching the faith which he once tried to destroy."** For obvious reasons, it had been extremely difficult for believers to accept the genuineness of Paul's conversion (see Acts 9:13-14, 21, 26). But when the Lord gave such great blessing to Paul's ministry, resulting in his own persecution (vv. 23-24, 29), his fellow Christians could no longer doubt he was a specially chosen and gifted man of God, and **they were glorifying God because of** him.

He and Barnabas only made two visits to Jerusalem, one to bring famine relief from Antioch (Acts 11:30) and another to discuss the relation of the Mosaic law to the gospel of grace (Acts 15). Since Paul's presence there was so scarce for fourteen years (Gal. 2:1), most of the people did not know him except by reputation. And though his gospel had not come from Jerusalem nor been refined there, still the believers there affirmed both it and the power of his apostleship as being cause for **glorifying God.** The fact that the people were praising God for the very same gospel they knew shows it was identical to that taught by the Jerusalem apostles and was truly from the Lord.

Paul's point through all of this detailed autobiography was that the charges of the Judaizers was absurd on the surface. The church in Jerusalem, which was still overseen by the other apostles and James, the Lord's half brother, had long since recognized his apostolic office and authority and glorified God because of him. James, Peter, and John—the three leading apostles among the Twelve—had specifically acknowledged that the grace of God had been given to Paul and they enthusiastically gave him "and Barnabas the right hand of fellowship" (Gal. 2:9). In his second letter Peter not only acknowledges Paul's divine authority but asserts that his epistles even at that early date were already recognized as scriptural (2 Pet. 3:15-16).

To reject Paul's teaching is to reject God's Word. Neither the testimony of Paul himself nor of the other apostles allows another conclusion.

Apostolic Commendation
(2:1-10)

4

Then after an interval of fourteen years I went up again to Jerusalem with Barnabas, taking Titus along also. And it was because of a revelation that I went up; and I submitted to them the gospel which I preach among the Gentiles, but I did so in private to those who were of reputation, for fear that I might be running, or had run, in vain. But not even Titus who was with me, though he was a Greek, was compelled to be circumcised. But it was because of the false brethren who had sneaked in to spy out our liberty which we have in Christ Jesus, in order to bring us into bondage. But we did not yield in subjection to them for even an hour, so that the truth of the gospel might remain with you. But from those who were of high reputation (what they were makes no difference to me; God shows no partiality)—well, those who were of reputation contributed nothing to me. But on the contrary, seeing that I had been entrusted with the gospel to the uncircumcised, just as Peter had been to the circumcised (for He who effectually worked for Peter in his apostleship to the circumcised effectually worked for me also to the Gentiles), and recognizing the grace that had been given to me, James and Cephas and John, who were reputed to be pillars, gave to me and Barnabas the right hand of fellowship, that we might go to the Gentiles, and they to the circumcised. They only asked us to remember the poor—the very thing I also was eager to do. (2:1-10)

As Jesus made clear in the parable of the wheat and tares (Matt. 13:24-30), wherever and whenever the good seed of God's truth is sown Satan will be there to sow his seed of falsehood. It was therefore inevitable that, as Paul faithfully and powerfully planted the truth of the gospel, Satan's false teachers would be on the apostle's heels planting lies.

Paul warned the Ephesian elders to "be on guard for yourselves and for all the flock, among which the Holy Spirit has made you overseers, to shepherd the church of God which He purchased with His own blood. I know that after my departure savage wolves will come in among you, not sparing the flock; and from among your own selves men will arise, speaking perverse things, to draw away the disciples after them" (Acts 20:28-30). He warned Timothy, "But the Spirit explicitly says that in later times some will fall away from the faith, paying attention to deceitful spirits and doctrines of demons, by means of the hypocrisy of liars seared in their own conscience as with a branding iron" (1 Tim. 4:1-2).

Throughout his long and widespread ministry Paul fought against the emissaries of Satan who always seek to discredit both the truth and its representatives. In Galatians 2:1-10 he continues defending himself against their accusation that he was a self-appointed apostle proclaiming a self-devised message that was different from that of Peter and the other apostles at Jerusalem. He devastatingly argues that, although he received his message independently of the other apostles, he preached a message identical to theirs, a fact they wholeheartedly acknowledged. His gospel was independent in terms of revelation but identical in terms of content.

Recounting his most significant trip to Jerusalem after his conversion, Paul shows by his coming, his companion, his commission, and his commendation that he was of one truth and one spirit with the other twelve apostles.

PAUL'S COMING

Then after an interval of fourteen years I went up again to Jerusalem with Barnabas, taking Titus along also. And it was because of a revelation that I went up; and I submitted to them the gospel which I preach among the Gentiles, but I did so in private to those who were of reputation, for fear that I might be running, or had run, in vain. (2:1-2)

Paul had already established that his contact with the other apostles was almost nil during the first years after his conversion. He did not see any of them until three years after his Damascus Road encounter with the Lord, and then only briefly. He had stayed with Peter for fifteen days in Jerusalem and had met James, Jesus' half brother (1:18-19; cf. Acts 9:26-28). He later went to Jerusalem a second time for probably an even briefer period, which he does not refer to in this text since it had no direct bearing on the issue of apostleship. During that brief second visit he helped Barnabas take the collection to Jerusalem from the church at Antioch for relief of famine-stricken believers in Judea (Acts 11:27-30; 12:24-25).

Then after an interval of fourteen years from the first visit when he met Peter and James, he **went up again to Jerusalem.** During the previous seventeen years he had preached the gospel without any human instruction, his message having been given to him entirely by God's direct revelation (Gal. 1:11-12, 16-17).

Paul and Barnabas had completed their first missionary tour (Acts 13:1–14:28) and returned to Antioch to report the miracles of Gentile conversion by grace through faith. Jewish legalists in Judea were upset when they heard the report and went to Antioch to teach that a Gentile had to become a Jew before becoming a Christian.

It seems probable, as many scholars believe, that this trip of Paul's **again to Jerusalem** was for the council (Acts 15) called to resolve the issue, and that **again** does not linguistically denote a second visit. (For a thorough treatment of the viability of that view of Acts 15 compared with the view that this text refers to Paul's second visit to Jerusalem for famine relief recorded in Acts 11:27-30; 12:24-25, see William Hendricksen's *New Testament Commentary: Exposition of Galatians* [Grand Rapids: Baker, 1971], pp. 69-77.)

According to Acts 15, those professing Jewish Christians from Judea went to Antioch, where Paul and Barnabas were ministering, "and began teaching the brethren, 'Unless you are circumcised according to the custom of Moses, you cannot be saved.' And when Paul and Barnabas had great dissension and debate with them, the brethren determined that Paul and Barnabas and certain others of them should go up to Jerusalem to the apostles and elders concerning this issue" (Acts 15:1-2). The whole debate was to be resolved in **Jerusalem.**

In addition to the leader Paul and his intimate Jewish friend and companion **Barnabas,** . . . **Titus,** a spiritual child of Paul and his co-worker (Titus 1:4-5), went **along also,** being among the "certain others" mentioned by Luke. Titus, as an uncircumcised Gentile and a product of the very ministry the Judaizers were attacking, was a fitting attendee to take along to the council. Consistent with their deceitful, self-serving methods of operation, the Judaizers likely claimed they sent the delegation from Antioch to Jerusalem to have Paul's and Barnabas's doctrine corrected. But both Luke and Paul make clear that such was not the case. Luke states that they were "sent on their way by the church" at Antioch (v. 3). Though there may have been some reluctance on the part of Paul in accepting the assignment to go to Jerusalem, a direct **revelation** by God affirmed his obligation. Paul says more specifically that **it was because of a revelation that I went up.** It is possible that the Holy Spirit spoke to the leaders of the Antioch church, along with Paul, just as He had done when Paul and Barnabas were commissioned for their first missionary venture (Acts 13:2). In any case, the matter was resolved when Paul, divinely commanded to go to Jerusalem, was obedient, and the Antioch church affirmed that command by giving their blessing.

When Paul reached Jerusalem, he simply **submitted** (from *anatithēmi,* to lay something before someone for consideration) **to them the gospel which** he had always preached **among the Gentiles,** the gospel of salvation by God's sovereign grace through man's penitent faith—a gospel utterly contrary to the works-righteous belief of the Judaizers that "unless you are circumcised according to the custom of Moses, you cannot be saved" (Acts 15:1).

Them refers first of all to the local church apostles and elders, including chiefly Peter, John, and James, our Lord's half-brother, and then to the whole assembled church at Jerusalem, composed of all the apostles and elders as well as other church members and possibly other visiting believers besides those sent by the Antioch church (Acts 15:4). Paul and Barnabas gave that group a general report on "all that God had done with them," after which "certain ones of the sect of the Pharisees who had believed, stood up, saying, 'It is necessary to circumcise them [Gentiles], and to direct them to observe the Law of Moses'" (vv. 4-5).

At that point the "apostles and elders came together to look into this matter" more thoroughly. After much debate, Peter addressed the group, declaring that God makes no distinction betweens Jews and Gentiles, saving them both by faith and granting them both the gift of His indwelling Spirit. Concerning the supposed necessity of being circumcised and of following all the Mosaic law in order to be saved, he said, "Why do you put God to the test by placing upon the neck of the disciples a yoke which neither our fathers nor we have been able to bear? But we believe that we are saved through the grace of the Lord Jesus, in the same way as they also are" (vv. 10-11).

It seems reasonable to assume that this private meeting occurred first because Paul wanted to be sure of the theology of the Jerusalem leaders before he spoke publicly. Therefore before any council appearance, Paul and Barnabas related **in private to those who were of reputation** "what signs and wonders God had done through them among the Gentiles" (Acts 15:12). In complete accord with what Peter was to say, Paul and Barnabas declared, first privately and then publicly, that God had saved Gentiles wherever they had proclaimed the gospel and that their message and those conversions were attested by God himself through means of miraculous "signs and wonders." That evidence was conclusive, because God does not confirm falsehood. When the Lord attested preaching and conversion with signs and wonders, there was no greater proof that the preaching was according to divine truth and the conversions were by the power of His Spirit.

That the Jerusalem church, and probably most of the church at large, had not been seriously devastated by the heretical teaching of the Judaizers is seen in the fact that the matter was quickly and decisively resolved at the Jerusalem Council. The entire body "kept silent" when Peter finished his address, and immediately after Paul and Barnabas spoke, James summarized their messages and proposed that the substance of what they said be sent as a directive to all the churches. After Peter, Paul, and Barnabas spoke there was no more debate (cf. v. 7). James's proposal "seemed good to the apostles and the elders, with the whole church," and a letter stating their decision was sent to "the brethren in Antioch and Syria and Cilicia who are from the Gentiles" (vv. 12-22). The believers at Antioch, having been thoroughly grounded in the true gospel by Paul and Barnabas, "rejoiced because of its encouragement" when the council's letter was read to them (vv. 30-31).

Paul's referring to the apostles with whom he spoke in private as **those who were of reputation** reflected the general attitude of the church toward those Christ-appointed leaders. The phrase describing them is used of authorities and implies a position of honor. But the fact that he refers to them in this way four times in eight verses (Gal. 2:2-9) suggests a tinge of sarcasm. It is not, however, directed at the apostles but at the Judaizers who had been claiming apostolic approval of their legalistic perversions of the gospel. In the letter sent out by the council the deceitful Judaizers are described as "some of our number to whom we gave no instruction" who had been disturbing the churches and "unsettling [their] souls" (Acts 15:24).

Although the Judaizers did not proclaim the same gospel taught by the Twelve, they knew they needed apostolic confirmation in order to be taken seriously. They therefore fabricated the lie that their message was approved by the apostles in Jerusalem and that they were among its acknowledged representatives. But that claim was absolutely denied by the apostles and elders at the council in Jerusalem.

The fact that Paul probably wrote Galatians some years after the Jerusalem Council shows that the decision and proclamation of that council had not stopped the Judaizers either from preaching their false doctrines or from claiming approval by the apostles, **those who were of reputation.** Paul was obviously not of any **reputation,** they told the Galatian believers, because his gospel conflicted with theirs and the apostles'.

But when Paul took Titus to Jerusalem and presented his gospel before these men **of reputation,** he was vindicated and the Judaizers were denounced. He had not sought vindication because he doubted the validity of his preaching. He had just declared emphatically that his message was by direct revelation from God and that it did not have and did not need any human clarification or confirmation (Gal. 1:11-19). He went to Jerusalem to prove that the gospel he preached was identical to that preached by the other apostles, having been revealed to him directly, though separately, by the Lord Jesus Himself. Paul did not go to confirm the apostolicity of his message in his own mind but in the minds of Galatian believers who were being confused and deceived by the Judaizers.

The Judaistic teachings were not simply misinterpretations or misapplications of the true gospel but the very antithesis of it. It was **for fear** that they might compromise with the teaching of the Judaizers and their perverse gospel that Paul sought in private to be certain that the teachers in Jerusalem agreed with his revelation of the gospel and would not be soft on legalism. Otherwise he **might** discover he was like an athlete who was **running, or had run, in vain** by seeing that all the spiritual effort in his ministry past and present was in conflict with them and was futile. The apostles affirmed Paul's gospel and added nothing to it (Gal. 2:6). That private confirmation set the stage for the decision in the public council that followed. It was of the greatest importance that believers in Galatia, and everywhere else, understand that his gospel of grace was identical to that of the other apostles and that it was the Satanic message of the Judaizers that was the aberration of God's saving truth.

Paul's Companion

But not even Titus who was with me, though he was a Greek, was compelled to be circumcised. But it was because of the false brethren who had sneaked

in to spy out our liberty which we have in Christ Jesus, in order to bring us into bondage. But we did not yield in subjection to them for even an hour, so that the truth of the gospel might remain with you. (2:3-5)

Although the Greek text of these verses may have been perfectly intelligible to the Galatians, it is almost impossible for modern scholars to translate. The noted biblical scholar J. B. Lightfoot called the passage "a shipwreck of Greek grammar." Perhaps Paul became so emotional while defending the very heart of the gospel and was so afraid that his beloved flocks would be corrupted by the Judaistic heresy that he used complex grammar and failed to complete his sentences.

But Paul's meaning is obvious, and there is no difficulty in understanding precisely what he is saying. As specific evidence in a test case showing that the Jerusalem apostles were in complete accord with him, Paul states that **not even Titus who was with me, though he was a Greek, was compelled to be circumcised** while at Jerusalem (cf. Acts 15:10, 19). **Titus,** a true Christian, was living and incontrovertible proof that circumcision and Mosaic regulations are not necessary for salvation. The Jerusalem Council refused to accede to the demands of the Judaizers to have Titus and all other Gentile believers circumcised, determining that they would "not trouble those who are turning to God from among the Gentiles" by compelling them **to be circumcised** (Acts 15:19, cf. v. 28).

It should be noted that some years after that occasion Paul circumcised Timothy "because of the Jews who were in those parts" (the region of Galatia), but he did so because Timothy was half Jewish (Acts 16:1-3). He was not making a concession to the Judaizers, but rather was giving Timothy closer identity with Jews to whom they might witness. Timothy was circumcised as a Jew, not as a Christian. His circumcision had no relationship to his salvation but simply gave him entrance to Jewish synagogues, from which he would otherwise have been excluded.

Titus, however, was a full Gentile, and to have had him circumcised would have undercut the gospel of grace and made him a monument of victory for the Judaizers. Paul may have intentionally brought **Titus** to Jerusalem to confound the Judaizing **false brethren who had sneaked in to spy out our liberty which we have in Christ Jesus, in order to bring us into bondage.** Paul was perfectly confident in the outcome of the Jerusalem Council and knew that afterward he would have a companion who would be personal proof that his gospel of grace apart from law was valid. He was confident that **Titus** would be allowed to leave Jerusalem uncircumcised, just as he had entered, with the full blessing of the apostles and elders. And if Gentile believers were not compelled to be circumcised in Jerusalem, which was still home base for most of the apostles, how could they be required to be circumcised in their home countries? Henceforth **Titus** was a living verification that the Judaizers taught a spurious gospel that was rejected by the rest of the church.

The Judaizers were marked as **false brethren** (*pseudadelphos*), a phrase that has also been translated "sham Christians" (NEB) and "pseudo-Christians" (Phillips). Those professing Jewish believers had developed a hybrid faith that was true neither to traditional Judaism (because it claimed allegiance to Christ) nor to apostolic Christianity (because it demanded circumcision and obedience to the Mosaic law for salvation).

It is impossible to be a legalist and a Christian. "If you receive circumcision, Christ will be of no benefit to you," Paul declares later in the letter. "Every man who receives circumcision . . . is under obligation to keep the whole Law. You have been severed from Christ, you who are seeking to be justified by law; you have fallen from grace" (Gal. 5:2-4). To do a single thing to earn salvation is to vitiate grace.

Some of the Judaizers no doubt sincerely believed their legalistic gospel was correct and that they were the only genuine Christians. But Paul refers to those **who had sneaked in to spy out** the **liberty** of true believers in terms that suggest enemies entering a camp by stealth with the objective of sabotage. Those men may not even have been honest Judaizers. Some scholars believe they were planted in the churches by Pharisees or priests in order to corrupt this threat to traditional Judaism. In any case, Satan, as always, was the primary instigator of the subterfuge. The Judaizers were first of all the devil's agents, whatever their human associations and loyalties.

Their specific purpose was to undermine the **liberty which** true believers **have in Christ Jesus, in order to bring** them **into** the **bondage** of legalism. The verb (*katadouloō*) is a compound and conveys the strong slavery of a works system. The Judaizers could not tolerate a gospel that was not tied to Mosaic ritual and law, because their view of salvation was centered in what they could self-righteously perform to earn favor from God rather than in what God could do for them.

In Christ Jesus believers have **liberty** from the law as the way of salvation and **liberty** from its external ceremonies and regulations as the way of living. Because Christ has borne that curse (3:13), they also have **liberty** from the curse for disobedience of the law, which God requires all men to obey but which no man is able to perfectly keep. Christians are under an entirely different kind of law, "the law of the Spirit of life in Christ Jesus [that sets them] free from the law of sin and of death" (Rom. 8:2).

Freedom is a much-repeated theme of the New Testament. In Christ believers "have been released from the Law, having died to that by which we were bound, so that we serve in newness of the Spirit and not in oldness of the letter" (Rom. 7:6), because "where the Spirit of the Lord is, there is liberty" (2 Cor. 3:17). "If therefore the Son shall make you free," Jesus said, "you shall be free indeed" (John 8:36).

Christian freedom is not license. When we become free in Christ we lose our freedom to sin, of which we were once a slave. In Christ, "having been freed from sin, [we] become slaves of righteousness" (Rom. 6:18). "For you were called to freedom, brethren," Paul explains; "only do not turn your freedom into an opportunity for the flesh" (Gal. 5:13). Peter expresses the same truth in these words: "Act as free men, and do not use your freedom as a covering for evil, but use it as bondslaves of God" (1 Pet. 2:16).

Paul **did not yield in subjection to** the legalistic bondage of the Judaizers **for even an hour, so that the truth of the gospel might remain with you** Galatian believers (and all others), untainted and unadulterated. **Remain** is from *diamenō* and emphasizes a permanent state. In regard to methods of ministry and issues of no spiritual importance, Paul became "all things to all men, that [he might] by all means save some" (1 Cor. 9:22). But in doctrinal matters, especially those relating to the heart of the gospel, he was intransigent. He would make considerable concessions in order to accommodate weak Christians, but he would not yield an inch of truth to accommodate false Christians. And the leaders of the church at Jerusalem were wholeheartedly in agreement with Paul's gospel, as their declarations in the council indicated (Acts 15:13-21).

PAUL'S COMMISSION

But from those who were of high reputation (what they were makes no difference to me; God shows no partiality)—well, those who were of reputation contributed nothing to me. But on the contrary, seeing that I had been entrusted with the gospel to the uncircumcised, just as Peter had been to the circumcised (for He who effectually worked for Peter in his apostleship to the circumcised effectually worked for me also to the Gentiles), and recognizing the grace that had been given to me, (2:6-9*a*)

Again Paul refers to the other apostles as **those who were of high reputation,** apparently a favorite phrase of the Judaizers. In going on to say, **what they were makes no difference to me,** he was not depreciating those godly men. He respected them or he would not have sought a private audience with them, nor would he have sought their public confirmation so that people would know he was not running in vain. He rather was defending himself against the depreciation of the Judaizers, who accused him of not comparing with the Jerusalem apostles and of being a false, self-appointed, and inferior apostle. His point here was that, although those twelve men were personally appointed apostles by Jesus Christ, so was he. He did not need their approval for his own confidence, nor did he need to seek their confirmation to convince himself, and in that regard who or **what they were** made **no difference** to him and his ministry. He had no doubts about his calling and revelations.

It may be that the Judaizers put Paul down by reminding him that the Twelve had been with Jesus for the entire course of His earthly ministry, whereas he had not (cf. 1:19). The twelve were also leaders in the Jerusalem church, which understandably was held in high regard by Christians as the first and leading congregation. But, Paul goes on to say, **God shows no partiality,** as Peter had learned with some difficulty (Acts 10:9-48). The unique privileges of the twelve therefore did not make their apostleship more legitimate or authoritative than Paul's.

Paul was not being proud or boastful but was simply stating a truth. He knew that all he was and had was entirely by God's grace (Gal. 2:9). He acknowledged himself as the foremost of sinners (1 Tim. 1:15) and "the least of the apostles, who [was] not fit to be called an apostle, because [he had] persecuted the church of God" (1 Cor. 15:9). But under God's grace he was equal to all other believers, and in his calling he was equal to all the other apostles. In 2 Corinthians 11:5 he affirmed, "I consider myself not in the least inferior to the most eminent apostles."

The Twelve had **contributed nothing** to Paul's knowledge or understanding of the gospel or to his authority to preach it. For seventeen years he had preached the gospel without their having had the least part in it. When he finally went to Jerusalem to testify to what he preached, it was not for approval or correction but simply for recognition—and that not for his own sake but for the sake of those who had been deceived by the false accusations against him being spread by the Judaizers.

But on the contrary, seeing that Paul **had been entrusted with the gospel to the uncircumcised, just as Peter had been to the circumcised,** the apostles in Jerusalem recognized he was entrusted with preaching the true gospel. At that point the Judaizers' contention that Paul was preaching a deviant message was refuted once and for all. As Luke explains, not only did the Jerusalem Council vindicate Paul's message of grace apart from law but they entrusted him with the primary responsibility of reporting their decision to the churches in Antioch, Syria, and Cilicia—areas where his work had been severely criticized by the Judaizers (Acts 15:22-24).

Because some versions, such as the King James, have translated "the gospel *of* the uncircumcised" and "*of* the circumcised," many liberal interpreters have suggested (for this and other reasons) that Peter and Paul preached different messages. But that idea is disproved by Galatians 1:6-9, by the decision of the Jerusalem Council, and by Greek grammar. The Greek article (*tēs*) is here an objective genitive and does not indicate definition ("of") but direction (**to**), as in our text and most modern translations.

For He who effectually worked for Peter in his apostleship to the circumcised, Paul continues, **effectually worked for me also to the Gentiles.** The same Holy Spirit (**He**) who energized (**worked,** from *energeō,* to be at work, to produce results) and empowered **Peter** energized and empowered **Paul,** and the Spirit has but one gospel. When Paul returned to Jerusalem several years later, "the brethren received [him and those with him] gladly," and when he "began to relate one by one the things which God had done among the Gentiles through his ministry," James and the other elders "began glorifying God" (Acts 21:17-20). After the Jerusalem Council there was never a question about Paul's message or apostleship. In his second letter Peter highly commended Paul as a wise and beloved brother and ranked Paul's letters with "the rest of the Scriptures" (2 Pet. 3:15-16).

Recognizing the grace that had been given to Paul, the other apostles and the church at large could only conclude that this man was a divinely commissioned and blessed instrument of God. Only God's **grace**—His free, sovereign, and undeserved blessing—could account for the mighty spreading of the gospel and building up of the church that the Lord had accomplished through this mortal.

PAUL'S COMMENDATION

James and Cephas and John, who were reputed to be pillars, gave to me and Barnabas the right hand of fellowship, that we might go to the Gentiles, and

they to the circumcised. They only asked us to remember the poor—the very thing I also was eager to do. (2:9b-10)

Still again Paul refers to the reputation of **James and Cephas** (Peter) **and John**—those **who were reputed to be pillars** (a Jewish term used to refer to great teachers). As already mentioned, the somewhat sarcastic reference does not reflect against these men but against the Judaizers. Because those false teachers apparently used the term **pillars** (emphasizing their role in establishing and supporting the church) when referring to the three Jerusalem leaders, Paul throws the term back in their faces. He demonstrates to them and to the Galatian believers they were trying to turn against him that he was in perfect doctrinal harmony with those three **pillars** and with all the other apostles and elders at Jerusalem.

He not only was in doctrinal harmony with them but in personal harmony with them as well. There is only one gospel, and those five men (who wrote 21 of the 27 New Testament books) demonstrate that truth. They **gave to me and Barnabas the right hand of fellowship,** Paul says as he continues to confound the false claims of the Judaizers. In the Near East, to clasp **the right hand** of a person was to make a solemn vow of friendship and was a mark **of fellowship,** or partnership. The "pillars" at Jerusalem recognized Paul not only as a true preacher and teacher of the gospel but also as a beloved partner with them in Christ's service. They had different fields of service—Paul and Barnabas ministered primarily **to the Gentiles** and the Jerusalem leaders primarily **to the circumcised**—but they proclaimed the same gospel and served the same Lord in the power of His Spirit. That act of affirmation both of Paul and of his message was a devastating blow to the Judaizers. In fact, Paul's apostolate to the Gentiles was recognized as the equal of Peter's apostolate to the Jews.

The only request made of Paul and Barnabas at Jerusalem was that they **remember the poor.** The request was not doctrinal but practical, a reminder about the special needs of believers in Judea, especially Jerusalem. Even before the widespread famine (see Acts 11:28) for which Paul was called to bring relief, the Jerusalem church faced a serious problem of feeding and caring for its members. Its ranks were swelled by hundreds, perhaps thousands, of believers who had been converted while visiting the city and who then decided to stay there rather than return home. Many had little money, and they soon discovered that, because they were Christians, it was sometimes difficult to find employment. In the early days of the church those who had money and other possessions generously shared what they had "with all, as anyone might have need" (Acts 2:45). But those resources were rapidly depleted as the number of converts grew. For many years, therefore, the church at Jerusalem had been economically pressed.

To take care of the poor is not only a practical but a spiritual responsibility, because to forsake that responsibility is to disobey God's Word. "Whoever has this world's goods," John declares, "and beholds his brother in need and closes his heart against him, how does the love of God abide in him?" (1 John 3:17). James says that it is a sham believer who says to "a brother or sister . . . without clothing and in need of daily food, . . . 'Go in peace, be warmed and be filled,' and yet [does] not give them what is necessary for their body" (James 2:15-16; cf. Ex. 23:10-11; 30:15; Lev. 19:10; Deut. 15:7-11; Jer. 22:16; Amos 2:6-7; Luke 6:36, 38; 2 Cor. 8-9).

Paul was therefore **eager to do** all he could to fulfill the request of James, Peter, and John, as his numerous and constant collections for the poverty-stricken saints in Judea attested. His command that "if anyone will not work, neither let him eat" (2 Thess. 3:10) pertained to the lazy, not the helpless and needy. He continually encouraged believers who were more prosperous to give financial aid to fellow believers who were in need; and he heartily commended those who were generous (Acts 11:29-30; 24:17; Rom. 15:25-26; 1 Cor. 16:1-4; 2 Cor. 8:1-6; 9:1-5, 12). "For if the Gentiles have shared in their [the Jerusalem saints'] spiritual things," Paul explained to the Roman church, "they are indebted to minister to them also in material things" (Rom. 15:27).

Justification by Faith Alone (2:11-21)

5

But when Cephas came to Antioch, I opposed him to his face, because he stood condemned. For prior to the coming of certain men from James, he used to eat with the Gentiles; but when they came, he began to withdraw and hold himself aloof, fearing the party of the circumcision. And the rest of the Jews joined him in hypocrisy, with the result that even Barnabas was carried away by their hypocrisy. But when I saw that they were not straightforward about the truth of the gospel, I said to Cephas in the presence of all, "If you, being a Jew, live like the Gentiles and not like the Jews, how is it that you compel the Gentiles to live like Jews? We are Jews by nature, and not sinners from among the Gentiles; nevertheless knowing that a man is not justified by the works of the Law but through faith in Christ Jesus, even we have believed in Christ Jesus, that we may be justified by faith in Christ, and not by the works of the Law; since by the works of the Law shall no flesh be justified. But if, while seeking to be justified in Christ, we ourselves have also been found sinners, is Christ then a minister of sin? May it never be! For if I rebuild what I have once destroyed, I prove myself to be a transgressor. For through the Law I died to the Law, that I might live to God. I have been crucified with Christ; and it is no longer I who live, but Christ lives in me; and the life which I now live in the flesh I live by faith in the Son of God, who

**loved me, and delivered Himself up for me. I do not nullify the grace of God;
for if righteousness comes through the Law, then Christ died needlessly."**
(2:11-21)

Guilt is a universal plague of sinful mankind. Every person feels guilty.
Consequently every person tries in some way to alleviate his guilt. Primitive tribesmen
seek to assuage their guilt by appeasing the imagined gods who are supposedly angry
with them. Cultured, sophisticated people may take the escape route of psycho-
analysis or some other form of human counseling. Some people try to salve their guilt
by positive thinking and self-confident, self-indulgent living. Others try to escape
through sex, alcohol, or drugs.

Millennia before Jesus Christ came to earth and died for man's sin, God
foreshadowed His perfect sacrifice through the offering of slain animals. He
apparently began by instructing Adam to offer blood sacrifices as symbols pointing to
the true and effective shedding of Christ's blood on the cross. The sacrifice of a ram,
goat, lamb, or other animal never had power to forgive and cleanse sin—nor was it
ever meant to. Such sacrifices were only outward, symbolic acts of obedience that,
unless accompanied by a humble and contrite heart, were not acceptable to God.
Without reverential trust in the God to whom he offered the sacrifice, the offerer
engaged only in meaningless ritual (Isa. 29:13).

When Cain offered his sacrifice of grain to the Lord, he sinned both by
disobediently bringing the wrong kind of offering and by offering it in the wrong
spirit. Rather than bringing an animal sacrifice as God had obviously commanded, he
brought the fruit of his own labor, proudly supposing that this offering of
disobedience was just as acceptable to God as the one He had prescribed. His was the
first act of works righteousness, the forerunner of every such act since his time. Every
person of every era who has tried to come to God on the basis of his own merits and
works, or by some humanly designed religious prescriptions, has followed in the
unbelieving, grace-rejecting steps of Cain. By rejecting God's prescribed animal
sacrifice, Cain rejected God's provision of substitutionary salvation in His Son toward
which that blood offering pointed.

Abel, on the other hand, by obediently offering the blood sacrifice God
required, in faith leaped across the centuries and touched the cross. God accepted his
offering not because it had any spiritual benefit in itself but because it was presented in
faith and obedience.

Since the time of Cain and Abel the two divergent lines of works and faith have
characterized man's religious life. The person who follows the way of man, whatever it
is, follows Satan's lie and the way of Cain. The person who follows God's way follows
the way of Abel, the way of grace and forgiveness.

Those two lines of approach to God can be followed throughout the Old
Testament. The builders of the tower of Babel followed the unbelieving and rebellious
way of Cain, whereas Noah and his family followed the believing and obedient way of

Abel. The vast majority of the ancient world followed the ungodly way of Cain, whereas Abraham and his household followed the godly way of Abel. Within the nation of Israel there were always the same two lines of human achievement and divine accomplishment, of trusting in what man can do for God or of trusting in what God has done for man. Those who follow the narrow way of faith are always a minority, but for that faithful remnant, God's blessings never cease and His promises never fail.

At the time Jesus was born the believing remnant included Mary, Joseph, Elizabeth, Zacharias, Anna, Simeon, and many others whose names are unknown to us. They placed their trust in the God of Israel for their salvation and implicitly believed the Old Testament as His divinely-revealed Word. They faithfully and willingly conformed their behavior to God's prescribed ceremonies and standards, all the while demonstrating that their trust was in the Lord Himself, not in the keeping of those ceremonies and standards, important as such outward testimony of obedience was under the Old Covenant.

But when Jesus was born the vast majority of Israelites, whether in Palestine or other parts of the Roman Empire, continued to pervert and add to Old Testament revelation and to put their trust in themselves, looking to their own goodness and accomplishments to make them acceptable to God. The great body of rabbinic traditions was grounded in works righteousness, in the idea of attaining merit before God through strict observance of an almost endless list of man-made regulations and ceremonies. Most Jewish leaders, epitomized by the self-righteous scribes and Pharisees, proudly believed their religious works placed them in God's special favor and gained them forgiveness for their sins.

It was from among that vast group of legalistic Jews that the Judaizers arose, claiming to follow Christ but teaching that a Gentile had to be circumcised and follow the Mosaic law before he could be saved and that all believers, Jew and Gentile alike, had to continue observance of that law in order to maintain their relation to God. Their teaching not only corrupted the gospel but also the teaching of the Old Testament, in which the way of salvation was always and only by obedient faith in God. At no time in history has a person been saved by his own merit. Both before and during the time of the Mosaic covenant men were saved by faith alone. Abel, Enoch, Noah, Abraham, Sarah, Isaac, Jacob, Joseph, Moses, Rahab, the godly judges, kings prophets, and every other Old Testament saint were saved only on the basis of faith. All of those people, whether man or woman, Jew or Gentile, "gained approval through their faith" (cf. Heb. 11:1-39).

The Judaizers were therefore not teaching Old Testament doctrine but the cardinal doctrine of Satan, that a person can by his own goodness and works gain favor with God. That is why Paul referred to the Judaizers as "dogs, . . . evil workers, . . . the false circumcision" (Phil. 3:2). "False circumcision" translates *katatomē,* which is used only there in the New Testament and refers to pagan sexual mutilation. Paul was declaring that for an unbeliever, no matter what his Jewish pedigree and attainments might be, circumcision amounted to no more than pagan mutilation. "For he is not a Jew who is one outwardly; neither is circumcision that which is outward in the flesh. But he is a Jew who is one inwardly; and circumcision is that which is of the heart, by the Spirit, not by the letter" (Rom. 2:28-29). Since the coming of Christ only Christians can be "heart circumcised." "We are the true circumcision," Paul explained to the Philippian believers, "who worship in the Spirit of God and glory in Christ Jesus and put no confidence in the flesh" (Phil. 3:3).

No person of his day had more reason than Paul to boast in his Jewish heritage and accomplishments. He was "circumcised the eighth day, of the nation of Israel, of the tribe of Benjamin, a Hebrew of Hebrews; as to the Law, a Pharisee; . . . as to the righteousness which is in the Law, found blameless. But whatever things were gain to me, those things I have counted as loss for the sake of Christ. More than that, I count all things to be loss in view of the surpassing value of knowing Christ Jesus my Lord, for whom I have suffered the loss of all things, and count them but rubbish in order that I may gain Christ, and may be found in Him, not having a righteousness of my own derived from the Law, but that which is through faith in Christ, the righteousness which comes from God on the basis of faith" (Phil. 3:5-9).

The Judaizers recognized Jesus as the Messiah, but because their view of the Messiah was corrupt so was their view of Jesus. They did not look to the Messiah as the Lamb of God who would take away their sin, because they did not believe they had sin that demanded such sacrifice in order to be forgiven. As circumcised, ceremonial Jews they were convinced they already had the full favor of God and were spiritually and morally acceptable to Him just as they were. That common Jewish view is reflected in the argument of the book of Hebrews, in which the writer goes to great lengths to persuade his Jewish readers that the Messiah (Christ) is superior to the prophets, to angels, and even to Moses (Heb. 1:1–3:6). He was not simply another great Jewish leader. He was of a completely different order, the very Son of God and Savior of the world, whose saving sacrifice was necessary for anyone to be right with God.

In Galatians 2:11-21, the scene changes from Jerusalem and the council there to Syrian Antioch, where the first church in a Gentile area was established and where Paul and Barnabas served as co-pastors, with help from three other men (see Acts 13:1). Paul continues the defense of his apostolic credentials by reporting his exercise of authority on one occasion even over Peter, whom most believers in the early church considered to be the preeminent apostle. And Paul did not hesitate to correct him when he was out of line with the truth. First he briefly explains Peter's deviation from the gospel and then, from that platform, presents it in its true form.

Peter's Deviation

But when Cephas came to Antioch, I opposed him to his face, because he stood condemned. For prior to the coming of certain men from James, he used to eat with the Gentiles; but when they came, he began to withdraw and hold himself aloof, fearing the party of the circumcision. And the rest of the Jews joined him in hypocrisy, with the result that even Barnabas was carried away by their hypocrisy. (2:11-13)

THE CLASH

But when Cephas came to Antioch, I opposed him to his face, because he stood condemned. (2:11)

Because the Judaizers had told believers in the Galatian churches that Paul was not a true apostle, the incident mentioned in this verse is especially significant. Paul not only was equal to the other apostles but had on this occasion even reprimanded Peter (**Cephas**), the one who was recognizably the leading apostle among the Twelve. Both Peter and Paul had experienced salvation by grace through faith, both were directly chosen by the resurrected Jesus Christ to be apostles, and both had been mightily used by the Holy Spirit in establishing and teaching the church. The book of Acts can be divided between the early church ministry that centered on Peter (1-12) and that which centered on Paul (13-28). But in **Antioch** these two men of God came into head-on collision.

Opposed is from *anistēmi,* which carries the meaning of hindering or forbidding, and was usually applied to defensive measures. By his withdrawal from the Gentiles, Peter had, in effect, joined the Judaizers in belittling Paul's inspired teaching, especially the doctrine of salvation by God's grace alone working through man's faith alone. Peter knew better, and Paul **opposed him to his face, because he stood condemned.**

Peter was not **condemned** in the sense of losing his salvation but in the sense of being guilty of sin by taking a position he knew was wrong. He no doubt also **stood condemned** as a sinner in the eyes of the Gentile believers in Antioch, who, because they were well-grounded in the gospel of grace, were perplexed and deeply hurt by his ostracism of them.

Before Peter's compromise with the Judaizers could do serious damage in the Antioch church, God used Paul to nip the error in the bud. In so doing He also provided Paul with perhaps his most convincing proof of apostolic authority. God has a purpose even in the worst of circumstances, and what could have been a tragedy He used for His glory and for the strengthening of His church.

THE CAUSE

For prior to the coming of certain men from James, he used to eat with the Gentiles; but when they came, he began to withdraw and hold himself aloof, fearing the party of the circumcision. (2:12)

Peter had been in Antioch for some time **prior to the coming of certain men from James,** and during that time **he used to eat with the Gentiles.** The **certain men** were Judaizers who had come to Antioch claiming to be **from James** but were not. As leader of the Jerusalem church, **James** (our Lord's half brother) had summarized the decision of the council against the Judaizers, saying, "It is my judgment that we do not trouble those who are turning to God from among the

Gentiles" (Acts 15:19). These **men** were of **the party of the circumcision** and not only taught a false gospel but also made false claims of support by the Jerusalem apostles and elders. Like Peter, **James** at times had difficulty giving up his lifelong adherence to the Mosaic rituals and regulations (see Acts 21:18-26), and he perhaps still had remnants of prejudice against Gentiles. But he would hardly have sent a delegation of heretics to Antioch to undermine the true gospel and cause the church there nothing but trouble. He would never have been the cause of discord and chaos where there was the pursuit of such Spirit-induced harmony and unity.

The imperfect tense of the Greek verb indicates that Peter's eating **with the Gentiles** was continuous, that is, habitual and regular over some period of time. He ate whatever was set before him with whoever was sitting beside him. He had no doubt participated in numerous love feasts with Gentile believers and joined them in the Lord's Supper. Until the **men from James** came to Antioch, he was participating with the church in a model fellowship of Jewish and Gentile believers who freely expressed and deeply cherished their love and liberty in Christ.

It is only a small digression within the broad boundaries of our discussion to say that the Christian church cannot be what it is called to be when ritual, race, class, or other distinctions separate members from each other. The labels men put on themselves and on others are irrelevant to God, and should also be irrelevant to His people. Before salvation, every person is equally separated from God, and after salvation every person is equally reconciled to God. Believers "are all sons of God through faith in Christ Jesus. . . . There is neither Jew nor Greek, there is neither slave nor free man, there is neither male nor female; for [they] are all one in Christ Jesus" (Gal. 3:26, 28). Because believers are all children of God, they are all brothers and sisters, with no exceptions or distinctions.

The claim of some Christian groups that the Bible forbids the mingling of races is totally spurious, and such a claim is a blight on the church, an offense before God, and even a reproach before the world. It is the antithesis of New Testament teaching. If Paul were alive today he would stand as steadfastly against such prejudiced, unscriptural teaching as he did against Peter and the others in Antioch who allowed their prejudices and fears to compromise God's truth.

Better than any other apostle, Peter should have known that in Christ all foods were clean and all believers equal. He had heard Jesus explain that "whatever goes into the man from the outside cannot defile him; because it does not go into his heart" (Mark 7:18-19). He had experienced the unique and dramatic vision of the unclean animals and the related encounter with the Gentile Cornelius, after which he declared, "I most certainly understand now that God is not one to show partiality" (Acts 10:34). At the Jerusalem Council Peter forcefully opposed the Judaizers, saying, "God, who knows the heart, bore witness to them [the Gentiles, v. 7] giving them the Holy Spirit, just as He also did to us; and He made no distinction between us and them, cleansing their hearts by faith. Now therefore why do you put God to the test by placing upon the neck of the disciples a yoke which neither our fathers nor we have been able to bear? But we believe that we are saved through the grace of the Lord Jesus, in the same way as they also are" (Acts 15:8-11).

Yet when the Judaizers came to Antioch, Peter **began to withdraw and hold**

himself aloof from the Gentiles, **fearing the party of the circumcision. Withdraw** is from *hupostellō,* a term used for strategic military disengagement. Polibius used it to describe troops drawing back from the enemy in order to secure shelter and safety. The imperfect tense may indicate that Peter's withdrawal was gradual and, if so, suggests the idea of sneaky retreat. Acquiescing to both the ritualism and racism of the Jews, he began to drift away from his Gentile brethren and stopped accepting their invitations to dinner. He found excuses not to join with them in other activities and finally held **himself aloof** from them altogether.

The old Peter—weak, fearful, and vacillating—had come to the fore again. Here was the same Peter who under divine inspiration declared Jesus to be "the Christ, the Son of the living God" but who a short while later rebuked his Lord for saying that He must suffer and die (Matt. 16:16, 22). Here is the same Peter who boldly declared he would die rather than deny his Lord but who, before the night was out, had denied Him three times (Mark 14:29-31, 66-72). Here was the same Peter who was called to preach but who disobediently went back to fishing even after he had encountered the resurrected Christ (John 21:3).

Peter was not **fearing the party of the circumcision** because they might threaten his life or freedom. The Judaizers claimed to be Christians and therefore obviously had no authority from the Sanhedrin to arrest, imprison, or put anyone to death—as the men did who stoned Stephen and as Paul himself once had done. The most the Judaizers could have done against Peter was to ridicule him and malign him in Jerusalem, as their fellow Judaizers would later malign Paul in Galatia. Peter was afraid of just that—losing popularity and prestige with a group of self-righteous hypocrites whose doctrines were heretical and whose tactics were deceitful.

Peter was not unlike most Christians in finding it difficult to be consistent in spiritual commitment. He would show great courage and conviction and then stumble. He would staunchly defend the faith and then succumb to compromise. When he did that in Antioch he played into the hands of the Judaizers, who must have been elated to have drawn this great apostle into their camp, by practice if not by precept.

Christians who refuse to share the Lord's table with other believers because of fear and prejudice fall into the same spiritual error as Peter did at Antioch. And in so doing they fracture the divine unity of Christ's own Body, the church.

THE CONSEQUENCE

And the rest of the Jews joined him in hypocrisy, with the result that even Barnabas was carried away by their hypocrisy. (2:13)

Peter not only withdrew from the Gentile believers himself but, by example, indirectly induced **the rest of the Jews** to join **him in hypocrisy.** The separation became so widespread and influential **that even** the godly **Barnabas,** who at this time was one of the pastors at Antioch, **was carried away** into the sin. Paul and **Barnabas** had recently been on a fruitful missionary journey together, had gone with each other to the Jerusalem Council (see the previous chapter), and were now co-pastors at Antioch. They had taught together, prayed together, ministered together, and suffered together. They were the closest of friends and loved each other deeply. It was **Barnabas** who had first befriended and defended Paul when he went to Jerusalem shortly after his conversion (Acts 9:27). Many times **Barnabas** had heard Paul preach the gospel of salvation by faith alone and had preached it many times himself. But even he **was carried away by** the legalistic **hypocrisy** of Peter and the others. It may have been Barnabas's hypocrisy on this occasion that began the eventual rift with Paul that a short while later resulted in their separation over taking John Mark on the next journey (Acts 15:37-40).

Peter was a natural leader, and his public action invariably took others with him. When he acted in his own wisdom the result was tragic, and when other believers put their faith in him as a man the tragedy was compounded. The effect on the Antioch church was disastrous.

The Greek term behind **hypocrisy** originally referred to an actor wearing a mask to indicate a particular mood or type of character. A hypocrite is someone who, like a Greek actor, masks his true self.

Peter and the other Jewish believers who withdrew with him knew that what they were doing was wrong, but they were intimidated by the Judaizers into going against the truth of their convictions and consciences. In seeking to please those hypocrites they became hypocrites themselves, and in so doing brought heartache to their Gentile brothers and to their Lord.

From Peter's failure at Antioch several important truths can be learned. The first is that even uniquely gifted ministers of the gospel can commit serious transgressions, sometimes becoming guilty of the very errors and sins they once strongly preached against.

In order to maintain the doctrine of the infallibility of the popes, who are claimed by the Roman system to be successors of Peter, some Catholic theologians have insisted that the Peter at Antioch was not the apostle. But he was the same Peter who preached the Spirit-empowered sermon at Pentecost and through whom the crippled man outside the Temple was healed. Despite his divine calling and giftedness, he manifested feet of clay.

Second, we learn that faithfulness involves more than believing the right doctrine. Right doctrine without right behavior always produces hypocrisy.

Third, we learn that truth is more important than outward harmony and peace. Christian fellowship and unity are built on truth, never falsehood. No matter what the beneficial prospect might seem to be from a human perspective, compromise can do nothing but weaken the church. Peace that is preserved by compromising God's truth is the pseudo-peace of the world and is not of God. "The bond of peace" (Phil. 4:3) is not peace at any price but peace based on God's Word and established by God's Spirit.

Fourth, we see that situation ethics is ungodly ethics. God's Word, not a given human situation, determines what is right and wrong. Christians do not make truth; and a group of believers, no matter how large or influential—even if they were to be apostles—who take a wrong position or indulge in a wrong practice are still wrong. Neither expediency, falsely defined love, nor majority vote have any bearing on truth and righteousness.

Fifth, we learn that falsehood is not to be ignored, regardless of the consequences that opposition to it may bring. When the falsehood strikes at the heart of the gospel, as did the heresy of the Judaizers, opposition is all the more imperative. Even leading Christians "who continue in sin" are to be rebuked "in the presence of all, so that the rest also may be fearful of sinning" (1 Tim. 5:20).

PAUL'S DOCTRINE

But when I saw that they were not straightforward about the truth of the gospel, I said to Cephas in the presence of all, "If you, being a Jew, live like the Gentiles and not like the Jews, how is it that you compel the Gentiles to live like Jews? We are Jews by nature, and not sinners from among the Gentiles; nevertheless knowing that a man is not justified by the works of the Law but through faith in Christ Jesus, even we have believed in Christ Jesus, that we may be justified by faith in Christ, and not by the works of the Law; since by the works of the Law shall no flesh be justified. But if, while seeking to be justified in Christ, we ourselves have also been found sinners, is Christ then a minister of sin? May it never be! For if I rebuild what I have once destroyed, I prove myself to be a transgressor. For through the Law I died to the Law, that I might live to God. I have been crucified with Christ; and it is no longer I who live, but Christ lives in me; and the life which I now live in the flesh I live by faith in the Son of God, who loved me, and delivered Himself up for me. I do not nullify the grace of God; for if righteousness comes through the Law, then Christ died needlessly." (2:14-21)

The actions of Peter, Barnabas, and the other Jewish believers in Antioch were not simply a matter of personal hypocrisy. Their capitulation to the Judaizers, by example if not by doctrine, was fracturing the church. The fact that Peter and Barnabas were spiritual leaders made the matter immeasurably worse. For years they had taught salvation by faith alone, and they had exemplified that teaching in their lives. The Antioch church had become a model of Jewish-Gentile fellowship and harmony, and almost overnight it had become the opposite.

HIS REACTION

But when I saw that they were not straightforward about the truth of the gospel, I said to Cephas in the presence of all, "If you, being a Jew, live like the Gentiles and not like the Jews, how is it that you compel the Gentiles to live like Jews? We are Jews by nature, and not sinners from among the Gentiles. (2:14-15)

As already noted, the withdrawal of the Jewish believers from the Gentiles was likely gradual; but as soon as Paul realized what was happening he immediately reacted against it. **When [he] saw they were not straightforward about the truth of the gospel,** he sharply rebuked Peter (**Cephas**). As an apostle Peter was the most accountable, and it was his wrong example that had drawn the others into the destructive hypocrisy.

Straightforward is from *orthopodeō,* a compound of *orthos* (straight) and *pous* (foot) that means to walk straight, or uprightly. One scholar translates verse 14*a* as, "They were not walking on the straight path towards the truth of the gospel." In withdrawing from their Gentile brethren, Peter and the others were not living parallel to God's Word, not walking a straight spiritual course.

Because Peter's offense was public, Paul rebuked him **in the presence of all,** unmasking his hypocrisy before the whole congregation. Every believer in Antioch, and doubtlessly many unbelievers as well, knew that Peter was no longer associating with Gentiles as he had once done so freely and openly. Augustine said, "It is not advantageous to correct in secret an error which occurred publicly." Unless the public sin of a believer is dealt with publicly, people will think the church does not take sin seriously and therefore gives tacit approval of it. A church that does not discipline sinning members (including the most prominent members) loses its credibility, because it does not take seriously its own doctrines and standards. A child who is not disciplined when he does wrong soon concludes that his parent's standards are not really very important, because they are not enforced.

After taking care to determine by several witnesses that a charge against an elder is true, Paul told Timothy, the elder should be rebuked "in the presence of all, so that the rest also may be fearful of sinning" (1 Tim. 5:20). Paul's rebuke of Peter shows that no Christian leader, regardless of his stature, is beyond discipline by the Body. Public sin demands public rebuke.

"If you, being a Jew," Paul said, **"live like the Gentiles and not like the Jews, how is it that you compel the Gentiles to live like Jews?"** In contrast to Peter's hypocrisy, Paul's indictment *was* straightforward. He simply pointed out the obvious inconsistency of Peter's behavior in Antioch. He reminded him that when he first arrived there, Peter had freely fellowshiped with Gentile believers and regularly ate with them (v. 12). He had openly visited in their homes and joined them in love feasts and Communion, showing no evidence of legalism or prejudice. He had lived **like the Gentiles and not like the Jews,** who were known throughout the world for their separatism.

Josephus reports that the Midianite woman who tried to seduce the Israelites said to them, "Your kinds of food are peculiar to yourselves, and your kinds of drink are common to no other." For centuries Jews had been known for their strict laws and separation from Gentiles. Under the Old Covenant God had established certain dietary laws and other restrictions for the purpose of keeping His chosen people from intermingling and intermarrying with pagan Gentiles and being corrupted by their idolatry and immorality. But during and after the time of the Exile, rabbinic tradition had made countless additions and amendments to the biblical regulations. For example, Jews were allowed to buy meat from a Gentile market only if the animal had been slaughtered by a Jew and had not been used in a pagan religious ceremony.

After his vision of the unclean animals and his experience with Cornelius, Peter had no longer lived **like the Jews,** having finally come to realize that even the God-given ceremonial separation taught in the Old Testament was no longer valid. But under the influence of the Judaizers in Antioch he faltered and slipped back into the old ways. When the winds of legalism blew in, he adjusted his sails accordingly and was blown along with them.

Paul had no desire to lord it over Peter or to build up his own reputation at the expense of a fellow apostle. His motive was not to humiliate Peter but to correct him in a serious error that had caused many other believers to stumble with him. He could tolerate nothing that threatened the integrity of the gospel, especially if that threat came from a prominent and influential leader such as Peter.

HIS STATEMENT

We are Jews by nature, and not sinners from among the Gentiles; nevertheless knowing that a man is not justified by the works of the Law but through faith in Christ Jesus, even we have believed in Christ Jesus, that we may be justified by faith in Christ, and not by the works of the Law; since by the works of the Law shall no flesh be justified. (2:15-16)

The heart of man's spiritual dilemma is that he is incapable of overcoming the total sinfulness that separates him from the holy God. Job's friend Bildad asked, "How then can a man be just with God?" (Job 25:4). How can a guilty and condemned sinner be made righteous and thereby acceptable to God? The provision of justification by faith is God's answer to that dilemma and need.

Paul's rebuke of Peter culminated in one of the most forceful statements in the New Testament on the doctrine of justification—the very doctrine that Peter and the others were in effect renouncing by their hypocritical separation from Gentile believers. In effect, Paul was saying, "Peter, I am rebuking you because you are violating the cardinal truth of Christianity. By your behavior you are condoning works-righteousness, a system of legalism that is contrary even to the covenant given by Moses, not to mention the New Covenant given by our Lord Jesus Christ."

In setting forth the true doctrine of justification Paul first states what it is (vv. 15-16) and then gives a defense of it (vv. 17-21). As noted in a previous chapter, because of his intense and emotional concern for the integrity of the gospel and the spiritual welfare of the Galatian believers, Paul's grammar in this epistle is sometimes difficult to reconstruct and his logic difficult to follow, though his meaning is always clear.

We is used four times in verses 15-17 and refers to Paul, Peter, and all other Jewish Christians. The first part of his argument here is that, even **we who are Jews by nature . . . have believed in Christ Jesus.** "As Jews," he was indicating, "we of all people know what it is to live by the system of law. We know the law as a way of life, what it is to function continually under the demands of religious rituals and regulations. Yet even **we** were saved by believing **in Christ Jesus,** not by the law. And if **we,** as **Jews,** cannot be saved by the law, how can we expect **sinners from among the Gentiles** to be?"

In referring to **the Gentiles** as **sinners,** Paul was not using the term in the behavioral sense of public immorality (as it is often used in the gospels), but in the legal sense in which it was frequently used by Jews. In the minds of most Jews, Gentiles were **sinners** by nature because they had no law to guide them in right living and in pleasing God. But with or without the law, Paul was saying, no person is saved who has not **believed in Christ Jesus.**

At the Jerusalem Council Peter declared that same truth in response to the Judaizers. "Why do you put God to the test by placing upon the neck of the disciples a yoke which neither our fathers nor we have been able to bear? But we believe that we are saved through the grace of the Lord Jesus, in the same way as they [the Gentiles] also are" (Acts 15:10-11).

Martin Luther said that if the article of justification by faith is lost, all Christian doctrine is lost. In this last section of chapter 2 Paul was inspired to introduce this most essential doctrine in the epistle, a doctrine he had preached and explained to the Galatians on many occasions. He uses the verb form of justification (*dikaioō*) four times in verses 16-17 and the noun form (*dikaiosunē*) once in verse 21, where it is rendered "righteousness." In the New Testament these and other forms of the same Greek term are variously translated by such English words as justify, justification, righteousness, just, righteous, and justified.

The basic term was originally used forensically of a judge's declaring an accused person not guilty and right before the law. It was the opposite of being declared guilty and condemned. Throughout Scripture justification refers to God's declaring a sinner to be guiltless on the basis of faith in Him. It is the free and gracious act by which God declares a sinner right with Himself—forgiving, pardoning, restoring, and accepting him on the basis of nothing but trust in the Person and work of His Son, Jesus Christ.

Knowing that a man is not justified by the works of the Law but through faith in Christ Jesus, Paul continues, **even we have believed in Christ Jesus, that we may be justified by faith in Christ, and not by the works of the Law; since by the works of the Law shall no flesh be justified.**

No amount of law-keeping can make a person righteous, because the root of sinfulness is in the fallenness of man's heart, not in actions. Man's basic problem is in what he is, not in what he does. Sinful acts are but the outward expression of a depraved nature that contains sinful thoughts. A person who hates is inwardly a murderer, whether or not he ever takes another person's life (Matt. 5:22). A man who has immoral thoughts about women is an adulterer, whether or not he ever commits the physical act of adultery (5:28).

Consequently, no amount of **works of the Law** can save a person, because even the best of human works cannot change the nature of the person doing them. "We know that whatever the Law says, it speaks to those who are under the Law, that every mouth may be closed, and all the world may become accountable to God; because by the works of the Law no flesh will be justified in His sight" (Rom. 3:19-20). The law is important as a mirror to show us our sinfulness; but it can only reveal sin, not remove it. "But now apart from the Law the righteousness of God has been manifested, being witnessed by the Law and the Prophets, even the righteousness of God through faith in Jesus Christ for all those who believe; for there is no distinction; for all have sinned and fall short of the glory of God, being justified as a gift by His grace through the redemption which is in Christ Jesus. . . . For we maintain that a man is justified by faith apart from works of the Law" (3:21-24, 28).

Only **faith in Christ Jesus** can bring a person the gracious gift of righteousness that provides forgiveness and salvation. **Faith in Christ** is not mere intellectual assent to the fact that Jesus died and rose for man's sin but is personal trust in His death to remove and forgive one's own sins. It is total commitment to submit to Him as Lord (cf. James 4:7).

Three times in Galatians 2:16 Paul declares that salvation is only through faith in Christ and not by law. The first statement is general: **a man is not justified by the works of the Law but through faith in Christ Jesus.** The second is personal: **even we have believed in Christ Jesus, that we may be justified by faith in Christ, and not by the works of the Law.** The third is universal: **by the works of the Law shall no flesh be justified** (cf. Ps. 143:2). All three affirm the same great reality.

All claims that salvation is through belief in Jesus Christ plus something else are blasphemous, satanic lies. There can be no effective or acceptable human addition to Christ's work. This passage is as forceful and unequivocal a statement of the doctrine of salvation by faith alone as can be found in Scripture. First Paul establishes it on the basis of his apostolic authority. Second, he establishes it on the basis of his own experience. And third, he establishes it on the basis of God's Word in the Old Testament.

HIS DEFENSE

But if, while seeking to be justified in Christ, we ourselves have also been found sinners, is Christ then a minister of sin? May it never be! For if I rebuild what I have once destroyed, I prove myself to be a transgressor. For through the Law I died to the Law, that I might live to God. I have been crucified with Christ; and it is no longer I who live, but Christ lives in me; and the life which I now live in the flesh I live by faith in the Son of God, who loved me, and delivered Himself up for me. I do not nullify the grace of God; for if righteousness comes through the Law, then Christ died needlessly." (2:17-21)

By their behavior, Peter and the other Jewish Christians at Antioch had given approval to the Judaizers' idea that it was necessary for a Gentile to keep the Jewish rituals before he could become a Christian. Paul's defense of justification by faith in verses 17-21 continues his contradiction of this Judaistic legalism to which Peter and the others had succumbed.

It is crucial to understand that, as in the previous two verses, **we** refers to Jewish Christians. **But if, while seeking to be justified in Christ, we ourselves,** as Jewish Christians, **have also been found sinners,** Paul asks rhetorically, **is Christ then a minister of sin?**

His first point was to show that, if the Judaizers were correct in their doctrine that believers are saved in part by keeping the ceremonial law of Moses and continue to be bound by that law to maintain their salvation, then, even before the Judaizers arrived in Antioch, Peter, Barnabas, and all the other Jewish believers, including Paul, had fallen back into the category of **sinners** by having freely eaten and fellowshiped with Gentile Christians.

Paul's second point was even more devastating. "If you became **sinners** because of fellowshiping with your Gentile brothers," he implies, "then **Christ** Himself became **a minister of sin,** did he not?" How? Jesus had clearly taught that no food can spiritually contaminate a person, because food cannot affect the heart (Mark 7:19). Through the vision of the unclean animals and the dramatic conversion and anointing of Cornelius, the Lord had given Peter direct evidence that Gentile believers are in every way equal to Jewish believers (Acts 10). On many other occasions and in many other ways Jesus had taught that all those who belong to Him are one with Him and therefore one with each other. Shortly before His arrest, trial, and crucifixion, Jesus earnestly and repeatedly prayed to His Father that those who believed in Him "may all be one; even as Thou, Father, art in Me, and I in Thee, that they also may be in Us . . . that they may be one, just as We are one; I in them and Thou in Me, that they may be perfected in unity" (John 17:21-23).

But if the Judaizers were right, Paul pointed out, Jesus was wrong; if they taught the truth, He had taught falsehood and was thereby **a minister of sin!** Such an accusation must have shaken Peter to his bones. To be called a hypocrite stung enough, but to be called a sinner was unthinkable, and to be accused of making Jesus **a minister of sin** was shocking and repulsive. Yet the logic of Paul's argument was inescapable. By his actions, Peter had in effect condemned Jesus Christ. He therefore had to forsake his Judaistic sympathies or continue to make His Lord a liar.

To his own question Paul immediately responded, **May it never be!** It must have been painful to Paul to suggest even hypothetically that Christ could participate in, much less promote, sin. But the drastic danger of Judaistic legalism demanded such drastic logic. He knew of no other way to bring Peter and the others to their senses.

By using the term *we* in the previous verses, Paul had graciously identified himself with the compromisers to a certain extent. Now he even more graciously and lovingly softens the blow to his friends by using himself as a hypothetical example. **For if I rebuild what I have once destroyed,** he said, **I prove myself to be a transgressor.** In other words, if anyone, including **myself,** tries to **rebuild** a system of legalism after he has **once destroyed** it by believing and preaching the gospel of God's powerful grace and man's sinful helplessness, he proves *himself,* not Christ, to be

a transgressor. He proves himself to be a hypocrite and a sinner by abandoning grace for law.

"I could never do such a thing," Paul asserts, "**for through the Law I died to the Law, that I might live to God.** The idea of legalism clashes with God's clearest truth and my own deepest convictions. Now that I have accepted grace and **died to the Law**, I could never go back to its system of rituals and ordinances. Otherwise I could not **live to God**." The law is not the believer's master; God is. It is not his relation to the law that saves him, but his relation to God.

"Do you not know, brethren," Paul asked the believers at Rome, "that the law has jurisdiction over a person as long as he lives? For the married woman is bound by law to her husband while he is living; but if her husband dies, she is released from the law concerning the husband. . . . Therefore, my brethren, you also were made to die to the Law through the body of Christ, that you might be joined to another, to Him who was raised from the dead that we might bear fruit for God" (Rom. 7:1-2, 4).

> What shall we say then? Are we to continue in sin that grace might increase? May it never be! How shall we who died to sin still live in it? Or do you not know that all of us who have been baptized into Christ Jesus have been baptized into His death? Therefore we have been buried with Him through baptism into death, in order that as Christ was raised from the dead through the glory of the Father, so we too might walk in newness of life. For if we have become united with Him in the likeness of His death, certainly we shall be also in the likeness of His resurrection, knowing this, that our old self was crucified with Him, that our body of sin might be done away with, that we should no longer be slaves to sin; for he who has died is freed from sin. Now if we have died with Christ, we believe that we shall also live with Him, knowing that Christ, having been raised from the dead, is never to die again; death no longer is master over Him. For the death that He died, He died to sin, once for all; but the life that He lives, He lives to God. Even so consider yourselves to be dead to sin, but alive to God in Christ Jesus.
>
> Therefore do not let sin reign in your mortal body that you should obey its lusts, and do not go on presenting the members of your body to sin as instruments of unrighteousness; but present yourselves to God as those alive from the dead, and your members as instruments of righteousness to God. For sin shall not be master over you, for you are not under law, but under grace. (Rom. 6:1-14)

In both Romans and Galatians, Paul is referring to the fact that when a person exercises faith in the Lord Jesus Christ, he is placed in transcendent spiritual union with Christ in the historical event of His death and resurrection, in which the penalty of sin was paid in full.

If a man is convicted of a capital crime and is put to death, the law obviously has no more claim on him. He has paid his debt to society. Therefore, even if he were to rise from the dead, he would still be guiltless before the law, which would have no claim on his new life. So it is with the believer who dies in Christ to rise in new life. He is free forever from any claim of the law on him. He paid the law's demand when he died in Christ. His physical death is no punishment, only a release to glory provided in his union with Christ.

Legalism's most destructive effect is that it cancels the effect of the cross. **I have been crucified with Christ,** Paul testifies, **and it is no longer I who live, but Christ lives in me.** To go back under the law would be to cancel one's union with Christ's sacrifice on the cross and therefore to go back under sin.

I died to the Law, Paul explains, because I was **crucified with Christ, and it is no longer I who live.** The old man, the old self, is dead, crucified with Christ, and the new man lives (cf. Col. 3:9-10). Now **I . . . live to God,** because **Christ lives in me** (cf. Rom. 8:9). The life I *received* by faith **I now** also **live by faith.** The Greek verb behind **live** is in the perfect tense, indicating a past completed action that has continuing results. When a believer trusts in Christ for salvation he spiritually participates with the Lord in His crucifixion and in His victory over sin and death.

That is why, the apostle continues, **the life which I now live in the flesh I live by faith in the Son of God.** The true Christian life is not so much a believer's living for Christ as Christ's living through the believer. Because in Christ "all the fulness of Deity dwells in bodily form" (Col. 2:9), the fulness of God also dwells in every believer, as "partakers of the divine nature" (2 Pet. 1:4).

I do not have such a divine life and the magnanimous privilege of being indwelt with the living, powerful Son of God because of anything I have done or merited, but only because He **loved me, and delivered Himself up for me.**

The surpassing motive, therefore, for all spiritual devotion and obedience is gratitude to the sovereign, gracious Lord. The statement **who loved me** refers to the motive behind God's saving grace. The New Testament is replete with teaching on this great truth (see, e.g., John 3:16; Rom. 5:8; Eph. 2:5). The gift of love was not taken from Christ, but **He delivered Himself up for me,** says the apostle. This is reminiscent of our Lord's words in John 10:17-18, "I lay down my life that I may take it again. No one has taken it away from Me, but I lay it down of My own initiative. I have authority to lay it down, and I have authority to take it up again."

All of this saving work is the gift of God's sovereign grace. Consequently, Paul concludes, **I do not nullify the grace of God; for if righteousness comes through the Law, then Christ died needlessly.** In effect he was saying to Peter, "By withdrawing from fellowship with your Gentile brothers you take your stand with the Judaizers and against Christ. You **nullify the grace of God** by denying the need for Christ's death, just as you did when you rebuked the Lord for declaring it was necessary for Him to suffer, be killed, and raised on the third day (see Matt. 16:21-22).

The two pillars of the gospel are the **grace of God** and the death of **Christ,** and those are the two pillars that, by its very nature, legalism destroys. The person who insists that he can earn salvation by his own efforts undermines the very foundation of Christianity and nullifies the precious death of Christ on his behalf.

Bewitched: A Defense of Justification by Faith from Experience (3:1-5)

6

You foolish Galatians, who has bewitched you, before whose eyes Jesus Christ was publicly portrayed as crucified? This is the only thing I want to find out from you: did you receive the Spirit by the works of the Law, or by hearing with faith? Are you so foolish? Having begun by the Spirit, are you now being perfected by the flesh? Did you suffer so many things in vain—if indeed it was in vain? Does He then, who provides you with the Spirit and works miracles among you, do it by the works of the Law, or by hearing with faith? (3:1-5)

Defection and desertion are contemptible because they involve disloyalty and betrayal. Few things are more tragic or disappointing than a Christian who deserts the purity of the gospel for a false form of Christianity that presumes to improve on the finished work of Christ. Yet that is what many believers in the Galatian churches had done or were in danger of doing because of the Judaizers.

Throughout the history of the church some believers have begun well but later have been pulled away from the truths they first believed and followed. They receive the gospel of salvation by grace and live for the Lord in humble faith, but then fall prey to some system of legalism and works righteousness that promises more but produces much less. Some fall into formalism, substituting external ceremonies and rites for the internal reality of personal growth in the Lord. Others fall into legalistic systems of do's and don'ts, proudly hoping to improve their standing before God by doing or not doing certain things. Still others look for a second blessing—a spiritual secret to unlock some higher plane of spirituality, an additional experience of grace—hoping to receive more of God than they imagine was granted to them at conversion.

Paul had been used by the Lord to introduce the gospel of sovereign grace to the Galatians, first to bring them the truth that salvation is received by faith in Christ's atoning work on the cross plus nothing else. Now they were drifting away from the way of pure grace and had accepted an inferior and impotent substitute based on the old Mosaic rituals and ceremonial standards that the New Covenant in Christ had made invalid—and that, even under the Old Covenant, had no power to save. The defecting believers had not lost their salvation, but they had lost the joy and freedom of it and had returned, deceived, to the uncertainty and bondage of a self-imposed legalism. They were still in Christ and right with God positionally, but they were not practically living in conformity to the truth by which they had been made righteous. They substituted a form of religion that had no power or joy for the fullness of life in Christ they once enjoyed. Because they allowed themselves to be deceived, they also projected to the deceived unbelievers around them the thinking that Christianity was a matter of law rather than faith. They had robbed themselves of the fullness of God's blessing and were in danger of robbing their world of the knowledge of the only way of salvation.

Satan never ceases his effort to destroy God's way of salvation, and because God's way is by His grace working through man's faith, Satan's is the opposite, the way of man's own effort and work. From the time of Cain's first works-righteous offering of a grain instead of an animal sacrifice, unbelieving man has sought to make himself right with God through his own goodness and merit.

When Paul first came to Galatia, he marvelled at his gracious reception. He was physically afflicted, yet "that which was a trial to you in my bodily condition," he said, "you did not despise or loathe, but you received me as an angel of God, as Christ Jesus Himself" (Gal. 4:14). Now the apostle marvelled at their defection from the gospel he had preached to them. "I am amazed that you are so quickly deserting Him who called you by the grace of Christ, for a different gospel; which is really not another; only there are some who are disturbing you, and want to distort the gospel of Christ" (1:6-7). Having received new life in Christ by faith, they had been persuaded to live out their new lives by the old way of works. They had turned back from grace to law, from faith to works, from Calvary to ceremony, from freedom to bondage.

In chapters 3-4 Paul gives a classic defense of the doctrine of justification by faith, a defense he had introduced in 2:16-21. In 3:1-5 he defends the doctrine from the standpoint of personal experience, and in 3:6–4:31 from the standpoint of scriptural revelation.

In 3:1-5 the apostle reminds his readers that a believer's experience of the Lord Jesus Christ, of the Holy Spirit, and of God the Father are incontrovertible evidence of having been graciously made acceptable to God through personal faith in the perfect, complete work of Christ, apart from any human supplement.

Although experience in itself is not entirely reliable evidence of spiritual reality, it is nevertheless a powerful apologetic when closely linked with and built on scriptural truth. Because genuine Christian experience verifies the gospel of grace, the inspired apostle was led by the Holy Spirit to use it as an effective means of defending the doctrine of justification by faith.

The Believer's Experience with Christ

You foolish Galatians, who has bewitched you, before whose eyes Jesus Christ was publicly portrayed as crucified? (3:1)

You foolish Galatians reflects a combination of anger and love mixed with surprise. Paul was incredulous, hardly able to believe what the **Galatians** had done. Like many believers before and after them, they had been victimized by Satan and induced to slip away from the moorings of the truth by which they had been saved. Those believers were especially **foolish** because they had been so carefully and fully taught, having been on many occasions over the years privileged to sit under the teaching of Paul himself, whose very heartbeat was the gospel of God's grace.

Anoētos (**foolish**) does not connote mental deficiency but mental laziness and carelessness. The believers in Galatia were not stupid; they simply failed to use their spiritual intelligence when faced by the unscriptural, gospel-destroying teaching of the Judaizers. They were not using their heads.

The Greek term frequently carried the idea of a wrong attitude of heart, a lack of faith that clouds judgment. Paul wrote of greedy people who think that a lot of money will enhance their lives and bring happiness and fulfillment. In seeking to get rich, such people "fall into temptation and a snare and many foolish and harmful desires which plunge men into ruin and destruction" (1 Tim. 6:9). Paul confessed that before salvation he, too, had been "foolish . . . , disobedient, deceived, enslaved to various lusts and pleasures, spending [his] life in malice and envy, hateful, hating" (Titus 3:3).

Jesus used the word to rebuke the two disciples He encountered on the road to Emmaus: "O foolish men and slow of heart to believe in all that the prophets have spoken!" (Luke 24:25). The disciples' basic problem was not mental but spiritual. Because they had not carefully studied to believe the prophets, they failed to understand that, as the Messiah, Jesus not only had to die but that He would be raised and return to His Father in heaven (see v. 26). Their understanding failed because their faith had failed.

The Galatians had foolishly fallen into Judaistic legalism because they had stopped believing and applying the basic truths of the gospel Paul had taught them and by which they had been saved. By sinful neglect of their divine resources, they compromised the gospel of grace. They followed their whims and impulses rather than God's revealed truth, and in so doing forsook the basic truth of the gospel, that men come to salvation and live out salvation only by faith in the Person and the power of Jesus Christ. The Christian life is neither entered nor lived on the basis of good feelings or attractive inclinations but on the basis of God's truth in Christ. Christians who rely on self-oriented emotions instead of Scripture-oriented minds are doomed to be "tossed here and there by waves, and carried about by every wind of doctrine, by the trickery of men, by craftiness in deceitful scheming" (Eph. 4:14). When they judge an idea on the basis of how good it makes them feel or how nice it sounds rather than on the basis of its harmony with God's Word, they are in serious spiritual danger.

Most cult members did not become involved because they were intellectually convinced the doctrines of the cult were true but because its teachings and practices were appealing. Their minds were not persuaded; their emotions were victimized.

Paul pleaded with the Roman believers, "I urge you therefore, brethren, by the mercies of God, . . . not [to] be conformed to this world, but be transformed by the renewing of your mind, that you may prove what the will of God is, that which is good and acceptable and perfect" (Rom. 12:1-2). He urged the Ephesian believers to "be renewed in the spirit of [their] mind" (Eph. 4:23) and the Colossians to "put on the new self who is being renewed to a true knowledge according to the image of the One who created him" (Col. 3:10). Godly faith and obedience are established by the mind, not by the emotions. Being told that one can please God by certain behavior is very appealing to the ego, which is always looking for means of glory, ways to tell itself and others how good it is.

The faithful, effective Christian life, however, is not simply a great emotional adventure filled with wonderful feelings and experiences. It is first of all the humble pursuit of God's truth and will and of conformity to it. The obedient Christian experiences joy and satisfaction beyond measure, far exceeding that of superficial believers who constantly seek spiritual "highs." Life in Christ is not sterile and joyless. But true joy, happiness, satisfaction, and all other such feelings are by-products of knowing and obeying God's truth.

The **Galatians** were actually **bewitched** by the Judaizers. **Bewitched** is from *baskainō*, which means to charm or fascinate in a misleading way, as by flattery, false promises, or occultic power, and clearly suggests the use of feeling over fact, emotion over clear understanding of truth. "**Who** tickled your fancy?" Paul asked rhetorically, fully aware of the answer. "Who could have dragged you away from the solid foundation of truth in which you were once so well grounded?" Although **bewitched** can carry the idea of sorcery, that is not the idea here. The Galatians were not victims of a magical spell or incantation, but were misled pupils of teachings they should have instantly recognized as false. They were willing victims who succumbed to the flesh-pleasing works righteousness of the Judaizers. They had been convinced that faith was not enough, that something was lacking that could be fulfilled by returning to the ceremonies and requirements of the Old Covenant. But as William Hendricksen has said in his Galatians commentary, "A supplemented Christ is a supplanted Christ."

The Galatians' own experience of salvation should have prevented their falling for the Judaizing falsehood. First of all, they had experienced the powerful, trans-forming, mind-changing truth of the gospel in the crucified Christ. They were people **before whose eyes Jesus Christ was publicly portrayed as crucified.** They saw clearly the meaning of the cross. The gospel had come to them with the full clarity and power of Christ's sacrifice on their behalf, and by faith they had believed and received it.

Publicly portrayed translates *prographō,* a word that was used of posting important official notices on a placard in the marketplace or other public location for citizens to read. **Jesus Christ** had been figuratively placarded before the Galatians by Paul himself for everyone to see clearly. Paul was a dynamic preacher, and perhaps dramatic as well. Those who sat at his feet perhaps could almost hear the ringing of the hammer as it drove the nails into Jesus' hands and feet. They may have been able to visualize the blood flowing from His thorn-pierced brow and wounded side. They were convinced of Jesus' atoning death, convicted of their sin, and ushered by grace through faith into the kingdom.

Paul's preaching of **Jesus Christ** and the Galatians' acceptance of Him by faith was all done **publicly.** The believers there were witnesses to each other's salvation by faith in Him alone. But by turning to legalism they were denying the absolute saving power of Christ and the cross by which He had paid the penalty for their sins and bought their salvation.

Crucified translates a perfect passive participle, indicating that the crucifixion was a historical fact that had continuing results. John declares that "if we confess our sins, He is faithful and righteous to forgive us our sins and to cleanse us from all unrighteousness" (1 John 1:9). A more literal translation is, "He is still righteous to keep on forgiving our sins." No ritual, ceremony, regulation, or any other thing devised or accomplished by men can pick up where the cross leaves off—because the cross never leaves off. The cross is the continuing and eternal payment for all sin, and every sinner who puts his trust in the cross is forever and continually being forgiven. A believer can no more stay saved by works than he could have been saved by works in the first place. The cross keeps moving powerfully and relentlessly through history, and it will stand forever as living proof that men cannot redeem themselves.

It is tragic that even much religion that goes under the name of Christianity rejects the substitutionary work of Christ and replaces it with some form of works righteousness. Churches who go by the Lord's name but reject His righteousness in favor of man's are guilty of establishing a form of godliness that has absolutely no power.

Paul had proclaimed that justification is only by faith in Jesus Christ from the time he first set foot in Galatia. "And by him [Christ] all that believe are justified from all things," he told his Jewish hearers in Antioch of Pisidia, "from which you could not be justified by the law of Moses" (Acts 13:39, KJV). That is essentially the message of the book of Hebrews, which was written primarily to Jewish believers, some of whom, like those in Galatia, were in danger of turning back to Judaism. "For, on the one hand," the writer says, "there is a setting aside of a former commandment because of its weakness and uselessness (for the Law made nothing perfect), and on the other hand there is a bringing in of a better hope, through which we draw near to God. . . . Jesus has become the guarantee of a better covenant" (Heb. 7:18-19, 22).

Later in the Galatian letter the apostle implores his readers, "Behold I, Paul, say to you that if you receive circumcision, Christ will be of no benefit to you. And I testify again to every man who receives circumcision, that he is under obligation to keep the whole Law. You have been severed from Christ, you who are seeking to be justified by law; you have fallen from grace" (Gal. 5:2-4). The person who puts his trust in the law obligates himself to keep the entire law, which is humanly impossible, and he also cuts himself off from the benefits of the cross, whereby sins are forgiven and obligation to the law is fulfilled.

The Believer's Experience with the Holy Spirit

This is the only thing I want to find out from you: did you receive the Spirit by the works of the Law, or by hearing with faith? Are you so foolish? Having begun by the Spirit, are you now being perfected by the flesh? Did you suffer so many things in vain—if indeed it was in vain? (5:2-4)

Paul's next appeal was to the Galatian believers' experience with the Holy Spirit. "Don't you remember what **the Spirit** accomplished in your lives when you trusted in Christ for salvation?" he asks. He narrows his focus right to the issue when he pleads, **"This is the only thing I want to find out from you:** when you received Christ, **did you receive the Spirit by the works of the Law, or by hearing with faith?** Did you have to fulfill some further requirements, go through some special ceremony, or perform some additional rites? Or did you **receive the Spirit** by God's grace at the same time you received Christ as Lord and Savior?" The question was rhetorical and the answer obvious: They received the righteousness of Christ and His Holy Spirit at the same time.

The gift of the Holy Spirit is the believer's most unmistakable evidence of God's favor, his greatest proof of salvation and the guarantee of eternal glory. "The Spirit Himself bears witness with our spirit that we are children of God" (Rom. 8:16), Paul assured the Roman Christians. Conversely, "If anyone does not have the Spirit of Christ, he does not belong to Him" (v. 9). John writes, "By this we know that we abide in Him and He in us, because He has given us of His Spirit" (1 John 4:13; cf. 3:24).

 It is therefore ludicrous to maintain, as some Christians do, that the full gift of the Holy Spirit comes through an additional work or experience. A person who does not have the fullness of the Holy Spirit does not need a second blessing; he needs salvation. The indwelling presence of the Holy Spirit is inseparable from the new birth. At no time before salvation can a person *have* the indwelling **Spirit**, and at no time after salvation can he *not* have Him. "Having also believed" in Christ, Paul explained to the Ephesians, "you were sealed in Him with the Holy Spirit of promise, who is given as a pledge of our inheritance" (Eph. 1:13-14). "Pledge" is from *arrabōn*, which originally referred to a down payment or earnest money given by a person intending to make a purchase, as a guarantee that the full amount would be paid. In modern Greek a form of the word is used for engagement ring. The Holy Spirit is the believer's divine guarantee that, as part of Christ's church, His bride, he will one day participate in the marriage feast of the Lamb.

When Paul met some disciples of John the Baptist at Ephesus, he sought to determine the completeness of their faith by asking, "Did you receive the Holy Spirit when you believed?" When they replied no, he presented the gospel of Jesus Christ to them and they then received the Spirit (Acts 19:1-6). In his speech before the Jerusalem Council, Peter said, "Brethren, you know that in the early days God made a choice among you, that by my mouth the Gentiles should hear the word of the gospel and believe. And God, who knows the heart, bore witness to them, giving them the Holy Spirit, just as He also did to us" (Acts 15:7-8). Peter had first witnessed Gentiles' receiving the Holy Spirit when he preached to Cornelius and his relatives and friends at Joppa. "While Peter was still speaking these words, the Holy Spirit fell upon all those who were listening to the message. And all the circumcised believers who had come with Peter were amazed, because the gift of the Holy Spirit had been poured out upon the Gentiles also" (10:44-45).

Though probably not in so dramatic a way, every true believer in Galatia had received the Holy Spirit the moment he received Jesus Christ as Savior. "Don't you remember," Paul asked, "that you received **the Spirit . . . by hearing with faith?** How, then, can you be duped by the Judaizers into thinking that He came to you, or will eventually come to you, **by works of the Law?"**

Like the Judaizers, many groups and movements today want to introduce special conditions or requirements that supposedly add blessings to the finished and perfect work of Christ—such as a greater fullness of the Spirit, speaking in tongues, or a more complete salvation. But all such things are forms of works righteousness, adding things that men can do to what Christ has already done and that only He could have done.

"There is therefore now no condemnation for those who are in Christ Jesus," Paul declared. "For the law of the Spirit of life in Christ Jesus has set you free from the law of sin and of death. For what the Law could not do, weak as it was through the flesh, God did: sending His own Son in the likeness of sinful flesh and as an offering for sin, He condemned sin in the flesh, in order that the requirement of the Law might be fulfilled in us, who do not walk according to the flesh, but according to the Spirit" (Rom. 8:1-4).

The Holy Spirit is not the goal of the Christian life but is its source. He is not the product of faithful living but is the power behind it. A higher level of living does not bring the Holy Spirit; rather submission to the Holy Spirit, who already indwells the believer, includes a higher level of living.

"Having begun by the Spirit," Paul continues, **"are you now being perfected by the flesh?** How could you think that your weak, imperfect, still sinful **flesh** could improve on what the divine **Spirit** of God began in you when you first believed?" Drifting from the provisions of grace into the efforts of law is ludicrous.

For the sake of balance it should be noted that James warns that a faith that does not produce good works is not saving faith at all. "What use is it, my brethren," he asks, "if a man says he has faith, but he has no works? Can that faith save him?" (James 2:14). That is, can *that* kind of faith bring salvation? No. "Faith, if it has no works, is dead, being by itself" (v. 17). When he later says that "a man is justified by works, and not by faith alone" (v. 24), he is speaking of works verifying, not producing, salvation. Works that are pleasing to God—such as visiting "orphans and widows in their distress" and keeping "oneself unstained by the world" (1:27)—give evidence that one's profession of faith in Christ is genuine.

The validity of good works in God's sight depends on whose power they are done in and for whose glory. When they are done in the power of His Spirit and for His glory, they are beautiful and acceptable to Him. When they are done in the power of the flesh and for the sake of personal recognition or merit, they are rejected by Him. Legalism is separated from true obedience by attitude. The one is a rotten smell in God's nostrils, whereas the other is a sweet savor.

The prayer offered in humble faith, seeking God's will and glory, is pleasing to the Father, whereas a prayer uttered by rote or to impress God or other people is anathema to Him (Luke 18:10-14). Going to church to worship God sincerely with fellow believers is pleasing to Him, whereas going to the same church service and being with the same fellow believers is not acceptable to Him if done in a self-righteous, self-serving, legalistic spirit.

Even the best and most acceptable works do not increase our standing before God or elevate us to a higher spiritual status. How would it be possible to be more than a child of God and fellow heir with Jesus Christ, who is the Heir of all things (Rom. 8:17; Heb. 1:2; cf. Gal. 4:7; 1 Pet. 3:7)?

Did you suffer so many things in vain? Paul asks next. **Suffer** is from *paschō*, a word that carries the basic idea of experience and sometimes that of pain or hardship. Since the context suggests nothing of suffering or hardship, it seems best to take the word here to refer to experience, the believers' personal experience with Jesus Christ, the Holy Spirit, and God the Father. Paul is asking, "**Did you** experience **so many things in vain?** Did you learn nothing at all from them? Can't you think things through and see that the claims of the Judaizers cannot possibly square with the gospel you have been taught and have experienced yourselves?"

Paul softens the blow by adding, **If indeed it was in vain,** leaving open the possibility and hope that it was not. In other words, "I hope what I have heard about you is not true or that you have come back to your senses." The apostle uses the same approach several other times in the letter, hitting hard at an error or failure and then softening his tone (see, e.g., 4:9-14, 20; 5:2-10).

THE BELIEVER'S EXPERIENCE WITH THE FATHER

Does He then, who provides you with the Spirit and works miracles among you, do it by the works of the Law, or by hearing with faith? (3:5)

The third appeal to experience is with God the Father, **He . . . who provides you with the Spirit and works miracles among you.**

Just before His ascension Jesus commanded the disciples "not to leave

Jerusalem, but to wait for what the Father had promised, 'Which,' He said, 'you heard of from Me'" (Acts 1:4). Through the Son, the Father had promised to give "the Holy Spirit to those who ask Him" (Luke 11:13). And "when He, the Spirit of truth, comes," Jesus explained on another occasion, "He will guide you into all the truth; for He will not speak on His own initiative, but whatever He hears, He will speak" (John 16:13).

Provides is from *epichorēgeō,* which means to supply abundantly and with great generosity. It was used of patrons of the arts who underwrote productions of Greek plays and of patriotic citizens who gave of their wealth to help support their country's army or government. It was also used of a groom's vow to love and care for his bride.

In His superabundant generosity to His children, God **provides** them **with the Spirit and works miracles among** them. **Miracles** translates *dunamis,* which refers basically to inherent power or ability. Paul may have been referring to miraculous events God had worked **among** the Galatian believers, or he may have been referring to the spiritual power over Satan, sin, the world, the flesh, and human weakness that the Father bestows on His children through His **Spirit.** Paul's preaching in Corinth was "in demonstration of the Spirit and of power" (1 Cor. 2:4). He even boasted in his own weaknesses in order that the power of Christ might dwell in him (2 Cor. 12:9). God, he says, "is able to do exceeding abundantly beyond all that we ask or think, according to the power that works within us" (Eph. 3:20). In each of those passages *dunamis* is rendered "power" and refers to the Father's divine gift to His children.

Paul's argument is itself powerful: If a person has received eternal salvation through trust in the crucified Christ, received the fullness of the Holy Spirit the same moment he believed, and has the Father's Spirit-endowed power working within him, how could he hope to enhance that out of his own insignificant human resources by some meritorious effort?

Blessed or Cursed? A Defense of Justification by Faith from Scripture (3:6-14)

7

Even so Abraham believed God, and it was reckoned to him as righteousness. Therefore, be sure that it is those who are of faith who are sons of Abraham. And the Scripture, foreseeing that God would justify the Gentiles by faith, preached the gospel beforehand to Abraham, saying, "All the nations shall be blessed in you." So then those who are of faith are blessed with Abraham, the believer. For as many as are of the works of the Law are under a curse; for it is written, "Cursed is everyone who does not abide by all things written in the book of the law, to perform them." Now that no one is justified by the Law before God is evident; for, "The righteous man shall live by faith." However, the Law is not of faith; on the contrary, "He who practices them shall live by them." Christ redeemed us from the curse of the Law, having become a curse for us—for it is written, "Cursed is everyone who hangs on a tree"—in order that in Christ Jesus the blessing of Abraham might come to the Gentiles, so that we might receive the promise of the Spirit through faith. (3:6-14)

When the Philippian jailer asked what he must do to be saved, Paul concisely answered, "Believe in the Lord Jesus, and you shall be saved" (Acts 16:31). Salvation is appropriated by faith; and that faith is personal, internal, and spiritual, having nothing to do with ceremonies, rituals, observances, good works, or externals of any sort.

71

Faith has always been the God-required response that brings salvation (Eph. 2:8-9). The saints of the Old Testament were saved by faith, just as the saints of the New. Abel had comparatively little revelation concerning God, but he believed in the truth of what he knew of God and was saved. Noah also had limited knowledge about God, and he, too, had faith in the truth He did know and was saved. Moses had considerably more revelation of God's nature and will, and by trusting in what he knew of God, he was saved. All three were justified, counted righteous and made acceptable to God, by their personal faith in Him. They "gained approval through their faith" (Heb. 11:4, 7, 23-29, 39).

After having shown the Galatian believers from their own experience that they were justified by faith and not by works of the law (Gal. 3:1-5), Paul now defends that doctrine from Scripture.

The Judaizers doubtlessly quoted many passages from the Old Testament in support of their legalistic claims. And because their interpretations of those passages were based on long-accepted and revered rabbinical tradition, many believing Jews in Galatia and elsewhere found the claims persuasive.

In Galatians 3:6-14, Paul exposes those misinterpretations, showing that the Judaizers were heretical in their doctrine because they were mistaken in their understanding of Scripture. His first line of argument from the Old Testament is positive, showing what true biblical faith does, and his second line of argument is negative, showing what works cannot do.

POSITIVE PROOF FROM THE OLD TESTAMENT

Even so Abraham believed God, and it was reckoned to him as righteousness. Therefore, be sure that it is those who are of faith who are sons of Abraham. And the Scripture, foreseeing that God would justify the Gentiles by faith, preached the gospel beforehand to Abraham, saying, "All the nations shall be blessed in you." So then those who are of faith are blessed with Abraham, the believer. (3:6-9)

Paul's positive proof that the Old Testament teaches salvation by faith rather than works revolves around Abraham, father of the Hebrew people and supreme patriarch of Judaism.

The Judaizers doubtlessly used Abraham as certain proof that circumcision was necessary to please God and become acceptable to Him. After first calling Abraham to leave his homeland of Ur of Chaldea, the Lord promised, "And I will make you a great nation, and I will bless you, and make your name great; and so you shall be a blessing; and I will bless those who bless you, and the one who curses you I will curse. And in you all the families of the earth shall be blessed" (Gen. 12:2-3). Abraham and his descendants were later commanded to be circumcised as a sign of God's covenant and a constant illustration of the need for spiritual cleansing from sin: "This is My covenant, which you shall keep, between Me and you and your descendants after you: every male among you shall be circumcised" (Gen. 17:10). (The cutting away of the foreskin on the male procreative organ signified the need to cut away sin from the heart—sin that was inherent, passed from one generation to the next; cf. Deut. 10:16; Jer. 4:4; Col. 2:11.)

Putting those two accounts together, the Judaizers argued, "Isn't it obvious that if the rest of the world, that is, Gentiles, are to share in the promised blessings to Abraham, they must first take on the sign that marks God's people, the Jews? If all the nations of the earth will be blessed in Abraham, they will have to become like Abraham and be circumcised."

"But that doesn't follow," Paul replied in effect. Quoting Genesis 15:6, he asked, "Don't you know that **even so Abraham believed God, and it was reckoned to him as righteousness?** Had they conveniently ignored the fact that Scripture precisely ascribed righteousness to Abraham by faith and that God commanded Abraham to be circumcised many years *after* He had **reckoned** Abraham to be righteous because he **believed God?**"

When some ten years passed after God's first promise and his wife, Sarah, was still childless, Abraham prayed, "O Lord God, what wilt Thou give me, since I am childless, and the heir of my house is Eliezar of Damascus?" The Lord then took Abraham "outside and said, 'Now look toward the heavens, and count the stars, if you are able to count them.' And He said to him, 'So shall your descendants be.' Then he believed in the Lord; and He reckoned it to him as righteousness" (Gen. 15:2, 5-6). It was at least fourteen years after that occasion (see Gen. 16:16; 17:1) before the command for his circumcision was given.

Paul used the same argument in his letter to the Roman church. Speaking of believers "whose lawless deeds have been forgiven, and whose sins have been covered, . . . whose sin the Lord will not take into account," he asked,

> Is this blessing then upon the circumcised, or upon the uncircumcised also? For we say, "Faith was reckoned to Abraham as righteousness." How then was it reckoned? While he was circumcised, or uncircumcised? Not while circumcised, but while uncircumcised; and he received the sign of circumcision, a seal of the righteousness of the faith which he had while uncircumcised, that he might be the father of all who believe without being circumcised, that righteousness might be reckoned to them, and the father of circumcision to those who not only are of the circumcision, but who also follow in the steps of the faith of our father Abraham which he had while uncircumcised. (Rom. 4:7-12)

The Judaizers, like most other Jews of that day, had completely reversed the relationship of circumcision and salvation. Circumcision was only a mark, not the means, of salvation. God established circumcision as a physical sign to identify His people and to isolate them from the idolatrous, pagan world around them during the time of the Old Covenant. Circumcision is an external, physical act that has no effect on the spiritual work of justification. God gave the sign of circumcision to Abraham long *after* He had already declared him to be righteous because of his faith.

It has always been true that "he is not a Jew who is one outwardly; neither is circumcision that which is outward in the flesh. But he is a Jew who is one inwardly; and circumcision is that which is of the heart, by the Spirit, not by the letter" (Rom. 2:28-29). Physical circumcision was a matter of earthly, ceremonial identity with God's people, whereas salvation is a matter of spiritual identity with Him; and if the earthly symbol had no genuine spiritual counterpart it was worthless. Even under the Old Covenant, circumcision itself carried no spiritual power.

Since the Fall, proud mankind has been naturally inclined to trust in himself, including his ability to please God by his own character and efforts. The Jews of Jesus' day put great stock in circumcision and physical descent from Abraham. When Jesus told a group of them, "If you abide in My word, then you are truly disciples of Mine; and you shall know the truth, and the truth shall make you free," they replied, "We are Abraham's offspring, and have never yet been enslaved to anyone" (John 8:31-33). Their answer was obviously absurd from a historical standpoint. The Jewish people had been in severe bondage many times throughout their history and were at that time under the iron rule of Rome. Even more foolish, however, was their thinking that mere physical descent from Abraham made them acceptable to God. In one of His most powerful denunciations of bankrupt Judaism, Jesus said: "I know that you are Abraham's offspring; yet you seek to kill Me, because My word has no place in you. . . . If you are Abraham's children, do the deeds of Abraham. But as it is, you are seeking to kill Me, a man who has told you the truth, which I heard from God; this Abraham did not do. . . . You are of your father the devil, and you want to do the desires of your father" (John 8:37, 39-40, 44).

By counting on ceremonial nationalism, legalistic Jews imagined they were in the spiritual as well as racial heritage of Abraham, whereas they were really in the spiritual heritage of Cain, who, in rejecting God's way, not only followed his own way but also Satan's. Jesus' point on that occasion was that, no matter what physical lineage a person may have, if he does not have faith in God he is not a spiritual descendant of Abraham. Abraham was secondarily the physical father of the Jewish people. He was first of all the spiritual father of everyone, of whatever race or nationality, who believes in God (Rom. 4:11). Just as with Abraham, "to the one who does not work, but believes in Him who justifies the ungodly, his faith is reckoned as righteousness" (v. 5).

It should be noted also that Abraham is not only the pattern for justification by faith but for obedient living by that faith.

> By faith Abraham, when he was called, obeyed by going out to a place which he was to receive for an inheritance; and he went out, not knowing where he was going. By faith he lived as an alien in the land of promise, as in a foreign land, dwelling in tents with Isaac and Jacob, fellow heirs of the same promise; for he was looking for the city which has foundations, whose architect and builder is God. . . . By faith Abraham, when he was tested, offered up Isaac; and he who had received the promises was offering up his only begotten son;

it was he to whom it was said, 'In Isaac your descendants shall be called.' He considered that God is able to raise men even from the dead; from which he also received him back as a type. (Heb. 11:8-10, 17-19)

By faith Abraham followed God to an unknown land and by faith he was willing to give back to God the son who alone could be the means of fulfilling the divine promise. Abraham, as every true believer before and after him, understood faith as "the assurance of things hoped for, the conviction of things not seen" (v. 1). By faith Abraham even looked forward to Christ. Jesus told the unbelieving Jews in Jerusalem, "Your father Abraham rejoiced to see My day, and he saw it and was glad" (John 8:56).

To reemphasize the absolute importance of what he was saying, Paul added, **Therefore, be sure that it is those who are of faith who are sons of Abraham.** He was making the same point to the believing Jews in Galatia that Jesus made to the unbelieving Jews in Jerusalem: Only genuine believers, **those who are of faith**, have any claim to a spiritual relationship to **Abraham,** or to God. Jews with no faith in the Lord Jesus Christ are not true **sons of Abraham,** whereas Gentiles who believe in Him are.

Lest Christians think that, because His chosen people have rejected Him, the Lord will reject them, Paul declares unequivocally, "I say then, God has not rejected His people, has He? May it never be!" Then he repeats the declaration, "God has not rejected His people whom He foreknew" (Rom. 11:1-2). God still has marvelous future plans for the Jews as a people. But at no time of history—before or after His special calling of the Jews—has *any* person been brought into saving relationship to God by any other means than faith.

Personifying God's Word, the apostle goes on to say, **the Scripture, foreseeing that God would justify the Gentiles by faith, preached the gospel beforehand to Abraham**—which is an exposition of Genesis 12:3: "**All the nations shall be blessed in you.**" **Gospel** means "good news," and God's good news to mankind has always been salvation by faith alone, prompted by the power of His grace. Salvation by works would not be good but bad news. **All the nations,** Jews and **Gentiles** alike, are justified and **blessed** for the same reason **Abraham** was justified and blessed: their **faith. So then those who are of faith are blessed with Abraham, the believer.** To be **blessed** means to be the recipient of all that divine love, grace, and mercy bestows on those who are in Christ (cf. Eph. 1:3; 2:6-7).

[handwritten margin note: Luke 2:10]

At the Jerusalem Council, James said, "Brethren, listen to me. Simeon [Peter] has related how God first concerned Himself about taking from among the Gentiles a people for His name. And with this the words of the Prophets agree, just as it is written, 'After these things I will return, and I will rebuild the tabernacle of David which has fallen, and I will rebuild its ruins, and I will restore it, in order that the rest of mankind may seek the Lord, and all the Gentiles who are called by My name'" (Acts 15:13-17; cf. Amos 9:11-12).

When Gentiles are saved, they are saved as Gentiles, just as Jews are saved as

Jews. But no one from either group is saved or not saved due to racial or ethnic identity. Those who are saved are saved because of their faith, and those who are lost are lost because of their unbelief. A Gentile has absolutely no advantage in becoming a Jew before he becomes a Christian. In fact, by expecting salvation through the rite of circumcision, a person, whether Jew or Gentile, nullifies the grace of God and declares, in effect, that "Christ died needlessly" (Gal. 2:21).

Negative Proof from the Old Testament

For as many as are of the works of the Law are under a curse; for it is written, "Cursed is everyone who does not abide by all things written in the book of the law, to perform them." Now that no one is justified by the Law before God is evident; for, "The righteous man shall live by faith." However, the Law is not of faith; on the contrary, "He who practices them shall live by them." (3:10-12)

The Judaizers also strongly advocated the necessity of keeping the Mosaic **Law** in order to be saved. But here again, simply the sequence of Old Testament events should have shown them the foolishness of that belief. Abraham not only was declared righteous about 14 years before he was commanded to be circumcised, but more than 500 years before God revealed His law to Moses at Sinai. Isaac, Jacob, Joseph, and countless other Hebrew believers lived and died long before the written law was given by God.

Just as the Judaizers and their Galatian victims should have known that justification is by faith and not circumcision, they should also have known it is not by **the Law.** Therefore after showing what faith *can* do, Paul now shows what works *cannot* do. As in verses 6-9, his argument is based on the Old Testament.

In his defense before King Agrippa in Caesarea, Paul states the scriptural foundation of all his preaching and teaching: "Having obtained help from God, I stand to this day testifying both to small and great, stating nothing but what the Prophets and Moses said was going to take place; that the Christ was to suffer, and that by reason of His resurrection from the dead He should be the first to proclaim light both to the Jewish people and to the Gentiles" (Acts 26:22-23).

The ancient rabbis were so absolutely convinced that salvation could only be earned through keeping the law that they tried to prove God had somehow revealed His law even to the patriarchs and other saints who lived before Moses and that those people found favor with Him because they kept His law. Because they could not bring themselves to consider limiting the supremacy of the law, the rabbis sought instead to reconstruct history and the clear teaching of God's Word.

But Paul turns the tables on them again. "Don't you realize," he says, "that **as many as are of the works of the Law are under a curse?**" That question would have utterly perplexed the Judaizers, who would have responded vehemently, "We know no such thing. How can you speak such foolishness?" "Have you forgotten Deuteronomy, the last book of **the Law?**" Paul asks, in effect; **"for it is written,**

'**Cursed is everyone who does not abide by all things written in the book of the law, to perform them**'" (see Deut. 27:26). A curse is a divine judgment that brings the sentence of condemnation.

The apostle's emphasis in the quotation was on the requirement to **abide by all things.** In other words, the fact that those who trust in **the works of the Law** are obligated to keep **all things** in the law, without exception, places them inevitably **under a curse**, because no one had the ability to **abide** by everything the divine and perfect law of God demands. Paul confessed his inability to keep the law even as a devout Pharisee. He testified that "this commandment which was to result in life, proved to result in death for me" (Rom. 7:10). Even as a believer he said, "I myself with my mind am serving the law of God, but on the other, with my flesh the law of sin" (Rom. 7:25)' If men proudly insist on living by the law, it will curse them, not save them, because they cannot possibly live up to it.

The legalistic Jews had "a zeal for God, but not in accordance with knowledge. For not knowing about God's righteousness, and seeking to establish their own, they did not subject themselves to the righteousness of God. For Christ is the end of the law for righteousness to everyone who believes" (Rom. 10:2-4). Consequently, they unwittingly placed themselves under God's wrath rather than His blessing, because they *could not* live up to His law and they *would not* submit to His grace.

Paul reminds his readers again of more teaching concerning God's way of justification: **Now that no one is justified by the Law before God is evident; for, "The righteous man shall live by faith,"** quoting this time from Habakkuk 2:4. The passage from Deuteronomy proves justification *cannot* be by **the Law**, and the passage from Habakkuk proves it *must* be **by faith**. The ways of law and faith are mutually exclusive. To live by law is to live by self-effort and leads inevitably to failure, condemnation, and death. To **live by faith** is to respond to God's grace and leads to justification and eternal life.

Quoting another Old Testament text (Lev. 18:5), Paul again turns Scripture against the Judaizers by showing them that salvation by works and salvation by believing are mutually exclusive: **However, the Law is not of faith; on the contrary, "He who practices them shall live by them."** God's written law itself marks the danger of trying to live up to its standard, which is perfection. If you are relying on works of the law as your means of salvation, then you have to **live by them** perfectly.

Pointing up that same truth in the Sermon on the Mount, Jesus destroyed the very foundation of legalistic Judaism. Because God's standard is perfection, He said; "You are to be perfect, as your heavenly Father is perfect" (Matt. 5:48). And He had already made clear that God's standard of perfection is inner virtue and perfection, not simply outwardly respectable behavior. To those who piously asserted they had never committed murder, He said, "Everyone who is angry with his brother shall be guilty before the court; and whoever shall say to his brother, 'Raca,' shall be guilty before the supreme court; and whoever shall say, 'You fool,' shall be guilty enough to go into the fiery hell" (Matt. 5:22). And to those who claimed they had never committed adultery, He said, "Everyone who looks on a woman to lust for her has committed adultery with her already in his heart" (v. 28).

Whether consulting the texts in Deuteronomy, Habakkuk, or Leviticus, the message is the same: perfection allows no exceptions, no failure of the smallest sort. To break the law in one place is to break it all, "for whoever keeps the whole law and yet stumbles in one point, he has become guilty of all" (James 2:10). No wonder the Holy Spirit inspired Paul to write that "by the deeds of the law there shall no flesh be justified in His sight" (Rom. 3:20, KJV).

A ship that is moored to a dock by a chain is only as secure as the weakest link in that chain. If a severe storm comes and causes even one link to break, the entire ship breaks away. So it is for those who try to come to God by their own perfection. They will be lost and forever wrecked.

POSITIVE HOPE IN JESUS CHRIST

Christ redeemed us from the curse of the Law, having become a curse for us—for it is written, "Cursed is everyone who hangs on a tree"—in order that in Christ Jesus the blessing of Abraham might come to the Gentiles, so that we might receive the promise of the Spirit through faith. (3:13-14)

Turning again to the positive, Paul reminds the Jewish believers in Galatia of the fact that **Christ redeemed us from the curse of the Law, having been a curse for us.**

Redeemed is from *exagorazō*, a word commonly used of buying a slave's freedom. **Christ** justifies those who believe in Him by buying them back from their slavery to sin. The price He paid was the only one high enough to redeem all of mankind, the "precious blood, as of a lamb unblemished and spotless, the blood of Christ" (1 Pet. 1:19).

The curse of the Law was the punishment demanded because no man could keep from violating its demands, but **Christ** took that curse upon Himself as a substitute for sinners and became **a curse for us** in His crucifixion, **for it is written** (Deut. 21:23), **"Cursed is everyone who hangs on a tree."**

In ancient Judaism a criminal who was executed, usually by stoning, was then tied to a post, a type of **tree**, where his body would hang until sunset as a visible representation of rejection by God. It was not that a person became cursed by being hanged on a tree but that he was hanged on a tree because he was cursed. Jesus did not become a curse because He was crucified but was crucified because he was cursed in taking the full sin of the world upon Himself. "He Himself bore our sins in His body on the cross, that we might die to sin and live to righteousness; for by His wounds you were healed" (1 Pet. 2:24; cf. Acts 5:30).

That truth was extremely hard for most Jews to accept, because they could not imagine the Messiah's being cursed by God and having to hang on a tree. First Corinthians 12:3 suggests that "Jesus is accursed" was a common, demon-inspired saying among unbelieving Jews of that day. To them, Jesus' crucifixion was final and absolute proof that He was not the promised Messiah.

But for those who trust in Him, the two words **for us** become the two most beautiful words in all of Scripture. Because God sent His Son to bear the penalty for man's sin, every person who puts his trust in the crucified Savior has had the **curse** borne **for** him.

Jesus' sacrifice was total and for all men, **in order that in Christ Jesus the blessing of Abraham might come to the Gentiles, so that we might receive the promise of the Spirit through faith.** On man's part, the curse is lifted by **faith,** which God, on His part and by grace, counts as righteousness on the believer's behalf, and the river of blessing begins to flow as the rushing water of God's grace engulfs the believer. Jesus Christ bore the **curse,** Paul affirms, to bring **the blessing of Abraham . . . to the Gentiles.** Salvation was for the purpose of God's blessing the world. All that God desired for and promised to Abraham of salvation and its benefits would spread to the nations. A coordinate purpose clause is added—**so that we might receive the promise of the Spirit through faith** (cf. Acts 1:4-5; Eph. 1:13), who comes as the resident, indwelling Person to bless us with power.

All of this blessing is **through faith.** Justifying **faith** involves self-renunciation, putting away all confidence in one's own merit and works. Like the Israelites who had Pharaoh's pursuing army behind them and the impassable Red Sea in front of them, the sinner must acknowledge his sinfulness and his total inability to save himself. When he sees God's justice pursuing him and God's judgment ahead of him, he realizes his helplessness in himself and realizes he has nowhere to turn but to God's mercy and grace.

Justifying **faith** also involves reliance on and submission to the Lord. When a sinner sees that he has no way to escape and no power in his own resources, he knows he must rely on God's provision and power. Finally, justifying **faith** involves appropriation, as the sinner gratefully receives the free gift of pardon Christ offers and submits to His authority.

Justifying **faith** does not have to be strong faith; it only has to be true faith. And true faith not only brings salvation to the believer but glory to the One who saves.

When a person receives Christ as Lord and Savior, he receives the promised **blessing** and the promised **Spirit,** which Paul describes in Ephesians as being "blessed . . . with every spiritual blessing in the heavenly places in Christ" (1:3). This blessing gives a testimony of praise to "the glory of His grace" (1:6). God receives glory when His attributes are on display, and nowhere is His grace more evident than in the sending of His only Son to be crucified on man's behalf, the Sinless paying the debt of the sinful. Believers are "raised . . . up with Him, and seated . . . with Him in the heavenly places, in Christ Jesus, in order that in the ages to come He might show the surpassing riches of His grace in kindness toward [them] in Christ Jesus" (2:6-7).

Men are redeemed in order to exhibit God's majestic being before all creation. His supreme purpose is to demonstrate His glorious grace against the backdrop of man's sinfulness, lostness, and hopelessness. The very purpose of the church is to "stand in the presence of His glory blameless with great joy" and to praise "the only God our Savior, through Jesus Christ our Lord, . . . [for His] glory, majesty, dominion and authority, before all time and now and forever" (Jude 24-25).

In Light of God's Promise, Why the Law? (3:15-22)

8

Brethren, I speak in terms of human relations; even though it is only a man's covenant, yet when it has been ratified, no one sets it aside or adds conditions to it. Now the promises were spoken to Abraham and to his seed. He does not say, "And to seeds," as referring to many, but rather to one, "And to your seed," that is, Christ. What I am saying is this: the Law, which came four hundred and thirty years later, does not invalidate a covenant previously ratified by God, so as to nullify the promise. For if the inheritance is based on law, it is no longer based on a promise; but God has granted it to Abraham by means of a promise. Why the Law then? It was added because of transgressions, having been ordained through angels by the agency of a mediator, until the seed should come to whom the promise had been made. Now a mediator is not for one party only; whereas God is only one. Is the Law then contrary to the promises of God? May it never be! For if a law had been given which was able to impart life, then righteousness would indeed have been based on law. But the Scripture has shut up all men under sin, that the promise by faith in Jesus Christ might be given to those who believe. (3:15-22)

In 3:1-14 Paul proves from Old Testament Scripture that Abraham was justified by faith and not by law and that every other believer, whether Jew or Gentile, is likewise saved only by faith, made effective by Christ's taking sin's curse upon Himself.

Now the apostle anticipates the probable argument his adversaries, the Judaizers, would likely make against what he has just proved. "Very well," they would argue. "But granted that Abraham and his pre-Sinai descendants were saved by faith, it is obvious that when God gave the law to Moses, the basis of salvation changed. A new covenant was made and a new means of salvation was then established. After Moses, the basis of salvation became law in place of faith or at least as a necessary supplement to faith. The covenant with Moses annulled and supplanted the covenant with Abraham, a temporary measure God provided until He gave Moses the more perfect and complete covenant of law. Abraham and others who lived before the law were saved by faith only because they did not have the law. Why else would God have given the Mosaic covenant of law?"

It is that anticipated, imaginary argument that Paul answers in 3:15-22. The heart of his answer is to show that the covenant with Abraham was an unconditional covenant of promise relying solely on God's faithfulness, whereas the covenant with Moses was a conditional covenant of law relying on man's faithfulness. To Abraham, God said, "I will." Through Moses He said, "Thou shalt." The promise set forth a religion dependent on God. The law set forth a religion dependent on man. The promise centers on God's plan, God's grace, God's initiative, God's sovereignty, God's blessings. The law centers on man's duty, man's work, man's responsibility, man's behavior, man's obedience. The promise, being grounded in grace, requires only sincere faith. The law, being grounded in works, demands perfect obedience.

In contrasting the covenants of promise and of law, Paul first shows the superiority of the one and then the inferiority of the other.

THE SUPERIORITY OF THE PROMISE

Brethren, I speak in terms of human relations; even though it is only a man's covenant, yet when it has been ratified, no one sets it aside or adds conditions to it. Now the promises were spoken to Abraham and to his seed. He does not say, "And to seeds," as referring to many, but rather to one, "And to your seed," that is, Christ. What I am saying is this: the Law, which came four hundred and thirty years later, does not invalidate a covenant previously ratified by God, so as to nullify the promise. For if the inheritance is based on law, it is no longer based on a promise; but God has granted it to Abraham by means of a promise. (3:15-18)

Four reasons are given for affirming the superiority of the covenant of promise: its confirmation, its Christ-centeredness, its chronology, and its completeness.

ITS CONFIRMATION

Brethren, I speak in terms of human relations; even though it is only a man's

covenant, yet when it has been ratified, no one sets it aside or adds conditions to it. (3:15)

First of all, the covenant of promise was superior because it was confirmed as irrevocable and unchangeable. This can be illustrated by reference to a human covenant. **In terms of human relations,** Paul says, **even . . . a man's covenant, . . . when it has been ratified,** allows **no one** to set **it aside** or add **conditions to it.** Even human beings hold their covenants to be inviolable and unamendable. Once **ratified,** they are irrevocable and unchangeable.

Diathēkē (**covenant**) is a general term for a binding agreement. It was often used to refer to wills or testaments, and in some Scripture passages the word is best translated with that meaning. A last will and testament expresses the desires and intent of but one party and may or may not involve other specific parties. A **covenant,** on the other hand, always involves two or more specific parties, although the terms may be stipulated and fulfilled by only one. In the Septuagint (the Greek Old Testament translated in the third century B.C.) the term is consistently used of God's covenants with His people—covenants that God alone initiated and established and that sometimes were conditional and sometimes not.

When God made the covenant with Abraham, whose name was then Abram, He promised, "'I am a shield to you, your reward shall be very great. . . . This man [Eliezer] will not be your heir; but one who shall come forth from your own body, he shall be your heir.' And He took him outside and said, 'Now look toward the heavens, and count the stars, if you are able to count them.' And He said to him, 'So shall your descendants be.' Then he believed in the Lord; and He reckoned it to him as righteousness. And He said to him, 'I am the Lord who brought you out of Ur of the Chaldeans, to give you this land to possess it'" (Gen. 15:1, 4-7).

When Abram asked, "O Lord God, how may I know that I shall possess it?" (v. 8), God ratified the covenant by a ceremony common to the ancient Near East. On the Lord's instructions, Abram took a heifer, a female goat, a ram, a turtledove, and a pigeon, then cut them in half and laid the two sides of each animal opposite one another, with a path in between. At sunset, God caused a deep sleep, as well as "terror and great darkness," to fall on Abram. After reassuring Abram of His promises, the Lord symbolically passed between the animals in the form of "a smoking oven and a flaming torch" (vv. 12-17).

Ordinarily, both parties to a covenant would walk between the slain animals, whose blood would symbolically ratify the agreement. But in this case, God alone walked through, indicating that the covenant, though involving promises to Abraham and his descendants, was made by God with Himself. The covenant was unilateral and entirely unconditional, the only obligation being on God Himself.

"If, therefore," Paul argued, "a man's covenant, when ratified, cannot be set aside or have conditions added to it, how much less can a covenant God makes with Himself be annulled or modified? Even God's own covenant with Moses did not nullify or amend His covenant with Abraham, because God had made the former covenant permanent and unchangeable."

ITS CHRIST-CENTEREDNESS

Now the promises were spoken to Abraham and to his seed. He does not say, "And to seeds," as referring to many, but rather to one, "And to your seed," that is, Christ. (3:16)

Second, Paul argues from the lesser figure of verse 15 to the greater figure of verse 16, that the covenant of promise was superior to the covenant of law because it was Christ-centered. The immutability of the covenant involving faith directly relates to God's last and final covenant established through His Son, Jesus **Christ**. The covenant of law could not possibly have interrupted or modified the previous covenant of promise, because the first one not only was inviolable and permanent in itself but was inseparable from God's supreme covenant, the New Covenant in the Messiah, the **Christ**.

Under the guidance of the Holy Spirit, who inspired the writing of both Genesis and Galatians, Paul exegetes the quoted Genesis passage. The term **seed**, he declares, is singular in Genesis 22:18. It was therefore not **referring to many, but rather to one, "And to your seed."**

Both the Greek term *sperma* (**seed**) and the corresponding Hebrew term (*zera'*) are like the English *seed* in that they can be either singular or plural. Apart from inspiration by the Holy Spirit, Paul could not have established such a crucial interpretation on the basis of grammar alone. Hebrew grammar, like Greek and English, allows, but does not necessitate, the singular.

In numerous Old Testament passages the term obviously applies to but one person. In Genesis 4:25 ("offspring") it refers to Seth alone, in Genesis 21:13 ("descendant") to Ishmael (see 16:11) alone, in 1 Samuel 1:11 ("son") to Samuel alone, and in 2 Samuel 7:12 ("descendant") to Solomon (see 12:24) alone. On the basis only of grammar and context, the meaning of **seed** in Genesis 22:18 could be either singular or plural. But in interpreting His own Word through the apostle, the Holy Spirit makes clear it is singular, **referring . . . to one.**

In an even earlier promise, a clearly singular use of *seed* also refers to Christ. To the serpent in the Garden of Eden, God said, "And I will put enmity between you and the woman, and between your seed and her seed; He [singular, referring to "her seed"] shall bruise you on the head, and you shall bruise him on the heel" (Gen. 3:15).

The one and only heir of every promise of God is Christ. Every promise given in the covenant with Abraham was fulfilled in Jesus Christ and only Jesus Christ. Therefore the only way a person can participate in the promised blessings to Abraham is to be a fellow heir with Christ through faith in Him.

Whether before or after Christ came to earth, salvation has always been provided only through the perfect offering of Christ on the cross. Believers who lived before the cross and never knew any specifics about Jesus were nevertheless forgiven and made right with God by faith in anticipation of Christ's sacrifice, whereas believers who live after the cross are saved in looking back to it. When Christ shed His blood, it covered sins on both sides of the cross. The Old Covenant goes to the cross; the New

Covenant comes from it. On the one hand faith pointed forward, whereas on the other it points back.

There has never been nor can there ever be salvation apart from the finished work of **Christ**. The covenant with Abraham was fulfilled in the covenant of Jesus Christ, and therefore the covenant of law, whatever its character and purpose, did not abrogate or modify those two covenants, which really merged into one.

ITS CHRONOLOGY

What I am saying is this: the Law, which came four hundred and thirty years later, does not invalidate a covenant previously ratified by God, so as to nullify the promise. (3:17)

Third, the covenant of promise was superior to the covenant of law because of chronology. **The Law, which came four hundred and thirty years later, does not invalidate a covenant previously ratified by God.** Because the covenant with Abraham was permanent and inviolate, no amount of time could **nullify the promise.**

The **four hundred and thirty years** refers to the time elapsed between God's last statement of the Abrahamic covenant and His giving of **the Law** to Moses. The Lord repeated the promise to Abraham's son Isaac (Gen. 26:24) and then to his grandson Jacob (28:15). **The Law** came 645 years after Abraham, but 215 years later God repeated the Abrahamic covenant to Jacob, exactly **four hundred and thirty years** prior to the Mosaic covenant at Sinai.

Even the covenant with Abraham did not *establish* the principle of salvation by faith but only verified and typified it. From the time of Adam's fall, faith had been the only means of man's becoming right with God.

As for **the promise** that **God** gave as part of the **covenant** with Abraham and that He Himself had **ratified** (the verb is a perfect passive participle, pointing to the lasting authority of the ratification), the mere passage of time could have no effect on it all, much less **nullify** it.

ITS COMPLETENESS

For if the inheritance is based on law, it is no longer based on a promise; but God has granted it to Abraham by means of a promise. (3:18)

Fourth, the covenant of promise is superior to the covenant of law because it is more complete. Paul's point is that an **inheritance . . . based on law** depends on man's performance, whereas the one **granted . . . to Abraham by means of a promise** depends on God's power. The term **granted** translates the perfect tense of *charizomai* (to give graciously) and points to the permanent character of the inheritance. The principles behind the two types of **inheritance** are incompatible.

One is by God's law and man's works and the other by God's grace and man's faith. Not only that, but the abilities to fulfill the covenants are of an infinitely different order. Man *cannot succeed* in perfectly keeping the **law,** and God *cannot fail* in perfectly keeping the **promise.** Because the covenant of **promise** is complete, the covenant of **law** can in no way improve or change it.

By definition, an **inheritance** is not earned but simply received, and to work for that which is already guaranteed is foolish and unnecessary. Trying to earn the **inheritance** God promises through faith in His Son is much worse than foolish. To add works of the **law** to faith in God's **promise** is to "nullify the grace of God" and to cause Christ to have "died needlessly" (2:21).

The Inferiority of the Law

Why the Law then? It was added because of transgressions, having been ordained through angels by the agency of a mediator, until the seed should come to whom the promise had been made. Now a mediator is not for one party only; whereas God is only one. Is the Law then contrary to the promises of God? May it never be! For if a law had been given which was able to impart life, then righteousness would indeed have been based on law. But the Scripture has shut up all men under sin, that the promise by faith in Jesus Christ might be given to those who believe. (3:19-22)

After showing the superiority of the covenant of promise, Paul shows the inferiority of the covenant of law—first in regard to its purpose, then in regard to its mediator, and finally in regard to its accomplishment.

ITS PURPOSE

Why the Law then? It was added because of transgressions, (3:19*a*)

In light of Paul's convincing argument up to this point, the obvious question would be, **Why the Law then?** If salvation has always been by faith and never by works, and if the covenant of promise to Abraham was fulfilled in Jesus Christ, what purpose did **the Law** have?

Paul's answer is direct and sobering: **It was added because of transgressions** (*parabasis,* stepping over the boundary). The purpose of the law was to demonstrate to man his total sinfulness, his inability to please God by his own works, and his need for mercy and grace. **The Law . . . was added** to show the depth of man's **transgressions** against God. It was given to drive him to desperate guilt and the awareness of his need for the Deliverer.

As the apostle explains a few verses later, the law was a "tutor to lead us to Christ, that we may be justified by faith" (3:24). The impossible demands of the law were meant to compel men to recognize their violation of God's standards and to seek His grace through faith in His Son. When a man looks at the law, he sees that his living is more than simply wrong; it is sin, an offense against the holy God, before whom no sinful person can stand. The law shows men their violation of the will of God, who rules the universe and holds them accountable for their sin.

The covenant of law is long past, but the moral demands of the law have not diminished, having neither begun nor ended with the Mosaic covenant. That is why preaching the moral, ethical standards of the law today is still imperative in driving men to Christ. Unless men realize they are living in violation of God's law and therefore stand under His divine judgment, they will see no reason to be saved. Grace is meaningless to a person who feels no inadequacy or need of help. He sees no purpose in being saved if he does not realize he is lost. He sees no need of forgiveness by God if he does not know he has offended God. He sees no need to seek God's mercy if he is unaware he is under God's wrath. ⟶thankful for Richard's class.

The purpose of the law was, and is, to drive men to despair over their sins and to a desire to receive the salvation that God's sovereign grace offers to those who believe. The purpose of the law was therefore not wrong, but it was inferior. "The Law is holy," Paul says, "and the commandment is holy and righteous and good" (Rom. 7:12). But the law merely points to what only grace can produce.

ITS MEDIATORS

Having been ordained through angels by the agency of a mediator, until the seed should come to whom the promise had been made. Now a mediator is not for one party only; whereas God is only one. (3:19b-20)

Second, the covenant of law was inferior to the covenant of promise because it was **ordained** (*diatassō*, a technical word for carrying out laws) **through angels by the agency of a mediator.** God gave the covenant of law through two sets of mediators, first **through angels** and then by them through Moses to the people.

God was the Author and Giver of the covenant of law, and He was present with Moses on Mt. Sinai when it was given (Ex. 19:18-24). But in a way not fully explained, the law was given by God to Moses **through angels** (cf. Acts 7:53; Heb. 2:2).

When God gave the law, the setting was awesome and forbidding. God warned the people not to come near the fiery mountain, "lest He break forth upon them" (Ex. 19:24). But God gave the covenant to Abraham as Friend to friend (see Gen. 12:1-3; 15:1-7; 18:1-33). The promise of salvation by faith was so precious to the heart of God that He gave it to Abraham in person. That is the way God desires to come to every person who will have His Son as Lord and Savior, **the seed** of Abraham who was to come and **to whom the promise had been made.**

Moses was great and the angels were great; but they were only mediators. Paul warned the Galatian believers not to exalt Moses or angels over God Himself as the Judaizers were doing.

The Greek text of Galatians 3:20 is difficult to translate and interpret, but Paul seems to be pointing out that **a mediator** (literally one who stands between two parties) is needed only when more than **one party** is involved. God gave the covenant directly to Abraham without **a mediator** because He was the **only one** involved in *making* the covenant. Abraham was a witness to the covenant and was a beneficiary, but he was not a party to it. Abraham had no part in establishing or keeping the covenant. That responsibility was God's alone.

The covenant of law, however, not only involved mediators (angels and Moses) but mutual obligations on the two parties (God and Israel). The stipulation of that covenant was, "You shall walk in all the way which the Lord your God has commanded you, that you may live" (Deut. 5:33). Man's part was to obey and God's was to give life, to save. The problem was that man could not keep His part, and therefore God could not grant salvation.

ITS ACCOMPLISHMENTS

Is the Law then contrary to the promises of God? May it never be! For if a law had been given which was able to impart life, then righteousness would indeed have been based on law. But the Scripture has shut up all men under sin, that the promise by faith in Jesus Christ might be given to those who believe. (3:21-22)

Finally, the covenant of law was inferior to the covenant of promise because of its accomplishments.

Again anticipating his readers' likely response, Paul asks rhetorically, **Is the Law then contrary to the promises of God?** The preposition *kata* (**contrary to**) seems better rendered "against" (KJV) or "opposed to" (NIV). God gave both the promise and the law, and He does not work against Himself.

As with other such questions (see 2:17; Rom. 6:1-2; 7:13), Paul immediately gives the strong negative answer himself: **May it never be!** The idea was unthinkable.

For if a law had been given which was able to impart life, then righteousness would indeed have been based on law. In other words, **the Law** was inferior because it could not save, it **was** not **able to impart life.** If it could have done so, it *would* have been against and **contrary to the promises of God,** because it would have provided an alternate and conflicting way of salvation. It would have made the death of Christ tragically unnecessary (2:21). God's grace, Christ's sacrifice, and man's faith would be superfluous, or at best, an optional means of salvation.

But that is not the case, because **the Scripture,** through the law, **has shut up all men under sin.** The phrase **shut up** translates *sunkleiō,* a strong term meaning to lock up securely, to enclose on all sides with no way of escape. "I was once alive apart from the Law," Paul said; "but when the commandment came, sin became alive, and I died" (Rom. 7:9), because the covenant with Moses brought "the law of sin and of death" (8:2). Not until a person smashes himself against the demands of the law and the accusations of conscience does he recognize his helplessness and see his need for a Savior. Not until the law has arrested and imprisoned him and sentenced him to death will he be driven to despair in himself and turn to Jesus Christ.

The ultimate purpose of shutting up men under sin and death was **that the promise by faith in Jesus Christ might be given to those who believe.** The law was given to bring **men under sin** to the point of saying, "Wretched man that I am! Who will set me free from the body of this death?" (Rom. 7:24). Grace is given to enable **those who believe** to say, "Thanks be to God through Jesus Christ our Lord!" (v. 25). God's saving purpose is the climax (cf. Luke 19:10; 1 Tim. 1:15).

Under the Law or in Christ? (3:23-29)

But before faith came, we were kept in custody under the law, being shut up to the faith which was later to be revealed. Therefore the Law has become our tutor to lead us to Christ, that we may be justified by faith. But now that faith has come, we are no longer under a tutor. For you are all sons of God through faith in Christ Jesus. For all of you who were baptized into Christ have clothed yourselves with Christ. There is neither Jew nor Greek, there is neither slave nor free man, there is neither male nor female; for you are all one in Christ Jesus. And if you belong to Christ, then you are Abraham's offspring, heirs according to promise. (3:23-29)

Continuing his discussion of works of the law as opposed to faith in the promise, Paul now contrasts the personal effects those two approaches have on people. After showing the historical relationship between the covenant of promise to Abraham and the covenant of works through Moses and then showing the redemptive superiority of the former over the latter (vv. 6-22), he now introduces the personal application of the two covenants. In doing so, he describes the before and the after of conversion, the character and orientation of a person's life before he trusts in God for salvation and after God grants him righteousness because of that trust. Before conversion a person is under the law and suffers the bondage that relationship brings; after conversion he is in Christ and enjoys the freedom that relationship brings.

UNDER LAW: BONDAGE

But before faith came, we were kept in custody under the law, being shut up to the faith which was later to be revealed. Therefore the Law has become our tutor to lead us to Christ, that we may be justified by faith. (3:23-24)

After using the third person for most of the chapter (vv. 6-22), Paul reverts to the first person (**we**). In using **we,** he first of all identifies himself with the Jewish people, to whom both covenants were given. But in a broader and more comprehensive sense he is also identifying himself with all of mankind, Jew and Gentile. Even the most pagan Gentile who has never heard of the true God is under obligation to keep His moral and spiritual standards and, if he disregards those standards, to face the judgment of God.

Paul uses two figures to represent God's **law** and its effect on unbelievers, first that of a prison and then that of a guardian.

THE LAW AS A PRISON

But before faith came, we were kept in custody under the law, being shut up to the faith which was later to be revealed. (3:24)

Prior to God's revealing salvation in Christ, men were in a spiritual prison. The powerful words of Paul in another epistle are a good place to begin the consideration of man's imprisonment **before faith came.**

Paul declared,

> The wrath of God is revealed from heaven against all ungodliness and unrighteousness of men, who suppress the truth in unrighteousness, because that which is known about God is evident within them; for God made it evident to them. For since the creation of the world His invisible attributes, His eternal power and divine nature, have been clearly seen, being understood through what has been made, so that they are without excuse. For even though they knew God, they did not honor Him as God, or give thanks; but they became futile in their speculations, and their foolish heart was darkened. (Rom. 1:18-21)

In the next chapter of the same epistle Paul further explains that "when Gentiles who do not have the Law do instinctively the things of the Law, these, not having the Law, are a law to themselves, in that they show the work of the Law written in their hearts, their conscience bearing witness, and their thoughts alternately accusing or else defending them" (2:14-15).

Whether through the written law of Scripture or the inward law of conscience, until a person acknowledges his basic sinfulness and inability to perfectly fulfill the demands of God's law, he will not come repentantly to seek salvation. Until he despairs of himself and his own sinfulness, he will not come in humble faith to be filled with Christ's righteousness. A person who says he wants salvation but refuses to recognize and repent of his sin deceives himself. Salvation is deliverance from sin, and a person cannot want to keep his sin and at the same time want be free from it. He cannot truly want the new Christ-life of righteousness without renouncing the old self-life of sin. (See James 4:7-10 for a clear delineation of the proper elements of saving faith.)

The purpose of **the law** is to reveal and convict men of sin. "I would not have come to know sin except through the Law," Paul declared; "for I would not have known about coveting if the Law had not said, 'You shall not covet.' . . . I was once alive apart from the Law; but when the commandment came, sin became alive, and I died" (Rom. 7:7, 9).

Forgiveness means nothing to a person who is either unaware he has done anything wrong or is unconvinced the wrong he knows he has done produces any serious consequences to him. Grace means nothing to a person who does not know he is sinful and that such sinfulness means he is separated from God and damned. It is therefore pointless to preach grace until the impossible demands of the law and the reality of guilt before God are preached.

In the opening chapter of his classic allegory *Pilgrim's Progress,* John Bunyan writes:

> As I walked through the wilderness of this world, I lighted on a certain place where was a den, and laid me down in that place to sleep; and, as I slept, I dreamed a dream. I dreamed, and behold, I saw a man clothed with rags, standing in a certain place, with his face from his own house, a book in his hand, and a great burden upon his back. I looked, and saw him open the book, and read therein; and as he read, he wept and trembled; and, not being able longer to contain, he brake out with a lamentable cry, saying, "What shall I do?"

A short while later the man encountered Evangelist, who asked, "Wherefore dost thou cry?" Pilgrim answered, "Sir, I perceive by the book in my hand that I am condemned to die, and after that to come to judgment." Evangelist then pointed the pilgrim toward a gate in the distance and to a light beyond it and a hill. With the great burden on his back and the book in his hand, Pilgrim started off toward the hill, crying out, "Life! Life! Eternal life!"

The burden on Pilgrim's back was his sin, the book in his hand was the Bible, and the hill toward which he journeyed was Calvary. It was in reading God's Word that he learned God's law condemned him to death and hell because of his sin, and it was that knowledge of sin and judgment that drove Him to the cross of Christ, where the penalty for his sin was paid in full and complete forgiveness offered.

Not only from the viewpoint of the history of redemption, but even in a personal way throughout all times, **before faith** comes, every person is, in the deepest sense, **kept in custody under the law** of God and the burden of sin. Every human being either continuously lives as a captive slave chained under the judgment of God's immutable, universal law, the demands of which he must pay by eternal death and hell, or he lives by faith as utterly free from judgment (Rom. 8:1) as a redeemed child of God under His sovereign and eternal grace.

The believer who looks back realizes that being **under the law** had a good effect, because it showed him his guilty helplessness, his moral and spiritual degeneracy, his fearful danger, and his need of a deliverer. The impossible demands of the law are not designed to save but to condemn sinners and drive them toward the Savior.

As a college football player, I wrenched my knee during practice but was determined to play in the next game. I went to a doctor and was given some cortisone shots and a bottle of ethyl chloride to deaden the pain by temporarily "freezing" the tissue around the knee. I played the entire game without mishap, periodically applying the ethyl chloride to eliminate the recurring pain. But the result of covering up the pain was a permanently damaged knee with more severe ligament injuries that still affect my mobility. By rejecting pain, the body's warning system, I paid serious consequences. The purpose of pain is to warn and protect. When that warning is ignored or covered up, the results are always bad. So it is with guilt. It is the divine warning system telling man he is destroying his soul. If ignored, the results are eternally bad.

In custody under the law, which he violates continually, sinful man is imprisoned. He is, as it were, on death row, sentenced to execution for his sin, the wages of which is death (Rom. 6:23).

Not only that, but he is **shut up to the faith which was later to be revealed.** Historically, the Jews were locked up under the covenant of **law** until the Messiah came and fulfilled the covenant of promise and **faith** given to Abraham. In a similar way, even the Gentile believers in Galatia, like Gentile believers of every age, were **in custody under the law** written in their hearts (Rom. 2:14-16). This custody, however, was not exactly the same as that of the Jews, who had received the revelation (cf. Rom. 3:2; 9:4-5). Again like the Jew, through personal **faith** in Jesus Christ, they are pardoned and freed.

The law had virtually dominated Jewish life from the time of Moses. And because its demands were so impossible, the spiritually-minded, conscientious Jew who sought to love God and serve Him was overwhelmed with a sense of guilt and inadequacy. He sincerely wanted to obey the whole law but knew he could not.

Even under the covenant of **law,** therefore, God's way of **faith** was always open (cf. comments above on 3:6, 11, 17, 18). The law was never a substitute for or barrier to faith. Under Moses, a Jew could be saved by faith and counted righteous by God, just as Abraham and many others had believed and been saved. They looked forward to the Savior, as we look back.

But despite the fact that they could not keep the law, most Jews rejected the way of faith. They began to play mental games with themselves, devising traditions they *were* able to keep in order to convince themselves they could attain righteousness before God.

The first thing Jesus did in the Sermon on the Mount was to undermine that false security. The Pharisees were the epitome of self-righteousness, and Jesus declared that their self-declared goodness was worthless in qualifying a person to enter the kingdom of God (Matt. 5:20). "Do you think you keep the law?" He asked, in effect. "If you have ever hated your brother, you are a murderer, and if you have ever looked lustfully at a woman, you have committed adultery" (vv. 22, 28). They could not become righteous by keeping the law, because their imperfect hearts prevented them from keeping it perfectly, as God requires (v. 48).

"I bear them witness," Paul said of self-righteous Jews, "that they have a zeal for God, but not in accordance with knowledge." Their unbelief kept them from "knowing about God's righteousness, and seeking to establish their own, they did not subject themselves to the righteousness of God" (Rom. 10:2-3).

Since Cain offered the first self-determined sacrifice, men have insisted on coming to God and pleasing Him in their own ways. Unwilling to acknowledge and relinquish their sin or to recognize their hopelessness in trying to save themselves by their religious efforts, they spurn God's offer of salvation through faith and refuse to humble themselves. By relying on their own understanding and efforts they become progressively more entrenched in spiritual and moral destitution. Saving grace has always been God's gift reserved for those who humble themselves, overwhelmed by their inability to do anything in their humanness to earn God's righteousness (see Prov. 3:34; James 4:6, 10; 1 Pet. 5:5).

Spiritual pride characterized Paul for many years before his conversion. By human standards he was the quintessence of the proud and self-righteous Jew, "circumcised the eighth day, of the nation of Israel, of the tribe of Benjamin, a Hebrew of Hebrews; as to the Law, a Pharisee; as to zeal, a persecutor of the church; as to the righteousness which is in the Law, found blameless" (Phil. 3:5-6). But when the Lord confronted him with the gracious way of salvation by faith, Paul "counted as loss for the sake of Christ" all those things he had prized so highly. "More than that," he said, "I count all things to be loss in view of the surpassing value of knowing Christ Jesus my Lord, . . . and count them but rubbish in order that I may gain Christ, and may be found in Him, not having a righteousness of my own derived from the Law, but that which is through faith in Christ, the righteousness which comes from God on the basis of faith" (vv. 7, 8-9).

The law, even when kept to the best of a person's ability, is nothing but a prison, a death row cell where one waits for eternal execution.

THE LAW AS GUARDIAN AND GUIDE

Therefore the Law has become our tutor to lead us to Christ, that we may be justified by faith. (3:24)

Second, **the Law has become** a guardian and guide to the Jews and, in a less unique and more general sense, to all mankind.

A *paidagōgos* (**tutor**) was not a teacher or schoolmaster proper (KJV) but rather a slave employed by Greek or Roman families, whose duty was to supervise young boys in behalf of their parents. They took their young charges to and from school, made sure they studied their lessons, and trained them in obedience. They were strict disciplinarians, scolding and whipping as they felt it necessary. Paul told the Corinthian believers—who often behaved liked spoiled children—that, even if they "were to have countless tutors [*paidagōgous*] in Christ," he would be their only "father through the gospel" (1 Cor. 4:15). Continuing the contrast of *paidagōgos* and father, he later asks, "Shall I come to you with a rod or with love and a spirit of gentleness?" (v. 21).

The role of the *paidagōgos* was never permanent, and it was a great day of deliverance when a boy finally gained freedom from his *paidagōgos*. His purpose was to take care of the child only until he grew into adulthood. At that time the relationship was changed. Though the two of them might remain close and friendly, the *paidagōgos*, having completed his assignment, had no more authority or control over the child, now a young man, and the young man had no more responsibility to be directly under the *paidagōgos*.

The sole purpose of **the Law,** God's divinely appointed *paidagōgos,* was **to lead** men **to Christ, that** they might **be justified.** After a person comes to Him, there is no longer need for the external ceremonies and rituals to act as guides and disciplinarians, because the new inner principles operate through the indwelling **Christ,** in whom is "hidden all the treasures of wisdom and knowledge" (Col. 2:3). The **law** in the ceremonial sense is done away with, though in the moral sense it remains always an intimate friend that one seeks to love and favor.

Before Christ came, the law of external ritual and ceremony, especially the sacrificial system, pictured the once-for-all, perfect, and effective sacrifice of **Christ** for the sins of the world. When the perfect **Christ** comes into the believer's heart, those imperfect pictures of Him have no more purpose or significance.

IN CHRIST: FREEDOM

But now that faith has come, we are no longer under a tutor. For you are all sons of God through faith in Christ Jesus. For all of you who were baptized into Christ have clothed yourselves with Christ. There is neither Jew nor Greek, there is neither slave nor free man, there is neither male nor female; for you are all one in Christ Jesus. And if you belong to Christ, then you are Abraham's offspring, heirs according to promise. (3:25-29)

The Judaizers refused to relinquish the ceremonial law even after making a profession of belief in Christ. To them, trust in Christ was merely added to works of the law. And because they held onto the bondage of the law, they could not receive the freedom of **faith.** Because they insisted on remaining **under** the **tutor,** they never advanced to the care of the Savior.

The law was never intended to be anything more than a temporary means of showing men their sin and of leading them to the Savior. Its internal, moral demands left men ridden with guilt; its external ceremonies (circumcision, offerings, washings, sabbaths, feasts, etc.) symbolized the need for cleansing from that guilt. **Now that faith** in Jesus Christ **has come,** a person is **no longer under** the law as **a tutor.** He is now out from under the law's symbolism, the law's bondage, and the law's discipline. The law's purpose has been fulfilled, and the person is no longer "under law, but under grace" (Rom. 6:14). God's moral standards, however, do not change, and the New Testament reiterates them, and the power of the resident Holy Spirit in the believer enables obedience to them (see Eph. 2:10).

As he unfolds the result of being rightly related to God **through faith in Christ Jesus,** Paul shows three aspects of the freedom of that relationship. Those who believe in Him and thereby become one with Him are sons of God, are one with every other believer, and are heirs of the promise.

SONS OF GOD

For you are all sons of God through faith in Christ Jesus. (3:26)

Although God is the Father of all men creatively (cf. Acts 17:24-28; 1 Cor. 8:6), no doctrine is more unscriptural than that which teaches that God is the Father of all men redemptively. God's only true spiritual children are those who, **through faith in Christ Jesus,** become full-grown, spiritual **sons of God.** The **all** refers to believers of every race. Apart from saving faith in Jesus Christ, all human beings are enemies of God (Rom. 5:10) and "children of wrath" (Eph. 2:3). Like the self-righteous Pharisees in Jerusalem, every unbeliever is a child of the devil (John 8:44). No one belongs to the Father who does not belong to the Son. "I am the way, and the truth, and the life," Jesus said; "no one comes to the Father, but through Me" (John 14:6).

Because of his trust by many Arab tribes, the famous British scholar and soldier Lawrence of Arabia participated in the Paris peace talks after World War I. Several Arab leaders came with him to Paris and stayed in the same hotel. When they went into their bathrooms they were astounded to discover they could bring seemingly unlimited amounts of water into the bathtub or sink simply by turning the handle on a faucet. When preparing to leave Paris, they removed the faucets and packed them in their luggage, thinking that the faucets themselves magically created the vast amounts of water. When they told Lawrence what they had done, he explained that the faucets were useless unless connected to pipes that were, in turn, connected to a source of water.

In the same way, a person who is not connected to the Son is not connected to the Father and has no source of spiritual life or power. God has no **sons** who are not identified by **faith** with His only Son, **Christ Jesus.** No one comes to the Father except through His Son (John 14:6).

The ancient Romans had a coming-of-age ceremony called *toga virilis,* which was somewhat like the Jewish bar mitzvah. The ceremony signified a boy's reaching

97

the age of manhood (which varied between the ages of 14 and 17) and full Roman citizenship, with all its rights and privileges. He no longer had a *paidagōgos,* but was now a recognized adult, responsible for his own welfare and actions.

"You have all experienced a spiritual *toga virilis,*" Paul told the Galatian believers, in effect, "and in light of that stupendous truth, why would you consider going back under the tutorship of the law?"

Faith in Christ Jesus, the only begotten Son, brings believers into sonship with **God** the Father. "As many as received Him [Christ]," John wrote, "He gave the right to become children of God, even to those who believe in His name" (John 1:12).

A bit later in the Galatian letter Paul says, "And because you are sons, God has sent forth the Spirit of His Son into our hearts, crying, 'Abba! Father!'" (Gal. 4:6). Having indwelt the believer, "the Spirit Himself bears witness with our spirit that we are children of God" (Rom. 8:16). In other words, the first thing God gives the believer is Himself, in the form of His indwelling Holy Spirit. The Spirit, in turn, assures us that we belong to the Father. "Abba" is a diminutive of the Aramaic word for father and could be translated "daddy" or "papa." It was a warm, intimate term of endearment used by young children of their fathers. The Holy Spirit brings us into personal, intimate relation with our heavenly Father, whom we can approach at any time and under any circumstance, knowing that He lovingly hears us and cares for us. Because we **are all sons of God,** we can come with absolute confidence before His very "throne of grace, that we may receive mercy and may find grace to help in time of need" (Heb. 4:16).

For all of you who were baptized into Christ, Paul continues, **have clothed yourselves with Christ.** Though water baptism is the outward act of public confession of one's faith in Jesus Christ, Paul is not here speaking of that baptism. The Bible nowhere teaches salvation by physical baptism, especially not in Galatians, where the central message is salvation by faith alone, plus absolutely nothing else. Since it is here equated with being **clothed . . . with Christ,** the phrase **baptized into Christ** cannot refer to any water ceremony at all but rather to spiritual identification with and immersion **into** the life of **Christ.** It is precisely the spiritual immersing into the Person and work of Christ that Paul explains in his letter to the Romans:

> Or do you not know that all of us who have been baptized into Christ Jesus have been baptized into His death? Therefore we have been buried with Him through baptism into death, in order that as Christ was raised from the dead through the glory of the Father, so we too might walk in newness of life. For if we have become united with Him in the likeness of His death, certainly we shall be also in the likeness of His resurrection. (6:3-5)

That is a great mystery that the human mind cannot fathom. But in some spiritually supernatural way that transcends time and space, the person who places his trust in Jesus Christ is crucified, buried, and resurrected with his Savior, **baptized**

into Christ. "The one who joins himself to the Lord is one spirit with Him" (1 Cor. 6:17), so that when the Father looks at the sinful believer He sees His sinless Son. Faith appropriates the union that baptism symbolizes.

When Gideon faced the overwhelming forces of the Midianites and the Amalekites, "the Spirit of the Lord came upon" him (Judg. 6:34). "Came upon" literally means "clothed," indicating that Gideon was enshrouded, or mantled, with the Holy Spirit as a divine coat of armor. That is the concept Paul uses here. The believer who identifies himself with Jesus Christ through faith is divinely **clothed . . . with Christ.** That is a graphic way to describe how Christ's life, presence, and righteous nature envelop the believer.

Because believers are God's children and have the power and assurance of His indwelling Spirit and are enveloped in the life of Christ, they should bring honor to His name by the way they live. Being **clothed . . . with Christ,** they should live like Christ, "blameless and innocent, children of God above reproach in the midst of a crooked and perverse generation, . . . as lights in the world" (Phil. 2:15). "I have been crucified with Christ," the apostle had already said; "and it is no longer I who live, but Christ lives in me; and the life which I now live in the flesh I live by faith in the Son of God, who loved me, and delivered Himself up for me" (Gal. 2:20).

The simplest definition of a Christian is a person who is **clothed . . . with Christ.** Followers of Confucius, Buddha, or Mohammed are never said to be clothed with those men whose names they carry and whose teachings they follow. But there is no such thing as a Christian who is not **clothed . . . with Christ.** Following Christ's teachings is important, but that cannot save a person or keep him saved. It is only being **clothed . . . with Christ** that provides and preserves salvation. That truth is the heart of Christianity and is the emphasis of Galatians 3:26-29.

Whatever the Lord Jesus is and has becomes the believer's. Because **Christ** has the love of the Father, so do believers. Because Christ has full access to the Father, so do believers. And because Christ has the full resources of the Father, so do believers.

ONE WITH OTHER CHRISTIANS

There is neither Jew nor Greek, there is neither slave nor free man, there is neither male nor female; for you are all one in Christ Jesus. (3:28)

Paul focused on the existing, well-defined distinctions of his society that drew sharp lines and set up high walls of separation between people. The essence of those distinctions was the idea that some people—namely Jews, free men, and males in general—were better than, more valuable than, more significant than others. The gospel destroys all such proud thinking. The person who becomes one with Christ also becomes one with every other believer. There are no distinctions among those who belong to Christ. In spiritual matters, there is to be made no racial, social, or sexual discrimination—**neither Jew nor Greek, . . . slave nor free man, . . . male nor female.**

It is not, of course, that among Christians there is no such thing as a Jew, Gentile, slave, free person, man, or woman. There are obvious racial, social, and sexual differences among people. Paul, however, was speaking of spiritual differences—differences in standing before the Lord, spiritual value, privilege, and worthiness. Consequently, prejudice based on race, social status, sex, or any other such superficial and temporary differences has no place in the fellowship of Christ's church. All believers, without exception, **are all one in Christ Jesus.** All spiritual blessings, resources, and promises are equally given to all who believe unto salvation (cf. Rom. 10:12).

It was only with great difficulty that Peter finally learned that there are no racial distinctions in Christ, "that God is not one to show partiality" among **Jew** or **Greek,** "but in every nation the man who fears Him and does what is right, is welcome to Him" (Acts 10:35). Among the five prophets and teachers in the church at Antioch was "Simeon, who was called Niger," which means black (Acts 13:1). Paul's beloved son in the faith was Timothy, whose father was Gentile and whose mother and grandmother were Jewish (Acts 16:1; 2 Tim. 1:5).

Likewise there are no distinctions according to social or economic status. Paul told the Christian **slave** to be obedient to his master, "as to Christ," and he told the Christian master, a **free man,** to "give up threatening, knowing that" the Master of both "is in heaven, and there is no partiality with Him" (Eph. 6:5, 9).

James warned, "My brethren, do not hold your faith in our glorious Lord Jesus Christ with an attitude of personal favoritism. For if a man comes into your assembly with a gold ring and dressed in fine clothes, and there also comes in a poor man in dirty clothes, and you pay special attention to the one who is wearing the fine clothes, and say, 'You sit here in a good place,' and you say to the poor man, 'You stand over there, or sit down by my footstool,' have you not made distinctions among yourselves, and become judges with evil motives? . . . If you show partiality, you are committing sin" (James 2:1-4, 9). The oneness of the Body of Christ focuses on common spiritual life and privilege, as Paul wrote to the Ephesians: "Being diligent to preserve the unity of the Spirit in the bond of peace. There is one body and one Spirit, just as also you were called in one hope of your calling; one Lord, one faith, one baptism, one God and Father of all who is over all and through all and in all. But to each one of us grace was given according to the measure of Christ's gift" (Eph. 4:3-7).

Nor are there spiritual distinctions according to sex. **There is neither male nor female.** In recognizing believing women as the full spiritual equals of believing men, Christianity elevated women to a status they had never known before in the ancient world. In matters of rule in the home and in the church God has established the headship of men. But in the dimension of spiritual possessions and privilege there is absolutely no difference.

HEIRS OF THE PROMISE

And if you belong to Christ, then you are Abraham's offspring, heirs according to promise. (3:29)

The spiritual **promise** of eternal salvation and blessing given to **Abraham** belongs to all those who **belong to Christ.** They are all **heirs according to that promise,** which is fulfilled in **Christ.** This is not a reference to the promises given to Abraham regarding the land (Gen. 12:1; 13:14-15; 17:8), but refers to the spiritual blessings that come to all who, being justified by faith just as Abraham was (Gen. 15:6; Rom. 4:3-11), will inherit the spiritual promises given to Abraham. Not all the physical seed of Abraham will receive the promises of salvation (Rom. 9:6-11), but many who are not physical seed of Abraham will receive them by coming to God by faith as he did, thereby becoming his spiritual **offspring.**

Those who are children of God are "heirs also, heirs of God and fellow heirs with Christ" (Rom. 8:17). Christ's inheritance belongs to "all those who are sanctified" (Acts 20:32), His fellow "heirs according to the hope of eternal life" (Titus 3:7). They are "sealed in Him with the Holy Spirit of promise" (Eph. 1:13), the **promise** of inheriting God Himself. "The Lord is the portion of my inheritance and my cup," exulted David (Ps. 16:5).

In his vision on Patmos, John "heard a loud voice from the throne, saying, 'Behold, the tabernacle of God is among men, and He shall dwell among them, and they shall be His people, and God Himself shall be among them, and He shall wipe away every tear from their eyes; and there shall no longer be any death; there shall no longer be any mourning, or crying, or pain. . . . He who overcomes shall inherit these things, and I will be his God and he will be My son'" (Rev. 21:3-4, 7).

John Stott lucidly summarizes his comments on this passage in the following words: "We cannot come to Christ to be justified until we have first been to Moses to be condemned. But once we have gone to Moses, and acknowledged our sin, guilt and condemnation, we must not stay there. We must let Moses send us to Christ" (*The Message of Galatians* [London: Inter-Varsity, 1968], p. 102).

Sons of God (4:1-11)

10

Now I say, as long as the heir is a child, he does not differ at all from a slave although he is owner of everything, but he is under guardians and managers until the date set by the father. So also we, while we were children, were held in bondage under the elemental things of the world. But when the fulness of the time came, God sent forth His Son, born of a woman, born under the Law, in order that He might redeem those who were under the Law, that we might receive the adoption as sons. And because you are sons, God has sent forth the Spirit of His Son into our hearts, crying, "Abba! Father!" Therefore you are no longer a slave, but a son; and if a son, then an heir through God.

However at that time, when you did not know God, you were slaves to those which by nature are no gods. But now that you have come to know God, or rather to be known by God, how is it that you turn back again to the weak and worthless elemental things, to which you desire to be enslaved all over again? You observe days and months and seasons and years. I fear for you, that perhaps I have labored over you in vain. (4:1-11)

Continuing his basic argument that salvation is not gained by man's merit or works but solely by God's sovereign grace working through man's faith, Paul further develops the analogy of a child becoming an adult (see 3:23-26). He compares the position and privileges of a child to those of a servant, with the figures of child and servant representing life under the law and the figures of adult and son representing life in Christ.

The analogy continues to contrast man before salvation, when, whether Jew or Gentile, he is under God's law, and man after salvation, when he is in Christ. The central truths of 4:1-11 are that life under law is meant by God to be preparation for divine sonship and that trust in His grace brings realization of that sonship.

PREPARATION FOR SONSHIP: UNDER LAW

Now I say, as long as the heir is a child, he does not differ at all from a slave although he is owner of everything, but he is under guardians and managers until the date set by the father. So also we, while we were children, were held in bondage under the elemental things of the world. (4:1-3)

In the ancient world the division between childhood and adulthood was much more definitive than it is in most societies today. Although ancient customs varied, there was usually a prescribed age when **a child**, especially a boy, would officially come of age and take on the privileges and responsibilities of adulthood. As mentioned in the previous chapter, the Roman ceremony marking that change in status was called *toga virilis,* and the Jewish ceremony was (and still is) called bar mitzvah.

Until the age of twelve, a Jewish boy was under the direct and absolute control of his father. But at the bar mitzvah, observed on the first Sabbath after his twelfth birthday, the boy's father would pray, "Blessed be thou O God who hath taken from me the responsibility of this boy," and the boy would pray, "O my God and God of my father, on this solemn and sacred day which marks my passage from boyhood to manhood, I humbly raise my eyes unto Thee and declare with sincerity and truth that henceforth I will keep Thy commandments and undertake to bear the responsibility of my actions toward Thee."

In ancient Greece a boy was under his father's control until about the age of eighteen. At that time a festival called an *apatouria* would be held in which the boy was declared an *ephebos,* a type of cadet, with special responsibilities to his clan or city state for a period of two years. During the coming-of-age ceremony, the boy's long hair would be cut off and offered to the god Apollo.

At the Roman ceremony boys would take their toys—and at a similar ceremony girls would take their dolls—and offer them in a sacrifice to the gods as a symbol of putting childhood behind them. It was to that custom that Paul alludes in his comment, "When I became a man, I did away with childish things" (1 Cor. 13:11).

The illustration of a **child** (*nēpios,* infant, one without understanding, or a minor) coming of age was therefore easily understood by both Jews and Gentiles to whom Paul wrote. They were well aware that **as long as the heir** was **a child, he** was under conditions that did **not differ at all from** those of **a slave.** As son and **heir** of all his father's possessions and duties, a boy was the potential and rightful **owner of**

everything that belonged to his father. But as William Hendricksen points out, he was only an *heir de jure,* not an *heir de facto;* he was heir by legal right but not heir in fact.

While **a child,** he was **under guardians and managers until the date set by the father.** Families would assign certain capable and trusted slaves to act as **guardians** (a general term for a person who cared for underage boys) **and managers** (house stewards) over the child until he was grown. Along with his tutor (*paidagōgos,* see the discussion of 3:24-25), those family slaves would have virtually full charge of the child's education, training, and welfare. The **child** was subservient to them and could do nothing without their permission and go nowhere without their companionship. For all practical purposes, the **child** did **not differ at all from a slave** under whom he was being trained. Just as **a slave** had masters, so he had masters.

But at the **date set by the father,** the child's status changed radically. He was no longer simply an *heir de jure* but became an *heir de facto.* He was no longer **a child** or like **a slave,** but a responsible adult and citizen.

In a similar way, **so also we, while we were** under the law as unbelieving **children, were held in bondage.** For an unbeliever there is potential salvation and fulfillment of the promise given to all the world through Abraham (Gen. 12:3). But unless and until he spiritually "comes of age" through saving trust in Jesus Christ, every unbeliever is a kind of slave and is imprisoned **under the elemental things of the world.**

Elemental things is from *stoicheion,* which has the root meaning of "row" or "rank," signifying foundational and rudimentary orderliness. It was used, for instance, of the letters of the alphabet, the elemental building blocks of writing.

Paul does not specify what **the elemental things of the world** represent, and Bible scholars have offered many suggestions. Some hold that it refers to the demon spirits who rule the present **world** system. Others say it refers to stars and therefore to pagan systems of astrology. Still others believe it refers to the basic, **elemental things** of human religion; and that interpretation seems appropriate in this context, especially in light of the fact that in 4:9 the same phrase is connected with the ceremonial rituals of human religion.

In Colossians 2:8 Paul warns: "See to it that no one takes you captive through philosophy and empty deception, according to the tradition of men, according to the elementary principles of the world, rather than according to Christ." Here Paul clearly associates "elementary principles of the world" with deceptive human tradition and philosophy. The heart of Jewish religion during New Testament times was the system of rabbinic traditions that had superceded and stifled the revealed truth of the Old Testament. In the Gentile world of that day, human philosophy and pagan religions were closely interrelated. And both Jewish traditions and pagan religions centered in man-made systems of works. They were filled with rules and regulations, the obeying of which were thought to make a person right with deity. **The elemental things** of all human religion, whether Jewish or Gentile, ancient or modern, inevitably involve the idea of achieving divine acceptance by one's own efforts. And they are **elemental** in that they are only human, never rising beyond the mundane to the divine.

John Wesley was an honor graduate of Oxford University, an ordained clergyman in the Church of England and orthodox in theology. He was active in practical good works, regularly visiting the inmates of prisons and workhouses in London and helping distribute food and clothing to slum children and orphans. He studied the Bible diligently and attended numerous Sunday services as well as various other services during the week. He generously gave offerings to the church and alms to the poor. He prayed and fasted and lived an exemplary moral life. He even spent several years as a missionary to American Indians in what was then the British colony of Georgia. Yet upon returning to England he confessed in his journal, "I who went to America to convert others was never myself converted to God." Later reflecting on his preconversion condition, he said, "I had even then the faith of a servant, though not that of a son."

Wesley tirelessly did everything he could to live a life acceptable to God, yet he knew something vital was missing. It was not until he went "very unwillingly to a society in Aldersgate Street" one evening that he discovered and claimed true Christian life. "I felt my heart strangely warmed," he wrote. "I felt I did trust in Christ, Christ alone, for salvation; and an assurance was given me that He had taken away my sins, even mine, and saved me from the law of sin and death." Things were no longer **elemental** for Wesley. He had entered "the heavenlies."

REALIZATION OF Sonship

But when the fulness of the time came, God sent forth His Son, born of a woman, born under the Law, in order that He might redeem those who were under the Law, that we might receive the adoption as sons. And because you are sons, God has sent forth the Spirit of His Son into our hearts, crying, "Abba! Father!" Therefore you are no longer a slave, but a son; and if a son, then an heir through God.

However at that time, when you did not know God, you were slaves to those which by nature are no gods. But now that you have come to know God, or rather to be known by God, how is it that you turn back again to the weak and worthless elemental things, to which you desire to be enslaved all over again? You observe days and months and seasons and years. I fear for you, that perhaps I have labored over you in vain. (4:4-11)

In these 8 verses Paul plunges into the source, the confirmation, the consummation, and the obligation of the divine sonship realized by those who have personal faith in Jesus Christ.

ITS SOURCE

But when the fulness of the time came, God sent forth His Son, born of a woman, born under the Law, in order that He might redeem those who were under the Law, that we might receive the adoption as sons. (4:4-5)

The source of divine sonship is the true **Son**, Jesus Christ. Just as a human father in ancient times set the time of his son's coming of age, so did **God** the Father set **the time** to send **forth His** incarnate **Son** to earth as man's Redeemer. It was in **the fulness of the time** that Jesus Christ **came,** exactly as and when the Father had established.

Even the most godly Jews of the Old Covenant died without receiving the fulfillment of God's promise to Abraham. "All these, having gained approval through their faith, did not receive what was promised" (Heb. 11:39). Like believers of every age, they will ultimately receive the fullness of the promise. But during their lifetimes they too lived as heirs *de jure,* not heirs *de facto.*

When **God sent forth His Son,** He provided the guarantee that those believers and all others would become joint heirs with the **Son.** Those who under the law are no better than slaves (4:1) will **receive** full and complete **adoption as sons.**

The fulness of time refers to the completion of the period of preparation in God's sovereign timetable of redemption. When the law had fully accomplished its purpose of showing man his utter sinfulness and inability to live up to God's perfect standard of righteousness, God ushered in a new era of redemption. When He **sent forth His Son,** He provided the righteousness for man that man could not provide for himself.

When Jesus was born, everything was right for the coming of the Messiah. First of all, the time was right religiously. During the Babylonian captivity, Israel once and for all forsook the idolatry into which she had so often fallen. Despite their many other sins and failures, including the national rejection of their own Messiah, no significant number of Jews has ever again turned to idolatry.

Also during the Exile, Jews developed synagogues, which they used as places of worship, as schools, and as courts. In addition to that, they at last had the completed Old Testament, assembled by Ezra and others after the return from Babylon. Those features facilitated the proclaiming of the Messiah's gospel among the people of Israel.

Second, the time was right culturally. Christians who propagated the gospel during the first several centuries had a common language with those to whom they witnessed and with whom they worshiped. Alexander the Great had thoroughly established Greek culture and language throughout the known world, and these continued their dominating influence long after Rome succeeded Greece as world ruler.

Third, the time was right politically. Rome had instituted the *pax Romana* (Roman peace), which provided economic and political stability. The apostles and other early preachers and teachers could travel freely and safely throughout the empire and could do so on the magnificent system of roads built by the Romans.

Each of those factors was in some unique way a key to the spread of the gospel. God's timing was perfect.

When God's propitious **time came,** He **sent forth His Son. Son** does not refer to Jesus' divine essence. He was not by nature eternally subordinate to **God** the Father but was equal to Him, yet He willingly submitted Himself to the Father during His incarnation, as an obedient son does to an earthly father. It seems that Jesus had not been eternally subject to the Father but was subject only during the time of His humanity. Paul makes that fact clear when he refers to the kenosis (emptying): "Although He existed in the form of God, [He] did not regard equality with God a thing to be grasped, but emptied Himself, taking the form of a bond-servant, and being made in the likeness of men" (Phil. 2:6-7). Jesus is eternally "the radiance of [God's] glory and the exact representation of His nature, and upholds all things by the word of His power" (Heb. 1:3).

Some 900 years before Jesus was born God prophesied, "I will be a Father to Him, and He shall be a Son to Me" (Heb. 1:5; 2 Sam. 7:14), indicating that in eternity past that, though there were always three persons in the Trinity, there were not yet the roles of Father and Son. Those designations apparently came into being only at the incarnation. In the announcement of Jesus' birth to Mary, the angel Gabriel declared, "He will be great, and *will be called* the Son of the Most High; . . . the holy offspring *shall be called* the Son of God" (Luke 1:32, 35; emphasis added). **Son** was a new name, never before applied to the second person of the Godhead except prophetically, as in Psalm 2:7, which is interpreted in Hebrews 1:5-6 as referring to the event of His incarnation. John wrote, "In the beginning was the Word, and the Word was with God, and the Word was God" (John 1:1). Only when "the Word became flesh, and dwelt among us" as "the only begotten God" (John 1:14, 18) did He take on the role and function of **Son.**

Born of a woman is not intended to be an exclusive statement emphasizing the absence of a man, and thus does not so much refer to Jesus' virgin birth, important as that great truth is, as to His complete humanity. He was fully man, **born of a woman** like all other men, yet He was fully God. Otherwise He could not have been Savior of the world. He had to be fully God in order for His sacrifice to have the infinite worth necessary to atone for the sin of mankind. He also had to be fully man in order to represent mankind and take the penalty of sin upon Himself in man's behalf. It was man who sinned, who was under the curse, and who was condemned to render his life forfeit to God. Jesus therefore could not have substituted for sinful man on the cross had He not taken upon Himself "the likeness of men" (Phil. 2:7). He had to be God to have the power of Savior, and He had to be man to have the position of Substitute.

Jesus not only came to earth as a man but was **born under the Law, in order that He might redeem those who were under the Law.** As Paul explains in Romans, "For what the Law could not do, weak as it was through the flesh, God did: sending His own Son in the likeness of sinful flesh and as an offering for sin, He condemned sin in the flesh, in order that the requirement of the Law might be fulfilled in us" (Rom. 8:3-4).

Like every other man, Jesus was **born under the Law.** Like every other Jew, He was **under** obligation to obey and be judged by conformity to God's written **Law** in the Old Testament; but unlike any other Jew, He satisfied the requirements of that law by living in perfect obedience to it. And because He lived in perfect obedience, He was able to **redeem** all other men **who were under the Law** but *not* obedient to it, provided they had saving faith in Him.

As explained in chapter 7 (under Gal. 3:13), **redeem** is from *exagorazō,* which literally means to buy out or buy back and was used of slaves whose freedom was purchased. Through payment of the required price, slaves were redeemed and became free men, and, more than that, they received **adoption as sons** (cf. Rom. 8:15, 23; 9:4; Eph. 1:5; 3:14-15). That completed their liberation.

Huiothesia (**adoption**) is a compound of *huios* (son) and *thesis* (a placing) and refers to a man's giving the status of sonship to someone who is not his natural child. Because men are not naturally the children of God, they can become His **sons** only by divine **adoption**. In the Roman world **adoption** was an honored custom that gave special dignity and family membership to those who were not born into a family. Often a wealthy, childless man would adopt a young slave, who would trade his slavery for sonship, with all its concomitant privileges.

ITS CONFIRMATION

And because you are sons, God has sent forth the Spirit of His Son into our hearts, crying, "Abba! Father!" (4:6)

God confirms believers as His adopted **sons** through the gift of the Holy Spirit, **the Spirit of His Son.** They not only have the knowledge of sonship through the truth of God's Word in their minds but the very essence of sonship through His indwelling **Spirit** in their **hearts.** A human father cannot give his own nature to an adopted child, but God can and does by sending His Holy Spirit to dwell within the **hearts** of believers.

The Lord tells His children that He "has blessed [them] with every spiritual blessing in the heavenly places in Christ," that "He chose [them] before the foundation of the world, that [they] should be holy and blameless before Him," that "He predestined [them] to adoption as sons through Jesus Christ to Himself," and that "in Him [they] have redemption through His blood, the forgiveness of [their] trespasses, according to the riches of His grace, which He lavished upon [them]" (Eph. 1:3-5, 7-8). But when believers experience trying circumstances or fail to live in obedience to God, it is easy for them to doubt their exalted position as His children.

One of the ministries of **the Spirit** to the **sons** of **God** is to enable them with full confidence to cry out to Him, **"Abba! Father!"** **The Spirit** offers subjective ministry that confirms the objective truth of Scripture. Declaring that same message to believers at Rome, Paul wrote, "For all who are being led by the Spirit of God, these are sons of God. For you have not received a spirit of slavery leading to fear again, but you have received a spirit of adoption as sons by which we cry out, 'Abba! Father!' The Spirit Himself bears witness with our spirit that we are children of God" (Rom. 8:14-16).

As mentioned in the previous chapter, **Abba** is a diminutive of the Aramaic word for father. It was a term of endearment used by young children of their fathers and could be translated "daddy" or "papa." The Holy **Spirit** brings us into a personal, intimate relationship with our heavenly **Father,** whom we may approach at any time and under any circumstance, knowing that He always hears us and lovingly cares for us, because we are truly His own.

"In Him, you also," Paul wrote to the Ephesians, "after listening to the message of truth, the gospel of your salvation—having also believed, you were sealed in Him with the Holy Spirit of promise, who is given as a pledge of our inheritance, with a view to the redemption of God's own possession, to the praise of His glory" (Eph. 1:13-14). The fact that a believer has an intimate relationship with God, and can confidently cry out to Him as **Father,** is beautiful and magnificent proof of sonship. Those who have the status of divine sonship through the **Son** also have the essence and the assurance of it through **the Spirit,** who draws them into intimate communion with their heavenly Father.

ITS CONSUMMATION

Therefore you are no longer a slave, but a son; and if a son, then an heir through God. (4:7)

The consummation of divine sonship is given in the promise of joint inheritance with Christ. The ultimate outcome of our relationship is inheritance of the Father's estate. In the spiritual realm, a person who believes in Jesus Christ is no longer under the law, **no longer** its **slave.** Because he is now in the Son, he is himself **a son; and if a son, then an heir through God.** Just as it was in the ancient laws of adoption, so it is in the family of God—sonship means heirship.

Because believers are God's children, they are "heirs also, heirs of God and fellow heirs with Christ" (Rom. 8:17). What an incomprehensible truth: that by giving ourselves to Jesus Christ in faith, God gives us everything His Son possesses!

ITS OBLIGATION

However at that time, when you did not know God, you were slaves to those which by nature are no gods. But now that you have come to know God, or rather to be known by God, how is it that you turn back again to the weak and worthless elemental things, to which you desire to be enslaved all over again? You observe days and months and seasons and years. I fear for you, that perhaps I have labored over you in vain. (4:8-11)

The gracious gift of sonship is free, but it brings serious obligation. Great blessing carries great responsibility (Luke 12:48). But the believer's great responsibility is not to the ceremonial and ritual features of the law, from which salvation sets him free. It is that truth that the Galatian believers had forgotten under the seductive influence of the Judaizers.

Paul reminds those believers of the **time, when** they **did not know God** and **were slaves to those which by nature are no gods.** Before they came to Christ their religion was that of works, and they were **slaves to** various man-made gods that were actually **no gods** at all. The unredeemed are slaves not only to the law but also to idols.

Several years ago, I visited a very large Buddhist shrine. Scores of men and women, and even some children, were bowing down to a giant stone image of Buddha, reciting prescribed prayers, going through various incantations, and making offerings of incense and food. My heart broke because of their spiritual darkness and hopelessness. I wanted to shout, "Why are you doing all this? Don't you know that image is only a piece of stone carved by men? There is no god here. Buddha can't help you. He himself is long dead—physically and spiritually—and will eternally remain dead. If you continue to trust in him, you too will die and forever remain dead." There are many false gods men put their trust in, but none can save.

While those people were pitiable because of their ignorance of God, they were also condemned because of their rebelliousness against God. "That which is known about God is evident within them," Paul says of such people; "for God made it evident to them. For since the creation of the world His invisible attributes, His eternal power and divine nature, have been clearly seen, being understood through what has been made, so that they are without excuse. For even though they knew God, they did not honor Him as God, or give thanks; but they became futile in their speculations, and their foolish heart was darkened. . . . For they exchanged the truth of God for a lie, and worshiped and served the creature rather than the Creator" (Rom. 1:19-21, 25).

But now that you have come to know God, or rather to be known by God, Paul asks in bewilderment, **how is it that you turn back again to the weak and worthless elemental things** to which you once gave your devotion? Why do you **desire to be enslaved all over again?** Now that you are sons, he asks the wavering Galatians, why do you want to go back into slavery? Now that you are free adults through faith in Christ, why do you want to revert to your childhood servitude under the law?

Among the **weak and worthless elemental things** to which some of the Galatians were returning was the ritualistic observance of **days and months and seasons and years.** During his ministry in Galatia, Paul doubtlessly gave believers the same warning he gave to the church at Colossae: "Let no one act as your judge in regard to food or drink or in respect to a festival or a new moon or a Sabbath day— things which are a mere shadow of what is to come; but the substance belongs to Christ" (Col. 2:16-17). "If you have died with Christ to the elementary principles of the world," he continues, "why, as if you were living in the world, do you submit yourself to decrees, such as, 'Do not handle, do not taste, do not touch!' (which all refer to things destined to perish with the using)—in accordance with the commandments and teachings of men? These are matters which have, to be sure, the appearance of wisdom in self-made religion and self-abasement and severe treatment of the body, but are of no value against fleshly indulgence" (vv. 20-23).

In his commentary *The Message of Galatians,* John Stott mentions the wonderful account of John Newton, author of the beloved hymn "Amazing Grace." Newton was an only child and lost his mother when he was seven. At the age of eleven he went to sea as a sailor and became involved in the inhuman African slave trade. Soon hardened by his evil surroundings, he outdid his companions in immorality, vulgarity, and blasphemy. But when he was twenty-three his ship was caught in a severe storm, and when he began to fear for his life he cried out to God for mercy and was marvelously saved. Not wanting ever to forget the depths of sin from which he had been rescued by God's grace, Newton later inscribed the words of Deuteronomy 15:15 above his mantel: "And thou shalt remember that thou wast a bondman in the land of Egypt, and the Lord thy God redeemed thee."

Unlike John Newton, the Galatian Christians did not remember what they were once like, and Paul was inexpressibly disappointed with their immaturity and lack of discernment. He was not able to fathom how they could so quickly forget their former bondage in unbelief and so easily surrender their new freedom and blessings in Christ. **I fear for you,** he lamented, **that perhaps I have labored over you in vain.**

How sad for such a faithful servant of the Lord to believe that all the life-threatening, sacrificial service he had given in behalf of the people of Galatia was worthless. All the travel, illness, loneliness, struggles, even the stoning he received in Lystra that left him for dead, was for nothing if they reverted to their old slavery.

No wonder this is such an impassioned epistle. The thought of all that effort being void compelled Paul to write as he did.

Till Christ Be Formed in You

(4:12-20)

I beg of you, brethren, become as I am, for I also have become as you are. You have done me no wrong; but you know that it was because of a bodily illness that I preached the gospel to you the first time; and that which was a trial to you in my bodily condition you did not despise or loathe, but you received me as an angel of God, as Christ Jesus Himself. Where then is that sense of blessing you had? For I bear you witness, that if possible, you would have plucked out your eyes and given them to me. Have I therefore become your enemy by telling you the truth? They eagerly seek you, not commendably, but they wish to shut you out, in order that you may seek them. But it is good always to be eagerly sought in a commendable manner, and not only when I am present with you. My children, with whom I am again in labor until Christ is formed in you—but I could wish to be present with you now and to change my tone, for I am perplexed about you. (4:12-20)

Until this point in the letter, Paul's approach has been confrontational and impersonal. He has been writing like a scholar or debater, marshaling every possible argument and illustration to get his message across. He has taken the stance of a determined lawyer in court or a learned theologian in the classroom, giving a dispassionate and irrefutable presentation. He has referred to the Old Testament to teach the Galatians the basic truth of the gospel he had taught them many times before: salvation is by God's grace alone, forgiving man's lawbreaking sin and becoming effective through man's faith alone. He has used both his own experience and that of the Galatians to reinforce his teaching. But for the most part, he has sounded detached, seeming to be more concerned about principles than people.

But the apostle's approach changes dramatically in verse 12 of chapter 4. His anger at the Judaizers subsides, and he moves from the purely doctrinal to the more personal. In fact, verses 12-20 are the strongest words of personal affection Paul uses in any of his letters. He does not so much preach or teach as simply pour out his heart in personal exhortation. He says, in effect, "I care about you more than I can say. I love you dearly just as you have loved me dearly. Please listen to what I'm saying, because it's so vitally essential."

Paul's source of gentleness was Christ Himself, as seen in his appeal to the immature and stubborn Corinthians, who continually tried his patience: "I, Paul, myself urge you by the meekness and gentleness of Christ" (2 Cor. 10:1).

The apostle's spirit here reminds us that there must be a gentle side to every faithful servant of God (see 2 Tim. 2:24). No matter how serious the doctrine he may have to defend or how corrupting the immorality he may have to expose, he dare not lose his sensitivity and compassion.

In the course of his intimate outpouring to the Galatians in 4:12-20, Paul first appeals to them, then fondly remembers their loving acceptance of him, warns them about the ulterior motives of the Judaizers, and finally tells them of his desire to be with them again in person.

HIS APPEAL TO THEM

I beg of you, brethren, become as I am, for I also have become as you are.
(4:12a)

Paul's appeal to his **brethren** in Christ was for them to recognize and live by the spiritual freedom all believers have in God's grace. That is the central truth of the epistle, a truth he had previously preached and taught to the Galatians but one the Judaizers had seduced them into doubting and forsaking.

I beg of you, . . . become as I am, he pleaded, free from trying to earn salvation by keeping the law and free from having to live by its outward symbols, ceremonies, rituals, and restrictions. "I died to the Law, that I might live to God," he had already written (2:19). Now he implored them to confess again that death to the law as a way of sanctification, which death they, too, had experienced when they trusted in Jesus Christ as Lord and Savior. While all believers are called to live in obedience to God's moral standards that never change (such living is the evidence of salvation, as indicated in Eph. 2:6-10), they can no more live by the law than they could have been saved by it. "It was for freedom that Christ set us free; therefore keep standing firm and do not be subject again to a yoke of slavery" (5:1).

For now, Paul presents no more arguments but rather gives a heartfelt exhortation. "You know how I have always lived since receiving Christ," he said in effect, "and how I lived while I ministered among you. That is the way I want you to live as well."

The reason for Paul's appeal is also personal: because **I also have become as you are.** When he came to Christ he had torn away every shred of legalism, in which he had been enmeshed more tightly than perhaps few other Jews of his day (see Phil. 3:4-6). Although he now willingly became like a Jew when among Jews and like a Gentile when among Gentiles, becoming "all things to all men, that [he might] by all means save some" (1 Cor. 9:20-22), Paul never represented himself nor thought of himself as anything but a sinner redeemed by Jesus Christ, in whom "there is neither Jew nor Greek, . . . slave nor free man, . . . male nor female" (Gal. 3:28). Upon the advice of the elders in the Jerusalem church, Paul agreed on one occasion to sponsor four men in taking a certain Jewish vow in the Temple, in order to keep from needlessly offending unbelieving Jews (Acts 21:23-26). But he did so as an act of his liberty as a Christian, not under the compulsion of the law.

The Jewish believers in Galatia knew well that Paul had abandoned his former subservience not only to the rabbinic traditions but even to the ceremonial law of Moses (cf. Acts 21:21). Many of those believers, like Paul himself, had paid a dear price when they turned from Judaism to Christ, being ostracized from their families and synagogues and treated as if dead. Yet they were now being intimidated by the Judaizers into returning to their former bondage under the law. "I introduced you to freedom," Paul was saying; "don't turn back to slavery."

His Remembrance of Them

You have done me no wrong; but you know that it was because of a bodily illness that I preached the gospel to you the first time; and that which was a trial to you in my bodily condition you did not despise or loathe, but you received me as an angel of God, as Christ Jesus Himself. Where then is that sense of blessing you had? For I bear you witness, that if possible, you would have plucked out your eyes and given them to me. Have I therefore become your enemy by telling you the truth? (4:12b-16)

The verse division here is unfortunate in that 12b obviously belongs with verse 13. Paul makes a rather abrupt change of emphasis, reminding the Galatians of how rich and deep their personal relationship with him had once been. They not only had **done** him **no wrong** but had openly and lovingly received him while he was in extremely adverse personal circumstances. "How then," he was wondering, "could you reject me now, after being so accepting of me then?"

When Paul first went to Galatia, many Jews turned against him when they realized his message was as much for Gentiles as Jews (Acts 13:45, 50; 14:19). But God used him in the salvation of many converts there, both Jews and Gentiles (13:43–14:1), and those who accepted his message also accepted him, despite a serious physical affliction he had at the time. It was, in fact, **because of a bodily illness that** Paul had **preached the gospel to** them **the first time.**

On his first missionary journey Paul apparently either became seriously ill while in Galatia or else went there to recuperate. Some suggest that he contracted malaria while traveling through the low, swampy regions of Pamphylia and decided to go up into the higher and healthier area of Galatia and minister there for a while until he was better (see Acts 13:13-14). Although malaria can be terribly painful and debilitating, those effects are not continuous. If Paul did have that disease, he would have still been able to do some preaching and teaching between attacks of fever and pain. This explanation is plausible.

Whatever the **illness**, it **was a trial to** the Galatians, because his **bodily condition** was such that the normal response to it was revulsion. But the believers there **did not despise or loathe** Paul's affliction, repulsive as it was. The Greek term behind **despise** means to count as nothing or worthless, and the term behind **loathe** literally means "to spit," which was often done as an act of contempt. Paul was treated neither as worthless nor with contempt.

In ancient times, without benefit of good medicines, sterile bandages, and other such modern care, diseases were often disfiguring and their stench nauseating. To most ancients, including Jews, physical affliction was considered a form of divine judgment. Jesus' disciples asked Him about the blind beggar in Jerusalem, "Rabbi, who sinned, this man or his parents, that he should be born blind?" (John 9:2). Theirs was the same assumption Job's three friends made regarding his tragedies (Job 4:7-9; 8:1-6; 11:13-20) and that the natives of Malta made regarding Paul's being bitten by a deadly viper (Acts 28:3-4).

The fact that Paul's affliction was not a barrier to his credibility either to the Jews or Gentiles of Galatia was totally unexpected. The apostle was amazed that they even **received** him **as an angel of God, as Christ Jesus Himself.** They did not question what he said or the way he looked. They had no doubt that he was God's messenger and the apostolic representative of the Lord Jesus and were grateful beyond measure for the blessing of spiritual life they had received because of his ministry. After only his second message in Pisidian Antioch, the Gentiles there "began rejoicing and glorifying the word of the Lord" (Acts 13:48).

From the human perspective, Paul's going to Galatia seemed purely circumstantial, necessitated by a tragic disease. Yet his reception by those who believed the gospel he preached was beyond anything he could have anticipated. During the first trip to Galatia, persecution had been severe, and Paul had even been stoned and left for dead by those hostile to the gospel (Acts 14:19). But as he later returned to Antioch with Barnabas, one can imagine how he must have marveled over the vastly contrasting love and kindness he had received from believers.

But now he asked them, **Where then is that sense of blessing you had? For I bear you witness, that if possible, you would have plucked out your eyes and given them to me.** *Makarismos* (**blessing**) can also be translated "happiness" or "satisfaction" and implies a feeling of joy, fulfillment, and contentedness.

"From the beginning you were satisfied and happy with me and with the message of grace I preached," Paul was saying. "What made you lose that satisfaction? Why have you turned against me and against the gospel of grace?" He refreshed their memories that once they loved him so much that **you would have plucked out your eyes and given them to me.**

Paul may simply have been using a common figure of speech, suggesting that the Galatians would have given up their very eyesight, the most precious and irreplaceable of the physical senses, if doing that could have helped him. If, as some interpreters speculate, Paul's bodily affliction was a form of eye disease, he may here have been referring to the Galatians' willingness to have literally exchanged their eyes for his, had such a transplant been **possible** in those days.

Eye disease was common in ancient times, as it still is in most underdeveloped countries today. If Paul had an eye affliction it could have been a condition of long standing, perhaps the "thorn in the flesh" that was "a messenger of Satan" the Lord allowed him to endure as a humbling reminder of His sufficient grace (2 Cor. 12:7-9). Because malaria sometimes attacks the optic nerve, causing loss of color recognition, atrophy, and even blindness, his affliction while in Galatia may have affected the way he saw as well as the way he looked. The possibility of poor eyesight is substantiated by the closing section of the Galatian epistle itself, which begins: "See with what large letters I am writing to you with my own hand" (6:11). Paul usually dictated his letters to an amanuensis, a type of stenographer (see Rom. 16:22), but often added a postscript or personal greeting in his own hand (1 Cor. 16:21; Col. 4:18; 2 Thess. 3:17). If he had limited vision, he would likely have used larger than normal letters in order to see what he was writing.

Whatever the specific nature of Paul's illness, his primary point here is clear: the Galatians had loved him with a love that would have compelled them to make any sacrifice on his behalf.

After only a few years, however, the situation had radically changed. Now Paul asked in bewilderment, **Have I therefore become your enemy by telling you the truth?**

The Galatian believers who had succumbed to the Judaizing heresy were guilty of spiritual defection. Nothing tears the heart of a faithful pastor, teacher, youth worker, or missionary so much as seeing someone he has led to the Lord turn away from the faith. How much more does such defection grieve the Lord Himself?

In confronting the spiritual defection of Judah, Isaiah asked on behalf of God: "What more was there to do for My vineyard that I have not done in it?" (Isa. 5:4). Jesus lamented over Jerusalem, "O Jerusalem, Jerusalem, the city that kills the prophets and stones those sent to her! How often I wanted to gather your children together, just as a hen gathers her brood under her wings, and you would not have it!" (Luke 13:34). God continually gave everything He could possibly give to His chosen people, Israel, including His own incarnate Son. They called themselves by God's name, but they refused to obey His will or come to Him in faith to have their sins forgiven.

"When Israel was a youth I loved him," God had said through the prophet Hosea. "And out of Egypt I called My son. The more they called them, the more they went from them; they kept sacrificing to the Baals and burning incense to idols. Yet it is I who taught Ephraim to walk, I took them in My arms; but they did not know that I healed them. I led them with cords of a man, with bonds of love" (Hos. 11:1-4). God had, as it were, given birth to Israel, taught her how to walk, bandaged her wounds, taken her in His arms to comfort her, and nurtured her—only to have her turn her back on Him and go her own way. "What shall I do with you, O Ephraim? What shall I do with you, O Judah?" God asked in dismay. "For your loyalty is like a morning cloud, and like the dew which goes away early" (6:4).

Yet throughout Israel's rebelliousness, God's gracious offer of forgiveness stood as a beacon to call her back to Himself. "Return, O Israel, to the Lord your God, for you have stumbled because of your iniquity. Take words with you and return to the Lord. Say to Him, 'Take away all iniquity, and receive us graciously'" (Hos. 14:1-2).

Paul admonishes believers not to "grieve the Holy Spirit of God, by whom [they are] sealed for the day of redemption" (Eph. 4:30). The Father, Son, and Holy Spirit alike experience grief when those who have been called to the freedom of gracious salvation defect. Just as there is great rejoicing in heaven when even one sinner turns to the Lord (Luke 15:7), there is also great heartbreak in heaven when even one believer sinfully turns away from Him.

The implication is that on a second trip to Galatia by Paul some of the church members there had already come under the influence of the Judaizers and had begun to doubt **the truth** of salvation by faith alone, which they had learned and accepted from him. The gospel of legalism had become more attractive to them than the gospel of grace, and the man who had been their beloved friend had become to them like an **enemy.**

Many people appreciate a preacher or teacher only as long as he says what they want to hear. The confused and defecting believers in Galatia had once greatly admired Paul, but now they looked on him as their **enemy,** because he confronted them with **the truth** about the genuine gospel of God, which had saved them, and the false teaching of the Judaizers, which led them back into the bondage of legalism.

There is little doubt that among the Galatians there were also some who had never really been saved and thus were easily turned back to self-righteous legalism.

A prostitute came to our church one day looking for help. She was quite successful financially but was plagued by tremendous feelings of guilt and anxiety. She drank heavily, took drugs, and realized her life was a mess. When I explained the gospel to her and assured her that God was eager to forgive her sins and give her new life if she trusted in Jesus Christ, she expressed great interest. During the course of our conversation she had told me of a little book in which she kept the names and phone numbers of her customers. I suggested that we take the book and burn it right then, as a symbol of her repentance and renunciation of her old life. But she balked at the idea, saying, "I can't do that! Those names are worth thousands of dollars. I guess I don't want Jesus as much as I thought I did." Like many people, she knew her way of life was wrong and ruinous, but she loved it more than the Lord and would not give it up.

His Warning to Them

They eagerly seek you, not commendably, but they wish to shut you out, in order that you may seek them. But it is good always to be eagerly sought in a commendable manner, and not only when I am present with you. (4:17-18)

Paul again warns the Galatians about their real enemies, the Judaizers (cf. 1:7, 9; 2:4). **They eagerly seek you,** but **not commendably.** The term translated **seek** carries the idea of taking a serious interest in someone and was often used of a man courting a woman. "The Judaizers talk like they really care for you," Paul was saying, "but they are false suitors who have no genuine love for or interest in you or your welfare."

Most cults show keen interest and even affection toward prospective members, promising them great personal fulfillment and happiness. As with the legalism of the Judaizers, the true nature of their spiritual enslavement is hidden.

The Judaizers had no interest in the Galatian believers beyond entrapping them in legalism. They were like the scribes and Pharisees to whom Jesus said, "You travel about on sea and land to make one proselyte; and when he becomes one, you make him twice as much a son of hell as yourselves" (Matt. 23:15). Their true **wish** and objective was to **shut . . . out** the Galatians from God's grace and gain recognition and acceptance for themselves (implied in the phrase **that you may seek them**). Their true motivation was "to make a good showing in the flesh" (6:12).

But it is good always to be eagerly sought in a commendable manner, Paul went on to explain. He himself had **eagerly sought** them when he first preached the gospel in Galatia. But it was **in a commendable manner,** out of love for Christ and a deep desire for their salvation. And such enthusiastic concern was appropriate **not only when** Paul was **present with** them. He was not jealous of the Judaizers. He did not oppose them in order to preserve his own popularity or leadership but to protect the Galatians' spiritual well-being. Some years later he wrote from prison, "Some, to be sure, are preaching Christ even from envy and strife, . . . [proclaiming] Christ out of selfish ambition, rather than from pure motives, thinking to cause me distress in my imprisonment. What then? Only that in every way, whether in pretense or in truth, Christ is proclaimed; and in this I rejoice, yes, and I will rejoice" (Phil. 1:15, 17-18).

Paul warned against the Judaizers not because they opposed him and personally wounded him, but because they opposed the glorious, saving gospel of Jesus Christ.

His Desire for Them

My children, with whom I am again in labor until Christ is formed in you— but I could wish to be present with you now and to change my tone, for I am perplexed about you. (4:19-20)

Speaking like a mother, Paul now addressed the Galatian believers as **my children, with whom I am again in labor until Christ is formed in you.** He was not arguing like a lawyer before a skeptical jury but pleading like a parent to a wayward child.

Children is from *teknion,* a diminutive that was used figuratively as a term of special affection. Literally, it referred to a small child, and therefore can be translated here as "little children," as in the King James Version. In light of Paul's figure of childbirth, both ideas are appropriate. The Galatian believers were extremely dear to Paul but were acting like infants who refused to be born.

Paul's compassion was always evident. For example, to the Thessalonian church he wrote, "We proved to be gentle among you, as a nursing mother tenderly cares for her own children. Having thus a fond affection for you, we were well-pleased to impart to you not only the gospel of God but also our own lives, because you had become very dear to us" (1 Thess. 2:7-8).

With the Galatians, however, after having spiritually nursed them in their new life in Christ, he became **again in labor** with them. "That is abnormal and unnatural," he implies. "You have already experienced the new birth, but now you are acting as if you need to be spiritually born all over again. You make me feel like a mother who has to deliver the same baby twice."

But however abnormal and tragic their spiritual condition, Paul would not forsake them **until Christ** was **formed in** them. The verb (*morphoō*) carries the idea of essential form rather than outward shape, and therefore refers to Christlike character. Christlikeness is the goal of the believer's life. "As you therefore have received Christ Jesus the Lord, so walk in Him," he exhorted the church at Colossae (Col. 2:6; cf. Rom. 13:14). God has predestined believers "to become conformed to the image of His Son" (Rom. 8:29). "We all, with unveiled face beholding as in a mirror the glory of the Lord, are being transformed into the same image from glory to glory, just as from the Lord, the Spirit" (2 Cor. 3:18). The Father sent the Son to earth not only to die that men might be saved but also to live as the divine example for those who are saved.

Paul's great desire was to deal more directly with these issues that would require him **to be present with** the Galatians in person and to be able to **change** his **tone** with them. He hardly knew what more to say or how to say it, because he was so **perplexed about** them. This verb (*aporeomai*) means to be at one's wits' end. He could not understand how they could have been taught the gospel so well, believed it so genuinely, and then appeared to have forsaken it so quickly (cf. 1:6).

Every Christian worker experiences times when he comes to an impasse and finds his own resources are completely exhausted. After saying and doing everything he knows to say and do, those he is trying to help—sometimes unbelievers, sometimes believers—remain completely out of reach and even turn against him.

As John R. W. Stott has commented in his *The Message of Galatians,* "The church needs people who, in listening to their pastor, listen for the message of Christ, and pastors who, in labouring among the people, look for the image of Christ" ([London: Inter-Varsity, 1968], p. 119).

Two Covenants
(4:21–5:1)

12

Tell me, you who want to be under law, do you not listen to the law? For it is written that Abraham had two sons, one by the bondwoman and one by the free woman. But the son by the bondwoman was born according to the flesh, and the son by the free woman through the promise. This is allegorically speaking; for these women are two covenants, one proceeding from Mount Sinai bearing children who are to be slaves; she is Hagar. Now this Hagar is Mount Sinai in Arabia, and corresponds to the present Jerusalem, for she is in slavery with her children. But the Jerusalem above is free; she is our mother. For it is written, "Rejoice, barren woman who does not bear; break forth and shout, you who are not in labor; for more are the children of the desolate than of the one who has a husband." And you brethren, like Isaac, are children of promise. But as at that time he who was born according to the flesh persecuted him who was born according to the Spirit, so it is now also. But what does the Scripture say? "Cast out the bondwoman and her son, for the son of the bondwoman shall not be an heir with the son of the free woman." So then, brethren, we are not children of a bondwoman, but of the free woman.

It was for freedom that Christ set us free; therefore keep standing firm and do not be subject again to a yoke of slavery. (4:21–5:1)

In this text Paul continues to contrast grace and law, faith and works. Under the guidance of the Holy Spirit he employs an Old Testament story as an analogy, which serves not so much as an argument as an illustration.

The translators of both the King James Version and the *New American Standard Bible* have chosen simply to transliterate rather than translate the term *allēgoreō* (**allegorically**, v. 24). This has led to difficulty in handling the passage, because usually an allegory is either a fanciful or fictional story carrying a hidden meaning or a true story in which the apparent meaning is meaningless.

But obviously the record of Abraham, Sarah, and Hagar is both historical and meaningful. Recognizing this, the *New International Version* translators have attempted to aid the understanding of what Paul intended by avoiding the term *allegorical* and rendering "These things may be taken figuratively." But that also can have the implication of something that is not literal. It is best to identify this literal, historical account as simply analogous to and illustrative of the spiritual truth that Paul elucidates with it. The dictionary defines analogy as "a partial similarity between like features of two things on which a comparison may be made." Paul is simply comparing the similarities between the story of Abraham and the spiritual truth he is teaching, and this interpretation is consistent with the meaning of *allēgoreō*.

Paul does not explain why, after the powerful and irrefutable arguments he has already used, he chose allegory as a means of further persuasion.

Allegory as such is a tenuous and dangerous means of interpretation. Because allegory does not need to be based on fact, it is limited only by an interpreter's imagination and is easily influenced by his personal predispositions. It frequently leads to biased and often bizarre conclusions.

The ancient rabbis regularly used an allegorical approach to interpret Scripture, often claiming to discover amazing, hidden, and extremely fanciful "truths" that supposedly lay behind the ordinary meaning of the words of a text. Numerology was especially popular and was made easier and more tempting by the fact that Hebrew numbers are represented by certain Hebrew letters, and sometimes they can be distinguished only by context. Because every word had a corresponding arithmetic number, those numbers were frequently interpreted as revealing certain esoteric truths about the person, place, or event the word represented. Also, repetition was often interpreted allegorically. For instance, "Abraham, Abraham" was claimed by some rabbis to mean that he was destined for a heavenly afterlife.

During the last several centuries before Christ, Jewish scholars in Alexandria developed a system of scriptural allegory that strongly influenced not only Judaism but also Roman Catholicism until the time of the Protestant Reformation. For example, the Euphrates River was seen as the outflowing of good manners. The journey of Abraham from Ur to the Promised Land pictured a stoic philosopher who left his sensual understandings and came to his spiritual senses. The two coins given by the Good Samaritan to the innkeeper symbolized baptism and the Lord's Supper. Pope Gregory the Great claimed that Job's seven sons represented the twelve apostles, his friends represented heretics, his 7,000 sheep represented God's faithful people, and his 3,000 camels represented depraved Gentiles!

Allegory is a Pandora's box that ignores the literal, historical meaning of Scripture and opens biblical interpretation to every extreme. Because of man's finiteness and fallenness, it inevitably leads to arbitrariness, absurdity, and futility.

The Holy Spirit directed Paul to use analogy on this occasion in order to show the Judaizers that God's plan of redemption has always been by grace. **The law** itself both teaches and illustrates that salvation has never been through the law.

The term **law** frequently referred to the whole of the Old Testament (see, e.g., Rom. 3:19), but here it refers particularly to the Pentateuch, the five books of Moses. The point Paul makes by drawing an analogy from Moses' writing is that **the law** cannot be a means of salvation but is instead the way of spiritual and moral bondage.

As an introduction to the analogy, Paul suggests that the Judaizers, and the Jewish Christians who had been misled by them, look carefully at the very law they so highly touted. **Tell me**, he asks, **you who want to be under law, do you not listen to the law?** "Since you insist on living **under law**," he was saying, "are you willing to **listen to** what **the law** really says?"

Jesus used a similar approach with the Jewish leaders on several occasions. In the Sermon on the Mount, after declaring unequivocally that He had not come to abolish God's law, He nevertheless warned that the legalistic practices of the scribes and Pharisees would never qualify a person for entrance into the kingdom of heaven (Matt. 5:17-20). The whole point of the sermon was to show that no person is able in his own power to fulfill the holy demands of the law, the first of which is a righteous and perfect heart (5:6, 8, 48; cf. Matt. 22:36-38). When the chief priests and scribes rebuked Jesus for not disclaiming the title Son of David ascribed to Him by the Palm Sunday crowd, which included many children, He reminded those religious leaders of a well-known saying from their own sacred Scriptures, on which they claimed to be the supreme authorities. "Have you never read," He asked derisively, "'Out of the mouth of infants and nursing babes Thou hast prepared praise for Thyself?'" (Matt. 21:9-16; cf. Ps. 8:2).

As Paul develops the analogy, he first gives its historical background, then its divine interpretation, and finally its personal application.

The Historical Background

For it is written that Abraham had two sons, one by the bondwoman and one by the free woman. But the son by the bondwoman was born according to the flesh, and the son by the free woman through the promise. (4:22-23)

Paul reminds his readers of their forefather **Abraham**, progenitor of the Hebrew race. It was in their racial descent from him that most Jews of Paul's day placed their trust for salvation. But as John the Baptist had declared to the Pharisees and Sadducees, for Jews to say, "We have Abraham for our father," did not make them right with God, who "is able from these stones to raise up children to Abraham" (Matt. 3:9). Jesus told another group of unbelieving Jews that being the physical descendants of

Abraham not only did not make them children of God but did not prevent them from being children of Satan, just like Gentile unbelievers (John 8:33-44).

Paul's first historical reminder about **Abraham** was that he **had two sons.** The **sons** were distinct in a number of ways, first of all in having different mothers, **one** who was a **bondwoman** and the other who was a **free woman.** The first son was Ishmael, whose mother was Hagar, an Egyptian slave of Sarah, Abraham's wife. The second son was Isaac, whose mother was Sarah.

Throughout the analogy, all distinctions between the two sons are based on the fact that they had two different mothers, not on the fact that they had a common father, **Abraham.** The heritage of the line through one mother is lostness and bondage, and the heritage of the line through the other mother is salvation and freedom.

Paul's second historical reminder was that **the son by the bondwoman was born according to the flesh, and the son by the free woman through the promise.**

Many years after God first promised a son to Abraham, Sarah had not yet conceived. When he was 86 and she 76, Abraham feared that, according to the custom of the day, his chief servant, Eliezer of Damascus, would be his only heir. He cried out to God in despair, and the Lord reaffirmed His original promise, saying, "This man will not be your heir; but one who shall come forth from your own body, he shall be your heir" (Gen. 15:1-4). But when, after several more years, Sarah still had not conceived, she induced Abraham to father a child by her female slave, Hagar.

The birth of that son, whose name was Ishmael, was **according to the flesh,** not because it was physical but because the scheme for his conception, devised by Sarah and carried out by Abraham, was motivated by purely selfish desires and fulfilled by purely human means.

The birth of Isaac, however, **the son by the free woman** Sarah, was **through the promise.** His conception was supernatural, not in the sense that he was conceived directly by the Holy Spirit, as Jesus was, but that the Holy Spirit miraculously enabled Abraham and Sarah to produce a child after she was far past normal childbearing age and had been barren all her life. "Sarah herself received ability to conceive, even beyond the proper time of life" (Heb. 11:11). When Isaac was born, his father was 100 and his mother was 90 (Gen. 17:17; 21:5).

The conception of Ishmael represents man's way, the way of **the flesh,** whereas that of Isaac represents God's way, the way of **promise.** The first is analogous to the way of religious self-effort and works righteousness; the second is analogous to the way of faith and God's imputed righteousness. The one is the way of legalism, the other the way of grace. Ishmael symbolizes those who have had only natural birth and who trust in their own works. Isaac symbolizes those who also have had spiritual birth because they have trusted in the work of Jesus Christ.

THE DIVINE INTERPRETATION

This is allegorically speaking; for these women are two covenants, one proceeding from Mount Sinai bearing children who are to be slaves; she is

Hagar. Now this Hagar is Mount Sinai in Arabia, and corresponds to the present Jerusalem, for she is in slavery with her children. But the Jerusalem above is free; she is our mother. For it is written, "Rejoice, barren woman who does not bear; break forth and shout, you who are not in labor; for more are the children of the desolate than of the one who has a husband." (4:24-27)

Paul here specifically states that his present illustration is an analogy. **This is** refers back to verses 22-23, where the analogy begins. **Allegorically**, the unfortunate transliteration taken from *allēgoreō*, is a compound of *allos* (other) and *agoreuō* (to speak in a place of assembly, that is, publicly), and means literally "to speak other than one seems to speak." It was used of a story that conveyed meaning other than what was apparent in the literal sense of the words. It has the idea of one thing being represented under the image of another. In this case, the spiritual truth is illustrated by the historical story, and translating "analogically" is consistent with the basic meaning of the Greek.

Under the inspiration of the Holy Spirit, the apostle explains that **these women,** the bondwoman Hagar and the free woman Sarah, **are** illustrations of **two covenants.** The two mothers and two sons lucidly and graphically represent **two covenants.** Hagar and Ishmael represent the covenant of law and works, and Sarah and Isaac represent the covenant of grace and faith.

The Old Covenant of law was given through Moses at **Mount Sinai** and required God's chosen people, the Jews, to keep all the commands He gave in conjunction with that covenant. Because the terms of the covenant were humanly impossible to keep, it produced a type of religious **slaves,** as it were, bound to a master from whom they could never escape. Anyone, including a Jew, who attempted to satisfy God and gain freedom from condemnation by trying to live up to that covenant in his own self-righteousness was spiritually like a child of **Hagar,** the bondwoman. He was a slave, struggling for a freedom he could not obtain by his own efforts.

The descendants of **Hagar** through Ishmael eventually moved into the desert areas to the east and south of the Promised Land. They came to be known broadly as Arabs and their territory as **Arabia,** and it is significant that **Mount Sinai** is located in what is still known today as the Arabian Peninsula.

It was between the sons of Hagar and Sarah that the modern Arab-Israeli animosity began some 4,000 years ago, producing a continual conflict between two peoples who both trace their lineage from Abraham.

Mount Sinai in Arabia, Paul continues to explain, **corresponds to the present Jerusalem.** Both **Mount Sinai** and **Jerusalem** are commonly associated with Jews, not Arabs, but a major emphasis throughout the Galatian epistle is that historical, geographical, racial, social, and all other superficial distinctions among men have no spiritual significance (see 3:28). In fact, on the spiritual level, one's identity as Jew, Gentile, Arab, or whatever makes no difference. What unbelieving members of those groups have in common is infinitely more important, and damning, than any of their differences. Spiritually, they are *all* lost, because they are all spiritual descendants of Hagar and Ishmael, religious slaves who live by the futile power and for the sake of their struggling and never-attaining flesh.

Paul refers to the first **Jerusalem** as **present,** showing he has in mind the earthly, historical city by that name. Just as God chose **Mount Sinai** as the geographical location to give the Old Covenant to Moses, He chose **Jerusalem** as the geographical location where the Old Covenant would be upheld, propagated, and exemplified. In this illustration *both* locations represent the Old Covenant of law and works and the bondage they produce.

It is obvious that the holy city was also the location for the consummation of the New Covenant in the death and resurrection of the Lord Jesus Christ, but because the people rejected that New Testament in blood, **the present Jerusalem,** like **Mount Sinai in Arabia,** is where Hagar still figuratively lives **in slavery with her** unbelieving **children**—self-righteous, Christ-rejecting, grace-ignoring Jews. Except for a relatively few believers, the Jewish inhabitants of geographical **Jerusalem** in Paul's day were truly in deep bondage to damning legalism. And the Judaizers in Galatia were trying to subvert believing Jews back into that bondage—to the ritual, ceremony, self-effort, and all other works of the flesh that constitute the hopeless **slavery** of the spiritual **children** of Hagar.

The spiritual descendants of Sarah through Isaac, on the other hand, live in **the Jerusalem above** and are **free,** because **she is our mother,** if we are among those who live by faith in God's gracious promise, given to Abraham and fulfilled in Jesus Christ.

The Christian's "citizenship is in heaven," **the Jerusalem above,** "from which also we eagerly wait for a Savior, the Lord Jesus Christ" (Phil. 3:20). Referring to Mount Sinai, the writer of Hebrews says to believers, "You have not come to a mountain that may be touched and to a blazing fire, and to darkness and gloom and whirlwind, . . . but you have come to Mount Zion and to the city of the living God, the heavenly Jerusalem" (Heb. 12:18, 22).

The inhabitants of the heavenly Jerusalem are **free** from law, from works, from bondage, and from the flesh. They are also **free,** as inhabitants of the present Jerusalem are not, to genuinely do good and to please God. Before coming to Christ, a person is free to do virtually whatever he wants that is wrong, but he is not free to do anything that is right in God's sight. The Holy Spirit not only delivers the believer from sin but enables him, for the first time, to do what is right. "If therefore the Son shall make you free," Jesus said, "you shall be free indeed" (John 8:36).

One day the heavenly Jerusalem will descend to earth (Rev. 21-22); but it already exists, even more surely and eternally than the present, earthly Jerusalem. "Born again" (John 3:3) can also be translated "born from above," and it is only those who are born from above who have spiritually ascended to the heavenlies to live in **the Jerusalem above.**

Quoting Isaiah 54:1, Paul continues, **For it is written, "Rejoice, barren woman who does not bear; break forth and shout, you who are not in labor; for more are the children of the desolate than of the one who has a husband."**

Those words were originally written to cheer the Jewish exiles in Babylon but are here applied to Sarah, the **barren woman** whose barrenness seemingly stood as an impenetrable barrier to the fulfillment of God's promise to her husband, Abraham. As freedom and greater fruitfulness came again to the nation in Babylonian captivity, so it would come to the people in captivity to the law and its death penalty.

As Zion was a mother of children by grace after captivity, so believers will multiply in grace in the heavenly Jerusalem, which was also figuratively barren for a long time. "The general assembly and church of the first-born" (Heb. 12:23) was not occupied until Jesus was crucified and resurrected, taking captivity captive and removing the spiritual barrenness that no human effort under the Old Covenant could remove. Heaven, **the Jerusalem above,** will continue to be populated with the born-from-above saints of God until every predestined believer has entered.

In one sweep Paul sets forth the common factor of divine power in behalf of Sarah, the captive Jews, and the church. The common element of all three is divine power granting freedom and fruitfulness. Everything in this trilogy is the result of regenerating grace, not human effort.

THE PERSONAL APPLICATION

And you brethren, like Isaac, are children of promise. But as at that time he who was born according to the flesh persecuted him who was born according to the Spirit, so it is now also. But what does the Scripture say? "Cast out the bondwoman and her son, for the son of the bondwoman shall not be an heir with the son of the free woman." So then, brethren, we are not children of a bondwoman, but of the free woman.

It was for freedom that Christ set us free; therefore keep standing firm and do not be subject again to a yoke of slavery. (4:28–5:1)

Again addressing the Galatian believers as **brethren** (cf. 1:11; 4:12), Paul tells them that, **like Isaac,** they **are children of promise.** Every believer, **like Isaac,** is supernaturally conceived, miraculously born, and the offspring of God's **promise** to Abraham fulfilled in Christ. Those who have begun to sink back into the trap of legalistic Judaism must remember that they **are children of promise,** who owe their life not to their own effort but to the miraculous power of God, just as **Isaac** did in the physical realm. God's sovereign power of grace gave them life, and to fall back under law was to deny that divine work and to dishonor God.

In 4:29–5:1 Paul mentions three results of being a spiritual Isaac, a redeemed child of promise through Sarah. First of all, just as in **that time,** when there was resentment of Isaac by Ishmael, the spiritual descendants of Isaac, **who was born according to the Spirit,** can still expect persecution by the spiritual descendants of Ishmael, **who was born according to the flesh.**

When Abraham held a feast to celebrate Isaac's weaning, Ishmael mocked the occasion (Gen. 21:9). He hated Isaac just as his mother hated Sarah (16:1-5). **So it is**

now also, Paul told the Galatians. Throughout history, and still today, the physical and spiritual descendants of Hagar and Ishmael have, respectively, opposed and persecuted the physical and spiritual descendants of Sarah and Isaac. Those who hold to salvation by works, trusting in their own performance of the law, hate those who proclaim salvation by grace without works.

In their own minds, the Judaizers thought of themselves as the legitimate, God-honored descendants of Abraham through Isaac. But Paul was saying something that would infuriate them more than anything else, namely, that they, and all other unbelievers, are as much the spiritual descendants of Ishmael as the Arabs are his physical descendants. "If you are Abraham's children," Jesus told the protesting Jews in Jerusalem, "do the deeds of Abraham. But as it is, you are seeking to kill Me, a man who has told you the truth, which I heard from God; this Abraham did not do" (John 8:39-40). Paul wrote the Romans, "He is not a Jew who is one outwardly; neither is circumcision that which is outward in the flesh. But he is a Jew who is one inwardly; and circumcision is that which is of the heart, by the Spirit, not by the letter; and his praise is not from men, but from God" (Rom. 2:28-29).

Whether within Judaism or Christianity, legalists have always been persecutors. Those who trust in God have always been persecuted by those who trust in themselves. True believers have always been more mistreated and oppressed by religionists than by atheists. It is the false religious system of Revelation 17:6 that is "drunk with the blood of the saints."

② Second, the spiritual children of Sarah and Isaac will receive an inheritance that the spiritual children of Hagar and Ishmael will not. Just as **the Scripture** says, **"Cast out the bondwoman and her son, for the son of the bondwoman shall not be an heir with the son of the free woman."** The persecutors are going to be thrown out, and the persecuted will receive their promised and rightful inheritance. As Sarah had Hagar and Ishmael **cast out** of Abraham's household (Gen. 21:10-14), so will their unbelieving descendants, those who live by works of the flesh, be **cast out** of God's household (cf. Matt. 7:22-23; 25:41). No one outside the covenant of grace will receive anything from God.   *No one will Boast*

③ Third, although believers are **brethren** in Jesus Christ and therefore **not children of a bondwoman, but of the free woman,** they are nevertheless under obligation to live faithfully for their Lord. **It was for freedom that Christ set us free,** Paul says. **Therefore keep standing firm and do not be subject again to a yoke of slavery** to the law and its impotence.

In light of what Paul has been saying throughout the letter, he also here implies a disturbing question: "Why, then, do some of you want to go back to being like Ishmael, who was a slave, an outcast, and separated from God?" It made no sense at all.

"Thanks be to God," Paul exclaimed to the Roman church, "that though you were slaves of sin, you became obedient from the heart to that form of teaching to which you were committed, and having been freed from sin, you became slaves of righteousness. I am speaking in human terms because of the weakness of your flesh. For just as you presented your members as slaves to impurity and to lawlessness, resulting in further lawlessness, so now present your members as slaves to righteousness, resulting in sanctification" (Rom. 6:17-19).

Paul says emphatically that God's stated purpose for redemption **was for freedom** of the believer. **Christ set us free** from the "guilt-establishing and deadening power of the law" through His death and resurrection. Going back into **a yoke of slavery** is absurd. Yet the believers in Galatia were being duped by the Judaizers to consider doing just that.

The spiritual descendants of Sarah and Isaac should live as they lived, by faith. "By faith even Sarah herself received ability to conceive, even beyond the proper time of life, since she considered Him faithful who had promised" (Heb. 11:11), and "by faith Isaac blessed Jacob and Esau, even regarding things to come" (v. 20).

Keep standing firm is the positive, and **do not be subject again** (lit., "do not subject yourselves") is the negative warning for believers to persevere in freedom. Like an animal loosed from pulling a plow, we should not seek to be hooked up again.

On the human and personal level, Galatians 4:21–5:1 continues to contrast the way of the Judaizers and the way of Paul. But on the immeasurably more important level of doctrine it is an extended series of contrasts between the way of law and the way of grace, the way of works and the way of faith, the way of man and the way of God. Following that same pattern, we also explicitly or implicitly see the contrasts of Hagar/Sarah, Ishmael/Isaac, children of Satan/children of God, commandments/promise, wrath/mercy, bondage/freedom, Old Covenant/New Covenant, Sinai/Zion, present Jerusalem/Jerusalem above, fleshly/spiritual, rejection/inheritance, and lostness/salvation. Throughout this letter, and indeed throughout all of Scripture, such contrasts reflect and demonstrate the contrast of the ages: the way of Satan and the way of God. But in God's ultimate and unchangeable plan, Satan and his way will be destroyed, and only the way of God will remain, forever and ever. Vacillating between the two is unacceptable.

Fallen from Grace

(5:2-12)

13

Behold I, Paul, say to you that if you receive circumcision, Christ will be of no benefit to you. And I testify again to every man who receives circumcision, that he is under obligation to keep the whole Law. You have been severed from Christ, you who are seeking to be justified by law; you have fallen from grace. For we through the Spirit, by faith, are waiting for the hope of righteousness. For in Christ Jesus neither circumcision nor uncircumcision means anything, but faith working through love. You were running well; who hindered you from obeying the truth? This persuasion did not come from Him who calls you. A little leaven leavens the whole lump of dough. I have confidence in you in the Lord, that you will adopt no other view; but the one who is disturbing you shall bear his judgment, whoever he is. But I, brethren, if I still preach circumcision, why am I still persecuted? Then the stumbling block of the cross has been abolished. Would that those who are troubling you would even mutilate themselves. (5:2-12)

This passage begins the third section of the letter. After defending his apostleship (chaps. 1-2) and his message of justification by faith (chaps. 3-4), Paul now applies that doctrine to practical Christian living (chaps. 5-6), emphasizing that right doctrine should result in right living. His subject is the sanctification that should result from justification. The life of genuine faith is more than the belief in divine truth; it is also the bearing of divine fruit.

Especially in chapter 5 (vv. 5, 16-18, 25), the apostle emphasizes the personal ministry of the Holy Spirit in the life of a believer, without which genuine Christian living would be impossible. It is the Holy Spirit who makes the life of faith work. Were it not for the indwelling power of the Holy Spirit, the life of faith would be no more spiritually productive or acceptable to God than the life of law.

The freedom for which Christ sets us free (v. 1) is the freedom to live a life of righteousness in the power of the Holy Spirit. God's standard of holiness has not changed. As Jesus makes clear in the Sermon on the Mount, it requires not simply outward performance but inner perfection. Through His Holy Spirit, believers have the ability to live internal lives of righteousness.

The final two chapters of Galatians are a portrait of the Spirit-filled life, of the believer's implementing the life of faith under the control and in the energy of the Holy Spirit. The Spirit-filled life thereby becomes in itself a powerful testimony to the power of justification by faith.

In making his appeal for living the Spirit-filled life of freedom rather than reverting to the futile works-bound life of legalistic self-effort, Paul begins with the negative, a warning first against false doctrine (vv. 2-6) and then against false teachers (vv. 7-12). He shows the spiritual dangers of the first and the corrupt character of the second.

THE DANGERS OF FALSE DOCTRINE

Behold I, Paul, say to you that if you receive circumcision, Christ will be of no benefit to you. And I testify again to every man who receives circumcision, that he is under obligation to keep the whole Law. You have been severed from Christ, you who are seeking to be justified by law; you have fallen from grace. For we through the Spirit, by faith, are waiting for the hope of righteousness. For in Christ Jesus neither circumcision nor uncircumcision means anything, but faith working through love. (5:2-6)

The basic doctrinal error of the Judaizers was works righteousness, the same error that is the heart of every other man-made religious system. Jews were often referred to simply as the circumcised (Acts 10:45; 11:2; Gal. 2:7), because that was their most distinctive outward mark and the one in which they had the greatest pride and confidence. Rather than looking on **circumcision** as God had given it—as a symbol of His covenant of promise (Gen. 17:9-10)—most Jews looked on it as having spiritual value in itself. To them it was not a reminder of God's gracious and sovereign blessing but a means of humanly guaranteeing His favor.

It should be noted that the symbolism of cutting off the male foreskin was to be a constant reminder to all generations of Jews, for whom God desired to cut away the evil from their hearts (cf. Deut. 30:6; Jer. 4:4; 9:24-26). Every child circumcised was a dramatic symbol of God's desire to cleanse the heart by faith in Him and to impute His grace to the believer.

Paul's objection here is not to **circumcision** in itself. Like all Jewish boys, he himself had been circumcised as an infant (Phil. 3:5). He did not object to a Christian's being circumcised if, as in the case of Timothy (Acts 16:1-3), the act would open doors for ministry. Because Timothy was half Jewish, Paul had him circumcised in order that they might together have greater opportunity to witness to Jews. And had he known of the possible health advantages of circumcision, he would not have objected to it for that purpose either.

Paul's warning about **circumcision** pertained only to the false idea that in itself it carried spiritual benefit or merit. The Judaizers were saying, in effect, that faith in Jesus Christ, although important, was not sufficient for complete salvation. They taught that what Moses began in the Old Covenant and Christ added to in the New Covenant had to be finished and perfected by one's own efforts—the centerpiece of which was **circumcision.**

The Jerusalem Council was convened to deal with this false teaching, which declared, "Unless you are circumcised according to the custom of Moses, you cannot be saved. . . . It is necessary to circumcise them [Gentiles], and to direct them to observe the Law of Moses" (Acts 15:1, 5).

As he combats that heretical notion, Paul points out four of its tragic consequences. The person who trusts in circumcision forfeits benefit from Christ's work on his behalf, places himself under obligation to keep the whole law, falls from God's grace, and excludes himself from God's righteousness.

CHRIST IS OF NO BENEFIT

Behold I, Paul, say to you that if you receive circumcision, Christ will be of no benefit to you. (5:2)

Behold I, Paul, say to you undergirds the apostolic authority (see 1:1) by which Paul makes this serious assertion. He may also have been emphasizing his own Jewishness, indicating that he, **Paul,** a former Pharisee and "Hebrew of Hebrews" (Phil. 3:5), was obviously not speaking against trust in **circumcision** because of any personal or racial bias against Jews. Both as an apostle and as a circumcised and redeemed Jew, he declared that to **receive circumcision** for the purpose of gaining merit before God was to make **Christ . . . of no benefit.** The atoning sacrifice of the Lord Jesus **Christ,** perfect and complete though it was, cannot **benefit** a person who trusts in anything else, because that something else, whether **circumcision** or any other human act or effort, then stands between him and **Christ.**

All the people to whom Paul was writing had made a profession of Jesus **Christ** as Savior and Lord or they would not have been part of the churches of Galatia. Many, perhaps most, of them had genuinely trusted in Him for salvation. The truth Paul presents here applied to both groups. To those who were not saved, he was saying that they could not be saved, they could not gain any eternal, saving **benefit** from **Christ** if they trusted in **circumcision**. To those who were saved he was saying that such behavior was inconsistent with their salvation and that certainly they could experience no **benefit** of growth in their spiritual lives if they began trusting in **circumcision** in addition to God's grace (cf. 3:1-3).

To trust in Jesus Christ for salvation is to acknowledge that one cannot save himself. To trust in **circumcision** or any other personal effort as a means of grace is to supplement His divine work with human work; and a supplemented **Christ** is a supplanted **Christ**. To trust in human effort is to trust in law, which is totally incompatible with grace.

A person becomes acceptable to God only by placing his full trust in His Son, Jesus **Christ,** and after he is saved he perseveres in living a life acceptable to God only by *continuing* to trust in **Christ** alone. Whether before or after conversion, trust in human works of any kind is a barrier between a person and Christ and results in unacceptable legalism.

Paul explained to Roman believers "that Gentiles, who did not pursue righteousness, attained righteousness, even the righteousness which is by faith; but Israel, pursuing a law of righteousness, did not arrive at that law. Why? Because they did not pursue it by faith, but as though it were by works" (Rom. 9:30-32). The Gentiles who were not seeking righteousness nevertheless found it when they believed in Jesus Christ, whereas the Jews who were zealously seeking righteousness did not attain it, because they were seeking it in themselves. The believing Gentiles gained Christ's righteousness, which is perfect, whereas the unbelieving Jews had only their self-righteousness, which was worthless.

OBLIGATED TO KEEP THE WHOLE LAW

And I testify again to every man who receives circumcision, that he is under obligation to keep the whole law. (5:3)

A second consequence of trusting in **circumcision** is that the person who does so obligates himself **to keep the whole law.** To live by part of the law as a means of attaining righteousness demands living by all of it.

Marturomai (**testify**) often carried the idea of strong protestation, and that seems to be Paul's meaning here. **Again** could refer to the previous verse, to a previous occasion, or to both. In any case, this declaration is given with added urgency.

"Whoever keeps the whole law and yet stumbles in one point," James says, "he has become guilty of all" (James 2:10). Because God's standard is perfect righteousness, fulfillment of only part of **the law** falls short of His standard. Even if a person were somehow able to keep all of the law for all of his life, if he broke a commandment during his last minute on earth, he would forfeit salvation. Or if he managed to keep all of the laws perfectly except one, he would suffer the same fate. It is easy to understand why Paul declared that "as many as are of the works of the Law are under a curse; for it is written, 'Cursed is everyone who does not abide by all things written in the book of the law, to perform them'" (Gal. 3:10). Because God's standard was so obviously impossible to attain, that truth quoted from Deuteronomy 27:26 should have driven every Jew to seek His mercy.

FALLEN FROM GRACE

You have been severed from Christ, you who are seeking to be justified by law; you have fallen from grace. (5:4)

A third consequence of **seeking to be justified by** circumcision or any other form of the **law,** is that it causes a person to become **severed from Christ** and thereby become **fallen from grace. Severed** is from *katargeō,* which, when followed by the preposition, means to be separated or loosed from (cf. Rom. 7:2, 6). **Fallen** is from *ekpiptō,* which means to lose one's grasp on something. Simply stated, a person cannot live by both law and grace. To attempt to be justified by law is to reject the way of grace.

Paul is not dealing with the security of the believer but with the contrasting ways of **grace** and **law,** works and faith, as means of salvation. He is not teaching that a person who has once been **justified** can lose his righteous standing before God and become lost again by being circumcised or otherwise legalistic. The Bible knows nothing of becoming unjustified. Those "whom [God] predestined, these He also called; and whom He called, these He also justified; and whom He justified, these He also glorified" (Rom. 8:30).

Paul's primary point in this passage, as throughout the letter, is that **law** and **grace** cannot be mixed. They are totally incompatible and mutually exclusive. To mix **law** with **grace** is to obliterate **grace.** For a believer to start living again under the **law** to merit salvation is, in fact, to reject salvation by **grace.** Contrary to the teaching of the Judaizers, to add circumcision and other works of the **law** to what Christ accomplished by **grace** is not to raise one's spiritual level but to severely lower it. Legalism does not please God but offends Him. It does not bring a person closer to God but rather drives him away.

Applied to one who was really an unbeliever, the principle of falling **from grace** has to do with being exposed to the gracious truth of the gospel and then turning one's back on Christ. Such a person is an apostate. During the time of the early church many people, both Jews and Gentiles, not only heard the gospel message but witnessed the miraculous confirming signs performed by the apostles. They became attracted to Christ and often made professions of faith in Him. Some became involved in a local church and vicariously experienced the blessings of Christian love and fellowship. They were exposed first hand to every truth and blessing of the gospel of grace but then turned away. They had "been enlightened," had "tasted of the heavenly gift," and had even "been made partakers of the Holy Spirit" by witnessing His divine ministry in the lives of believers. But they refused to stand fully with Christ by placing their trust in Him, and they fell away, losing all prospect of repentance and therefore of salvation (Heb. 6:4-6). They came to the very doorway of **grace** and then fell away, back into their works religion.

Applied to a believer, the principle of falling **from grace** has to do with a person who genuinely trusts in Christ for salvation but then outwardly reverts to a life of legalism, of living under external rituals, ceremonies, and traditions that he carries out in his own strength, instead of living with a spirit of obedience to Christ. He exchanges life by **grace** for life back under **law**, life by faith for life again by works, life in freedom for life back in bondage, life in the Spirit for life back in the flesh. It is a major matter of concern to God whether we live in outward obedience and submission to the externals of religion or in heart obedience and submission to the internals of righteousness. In the former way, a person is prompted and sustained by the flesh to try to earn righteousness. In the latter way, a person is prompted and sustained by the Spirit to demonstrate righteousness.

Obviously true Christians will not reject the true way of salvation, but they confuse themselves and others when they try to live by works, because the mark of true discipleship is continuing obedience to Christ (John 8:31). The security of salvation from the divine side is guaranteed by God to His own (cf. v. 10; Rom. 8:28-39; 11:29), but from the human side it is manifested by perseverance in grace (see John 8:31; 15:4-9; Acts 11:23; 13:43; 14:21-22; Rom. 2:7; Heb. 2:1; 3:14; 4:14; 10:23; 1 John 2:19). Paul is here calling for such perseverance in grace by the genuine believer.

Contrary to justifying grace, sanctifying grace is interruptible. Living by the flesh interferes with living by the Spirit, and living by the flesh may even involve doing the right things for the wrong reasons or in the wrong way. For example, to worship God from the heart and for His own sake is to live by the Spirit. But to worship Him only outwardly or to impress others with our supposed spirituality is to live by the flesh. To witness to a person while trusting in God to convict and convert him is to live by the Spirit. To witness with the intention of converting a person through our own knowledge of Scripture and powers of persuasion is to live by the flesh. No matter how worthy and God-ordained a person's outward activities may be, to perform them by the flesh is to live by the way of law and to forsake the way of grace.

EXCLUDED FROM RIGHTEOUSNESS

For we through the Spirit, by faith, are waiting for the hope of righteousness. For in Christ Jesus neither circumcision nor uncircumcision means anything, but faith working through love. (5:5-6)

A fourth consequence of trusting in works is to be excluded from the **righteousness** for which the believer has **hope**, to forsake the true life of blessing God desires for His children.

The Judaizers' **hope of righteousness** was based on adding imperfect and worthless works of law in a vain attempt to complete the perfect and priceless work of Christ, which they assumed to be incomplete and imperfect. **We**, that is, true believers, Paul says, **through the Spirit, by faith, are waiting for the hope of righteousness** that is based on God's grace.

Believers already possess the imputed **righteousness** of justification, but the yet-incomplete **righteousness** of total sanctification and glorification still awaits them. "For I consider that the sufferings of this present time are not worthy to be compared with the glory that is to be revealed to us. . . . The creation itself also will be set free from its slavery to corruption into the freedom of the glory of the children of God" (Rom. 8:18, 21). In this life, believers are still waiting for the completed and perfected **righteousness** that is yet to come.

Paul here mentions three characteristics of the godly life, the life that continues to live by the grace through which salvation was received. First of all, it is a life lived **through the Spirit** rather than the flesh. Second, it is a life lived by **faith** rather than works. And third, it is a life lived in patient **waiting** and **hope** rather than in the anxious uncertainty of bondage to the law.

Nothing that is either done or not done in the flesh, not even religious ceremony, makes any difference in one's relationship to God. **In Christ Jesus neither circumcision nor uncircumcision means anything.** The outward is totally unimportant and worthless, except as it genuinely reflects inner righteousness.

Life in the Spirit is not static and inactive, but it is **faith working through love,** not the flesh working through self-effort. Believers are "created in Christ Jesus for good works, which God prepared beforehand, that we should walk in them" (Eph. 2:10). But their **working** is the product of their **faith,** not a substitute for it. They do not work *for* righteousness but *out of* righteousness, **through** the motivating power of **love.** In so doing they "walk in a manner worthy of the Lord, to please Him in all respects, bearing fruit in every good work and increasing in the knowledge of God; strengthened with all power, according to His glorious might" (Col. 1:10-11).

Love needs neither the prescriptions nor the proscriptions of the law, because its very nature is to fulfill the law's demands. As Paul declares a few verses later, "the whole Law is fulfilled in one word, in the statement 'You shall love your neighbor as yourself'" (Gal. 5:14; cf. Rom. 13:8). A person does not, for instance, steal from or lie to someone he truly loves. He certainly does not kill someone he loves. The person who lives by **faith** works under the internal compulsion of **love** and does not need the outward compulsion of law.

The story is told of an aspiring artist who was commissioned to do a large sculpture for a famous museum. At last he had the opportunity to create the masterpiece he had long dreamed of. After laboring over the work for many years, he saw it grow not only in shape but in beauty. But when it was finished he discovered to his horror that it was much too large to be taken out a window or door and that the cost for tearing down part of the building in order to remove it was prohibitive. His masterpiece was forever a captive to the room in which it was created.

That is the fate of all human religion. Nothing a person does to earn God's favor can leave the room of this earth where his self-made works are created.

THE CHARACTER OF FALSE TEACHERS

You were running well; who hindered you from obeying the truth? This persuasion did not come from Him who calls you. A little leaven leavens the whole lump of dough. I have confidence in you in the Lord, that you will

adopt no other view; but the one who is disturbing you shall bear his judgment, whoever he is. But I, brethren, if I still preach circumcision, why am I still persecuted? Then the stumbling block of the cross has been abolished. Would that those who are troubling you would even mutilate themselves. (5:7-12)

After exposing the dangers of the false doctrines that threatened the Galatians, Paul exposes the wicked character of the men who espoused the doctrines.

Like his Lord, Paul had great patience with those who were caught in even the deepest moral sin. As much as they condemned the sin itself and warned against its consequences, their love for the sinner was always evident.

For the oft-divorced woman at Jacob's well and the woman caught in the act of adultery, Jesus' rebukes were gentle, and His offers of help were kind and encouraging (John 4:7-26; 8:3-11). And even before the hated and larcenous Zaccheus repented and came to saving faith, Jesus was not ashamed to eat with him (Luke 19:1-10). But for the self-righteous scribes and Pharisees—whose outward lives were ceremonially impeccable, but who refused to recognize their spiritual need and who continually corrupted the people's minds with their legalistic perversion of true Judaism—Jesus had only condemnation.

The scribes and Pharisees were the primary teachers and interpreters of Scripture. When a man was initiated into the scribal office, he was given a key that symbolized his qualification to teach. Yet Jesus called them hypocrites, deceivers, extortioners, misguided proselytizers, blind guides, fools, inwardly corrupt and foul, partners with those who killed the prophets and murderers themselves, serpents and vipers, and future persecutors of His church (Matt. 23:13-36). Their worst evil, however, was one that Isaiah had prophesied of them more than six hundred years earlier: "In vain do they worship Me, teaching as doctrines the precepts of men" (Matt. 15:9; cf. Isa. 29:13).

Paul, too, was longsuffering with those who were caught in sin, as his letters to the immature, factious, and immoral believers at Corinth attest. But also like the Lord, the apostle's most scathing denunciations were reserved for those who pervert God's truth and lead others into falsehood. In Galatians 5:7-12 he presents six characteristics of the Judaizers that are general enough to fit all other teachers of ungodliness, ancient or modern.

THEY HINDER THE TRUTH

You were running well; who hindered you from obeying the truth? (5:7)

The first and most obvious characteristic of the false teachers was that they distorted and **hindered . . . the truth.**

You were running well reflects the figure of a race, which Paul frequently used (see Rom. 9:16; 1 Cor. 9:24; Gal. 2:2). While Paul had ministered among them, the Galatian believers had no trouble living their Christian lives by faith. They **were running well** until, apparently soon after Paul left, the Judaizers began leading them away from the way of grace and faith back into the way of law and works (see 1:6-7), which was crippling in its inconsistency.

Because Paul had already made clear who their spiritual enemy was, the question **Who hindered you . . . ?** was rhetorical. The question was not about the identity of the false teachers but about their having been able so easily and quickly to deceive and mislead the Galatian believers. "How could you have allowed those men to overturn what I carefully taught and you eagerly accepted as God's Word?" he was asking. "**Who** do they think they are and **who** do you think they are, that they can arrogantly undermine my own apostolic authority (see 1:1; 5:2) and the clear teaching of the Old Testament (3:6-29; 4:21-31), which they claim to revere?"

Obeying the truth could refer to the true gospel, that is, the way by which men are saved (cf. Acts 6:7; Rom. 2:8; 6:17; 2 Thess. 1:8). Or the phrase could refer to the true way in which the saved live out their redeemed lives in obedience to God's Word and Spirit (cf. Rom. 6:17; 1 Pet. 1:22). Paul seems to be using the phrase in both senses, because the legalism of the Judaizers was preventing the unsaved from coming to Christ in faith and the saved from following Him in faith.

The church has always faced the danger of legalism, because the inclination of the flesh is always to live for its own purposes and in its own power. But "though we walk in the flesh, we do not war according to the flesh," Paul warns, "for the weapons of our warfare are not of the flesh, but divinely powerful for the destruction of fortresses" (2 Cor. 10:4).

The false teachers who were leading the Galatians astray were far from well-intentioned. Their purpose was to gain a following for themselves (Gal. 4:17) and "to make a good showing in the flesh" (6:12). They were forerunners of all the self-promoting false teachers who have plagued the church throughout its history and will continue to do so until the Lord returns. "There will also be false teachers among you," Peter warns, "who will secretly introduce destructive heresies, even denying the Master who bought them, bringing swift destruction upon themselves" (2 Pet. 2:1). Paul warns that "the Spirit explicitly says that in later times some will fall away from the faith, paying attention to deceitful spirits and doctrines of demons, by means of the hypocrisy of liars seared in their own conscience as with a branding iron" (1 Tim. 4:1-2). They are "always learning and never able to come to the knowledge of the truth. . . . These men also oppose the truth, men of depraved mind, rejected as regards the faith" (2 Tim. 3:7-8).

THEY ARE NOT OF GOD

This persuasion did not come from Him who calls you. (5:8)

The second characteristic of the false teachers was their ungodliness. Their legalistic **persuasion did not come from** God, from **Him who calls** true believers. God is here uniquely identified as the sovereign who has effectually called all who believe and are saved. The work of salvation is entirely God's doing and none of man's (Rom. 8:28-30), and any teaching that says the gracious work of God in saving men is insufficient is false.

Legalism is never from God, because He chose believers "from the beginning for salvation through sanctification by the Spirit and faith in the truth. And it was for this He called you through our gospel, that you may gain the glory of our Lord Jesus Christ" (2 Thess. 2:13-14). The Judaizers' gospel, which was not the gospel at all (Gal. 1:6-7), was not from God.

THEY CONTAMINATE THE CHURCH

A little leaven leavens the whole lump of dough. (5:9)

A third characteristic of the false teachers was that they contaminated the church, spreading their heresy among both true believers and would-be believers. Just as **a little leaven leavens the whole lump of dough,** so a small amount of falsehood can corrupt the thinking and living of a large group of people.

In Scripture, **leaven** often represents sin directly, as in Jesus' warning about "the leaven of the Pharisees and Sadducees," which referred to their false teaching (Matt. 16:6, 12). But the figure of **leaven** is generally used simply to indicate permeating power, whether of something good or evil. In this passage, as in his reference to the gross immorality of the Corinthians, Paul used the figure of leaven in both ways, as representing the actuality of sin as well as its power to infect and permeate that which is good (see 1 Cor. 5:6).

Just as a single cell of cancer can metastasize until it spreads throughout the physical body, a single false doctrine can multiply itself and spread throughout a body of believers. A great forest fire can be started by one spark. "For want of a nail the shoe was lost," wrote Benjamin Franklin; "for want of a shoe the horse was lost; for want of a horse the rider was lost; and for want of a rider the battle was lost."

THEY WILL BE JUDGED

I have confidence in you in the Lord, that you will adopt no other view; but the one who is disturbing you shall bear his judgment, whoever he is. (5:10)

A fourth characteristic of the false teachers of Galatia was their destiny of **judgment.**

Paul introduces this declaration with a word of encouragement to the true believers. **I have confidence in you in the Lord,** he said, **that you will adopt no other view,** that is, **no other view** than the true gospel of grace he had taught them when he ministered among them and that he was so strongly emphasizing in this letter. The apostle had a similar word of encouragement for the Philippian church: "I am confident of this very thing, that He who began a good work in you will perfect it until the day of Christ Jesus. For . . . you all are partakers of grace with me" (Phil. 1:6-7).

The destiny of believers is secure. "They shall never perish," Jesus said; "and no one shall snatch them out of My hand. My Father, who has given them to Me, is greater than all; and no one is able to snatch them out of the Father's hand" (John 10:28-29). They will not reject their true salvation for a false one (John 10:4-5, 14). They will both persevere and be preserved.

But that is not the destiny of ungodly teachers who lead the Lord's people astray. "Whoever causes one of these little ones who believe in Me to stumble," Jesus said, "it is better for him that a heavy millstone be hung around his neck, and that he be drowned in the depth of the sea" (Matt. 18:6).

The one who is disturbing you shall bear his judgment, Paul declared, whoever he is. Because the Judaizers stood against God and His truth, they would carry the full weight of their own judgment. False teachers often cause many others to "follow their sensuality, and because of them the way of the truth will be maligned; and in their greed they will exploit you with false words," Peter wrote. But "their judgment from long ago is not idle, and their destruction is not asleep. . . . The Lord knows how . . . to keep the unrighteous under punishment for the day of judgment" (2 Pet. 2:2-3, 9).

THEY PERSECUTE TRUE TEACHERS

But I, brethren, if I still preach circumcision, why am I still persecuted? Then the stumbling block of the cross has been abolished. (5:11)

A fifth characteristic of false teachers is that they persecute true teachers, in this case, Paul. False religion has always been and will continue to be the most aggressive and dominant persecutor of the church (cf. John 16:1-3; Rev. 17:5-6). Satan fights God, and satanic religion fights the true faith.

Among their other deceptions and lies, the Judaizers apparently claimed that Paul preached **circumcision** just as they did. Because Timothy was half Jewish, Paul had him circumcised in order to minimize criticism from Jews among whom they would minister together (Acts 16:1-3). But Paul never advocated circumcision as having any part in becoming or living as a Christian. "**If I still preach circumcision** as I did when I was a Pharisee," he asks, "**why am I still persecuted** by the Judaizers? If I preached circumcision, I would be one of them."

As Paul had already explained, he could never advocate **circumcision** as part of the gospel, because to do so would be to "nullify the grace of God; for if righteousness comes through the Law," which circumcision represented for the Judaizers, "then Christ died needlessly" (Gal. 2:21). **Then the stumbling block of the cross** would have **been abolished.**

The **cross** was a **stumbling block** to the Jews partly because they could not accept the idea of a suffering, much less crucified, Messiah. But it was even more an offense to them because it robbed them of their most distinctive outward signs of Jewishness, the Mosaic law and circumcision. If the **cross** obliterated even the true Judaism of the Old Covenant, how much more did it obliterate the false, man-made Judaism represented by the scribes, Pharisees, and Judaizers?

The early church Father Chrysostom commented that the cross was a stumbling block to Jews primarily because it failed to require obedience to their ancestral laws. When they attacked Stephen, he observed, they did not charge him with worshiping Christ but with speaking "against the holy place, and the law" (Acts 6:13).

Paul confessed that when he "used to persecute the church of God beyond measure, and tried to destroy it," he did so because he was "extremely zealous for [his] ancestral traditions" (Gal. 1:13-14). The Jews were scandalized by the **cross** because it nullified not only the Mosaic law but also their highly revered rabbinic traditions.

The **cross** still offends fallen men for the same basic reason. Whether Jew or Gentile, all men are prone to trust in what they can do for themselves and are offended when told they can do nothing at all to make themselves right before God. To preach **the cross** invites persecution because it is the supreme offense to works righteousness. But as Peter boldly proclaimed before the Jewish leaders in Jerusalem, "There is salvation in no one else; for there is no other name under heaven that has been given among men, by which we must be saved" (Acts 4:12).

THEY SHOULD BE CUT OFF

Would that those who are troubling you would even mutilate themselves. (5:12)

Paul closes his polemic against false teachers with one of the harshest statements to come from his pen or lips. He was so passionately opposed to the heresy of the Judaizers that he wished they **would even mutilate themselves.**

Apokoptō literally means "to cut off," especially a member of the body, and hence to **mutilate.** The word was often used of castration, and that is clearly Paul's meaning here. He is probably referring to the cult of Cybele, a popular pagan nature goddess in Asia Minor during Paul's day. Many devout male worshipers in the cult castrated themselves, and all its priests were self-made eunuchs.

Paul was not expressing a crude and cruel desire for the Judaizers' punishment. God would take care of that (v. 10). He spoke rather of their mutilating **themselves.** His point was, "If the Judaizers are so insistent on circumcision as a means of pleasing God, why don't they go all the way and castrate themselves as the supreme act of religious devotion? If, like the pagans, they believe human achievement can earn divine favor, why don't they go to the pagan extremes of self-mutilation, like the Cybelene priests?"

To add *any* human effort or act to God's gracious provision through the death of His Son is to exchange the saving gospel of Jesus Christ for the damning falsehood of paganism.

Called to Freedom

(5:13-15)

14

For you were called to freedom, brethren; only do not turn your freedom into an opportunity for the flesh, but through love serve one another. For the whole Law is fulfilled in one word, in the statement, "You shall love your neighbor as yourself." But if you bite and devour one another, take care lest you be consumed by one another. (5:13-15)

Ours is a day that cries for liberation. Men, women, and even children are demanding more freedom to do as they please. In the name of personal rights, authority is flouted and restrictions are resisted. Like the Israelites in the days of the judges, sinful people want to do what is right in their own eyes (see Judg. 17:6; 21:25; cf. Deut. 12:8).

But ours is also a day of addiction, not only to alcohol and drugs but also to sexual passions, violence, and many other forms of bondage in which a person eventually becomes powerless to escape. When people choose to persist in a sin, they develop less and less control over it until eventually they forfeit any choice entirely. Except for the extremity of their situations, debilitated addicts are no different from most of unsaved humanity. "Truly, truly," Jesus said, "everyone who commits sin is the slave of sin" (John 8:34). Fallen man is a slave to his sinful nature, an addict who cannot successfully control his sinful thoughts and actions even when he may want to.

And ironically, the more he asserts his self-centered freedom, the more he becomes enslaved to sin.

In the passage just quoted, Jesus gives the prescription for true freedom: "If therefore the Son shall make you free, you shall be free indeed" (v. 36). That is the great manifesto of Christianity and the theme of the Galatian letter: freedom in Jesus Christ. Christianity is liberation.

Paul has already spoken of the "liberty which we have in Christ Jesus" (2:4) and presented an analogy illustrating the believer's spiritual descent from Abraham's wife Sarah, a "free woman" (4:21-31). He has declared that "it was for freedom that Christ set us free" (5:1).

But because the idea of Christian freedom is so easily misinterpreted and misapplied, Paul knew the importance of understanding its true significance. In Galatians 5:13-15 he briefly explains freedom's basic nature and purpose, and in verse 16 explains how God makes provision for believers to live in it.

The apostle makes clear again (see 5:1) that **freedom** is at the very heart of the gospel and of godly living. It is not a side benefit or an adjunct to the Christian life. God has **called** all believers **to freedom**. His calls to particular areas of ministry and service vary from believer to believer, but His call to **freedom** is universal.

In the book of Galatians the primary **freedom** to which Paul refers is freedom from being bound to law as a system of government regulating daily life, including the Old Testament ceremonies, back into which—along with the rabbinic traditions—the Judaizers wanted to drag believers. He speaks about freedom from the frustrating, oppressive, condemning tyranny of a legal system that was impossible to keep. It is the freedom of knowing that one is accepted by God because of Christ's sufficient merit rather than of knowing that one's own insufficient merit is never enough to please Him. It is the freedom of a total cleansing that even the most godly Old Testament saints never fully understood. Their consciences were never completely clear, because they knew they could not totally and finally satisfy God's demands in the law and because the rituals and ceremonies were but outward temporary acts symbolic of a reality they never experienced permanently. Not until the work of Christ did believers have the sense of complete righteousness imputed to them, once and forever making them right with God.

For Christians to submit to Old Testament rituals and regulations, represented for the Jews by circumcision, was to go back to spiritual bondage (4:9), to exchange the new and glorious internal reality for the old and oppressive external shadows.

Because the traditions and the revering of God's law ran so deep in their minds, Paul's relentless proclamation of Christian freedom was a stumbling block even to some sincere believing Jews. And it was total scandal to the hypocritical Judaizers who merely professed to believe in Christ. Jews believed the law was the only restraint that kept sin from running rampant and bringing God's destruction of the earth. And apart from divine provision that was true. In light of man's natural inclination to sin, the only way to prevent him from totally unleashing his worst passions was to establish a system of laws that set boundaries on behavior and that carried penalties severe enough to promote conformity out of fear.

The Judaizers, and some of the immature Jewish believers, considered Paul to be antinomian, a lawless libertine. They did not realize that becoming a Christian involves having Christ's own nature and Spirit in personal residence and that motivation to obey the commands and restrictions of the New Testament is therefore not external. The Christian has the glorious privilege of living under the internal guidance, restraint, and power of the Holy Spirit, who energizes him to obey the will of God.

Because the opposite extremes of legalism and antinomianism are both man-centered, they have always been attractive to sinners. The legalist satisfies himself, and presumably God, by adhering to a strict external code of do's and don'ts, which he imagines demonstrate his self-righteous suitability for heaven. The antinomian, on the other hand, satisfies himself by rejecting all codes and living completely according to his personal lusts and desires.

Someone has pictured legalism and libertinism as two parallel streams that run between earth and heaven. The stream of legalism is clear, sparkling, and pure, but its waters run so deep and furiously that no one can enter it without being drowned or smashed on the rocks of its harsh demands. The stream of libertinism, by contrast, is relatively quiet and still, and crossing it seems easy and attractive. But its waters are so contaminated with poisons and pollutants that to try to cross it is also certain death. Both streams are uncrossable and deadly, one because of impossible moral and spiritual demands, the other because of moral and spiritual filth.

But spanning those two deadly streams is the bridge of the gospel of Jesus Christ, the only passage from earth to heaven. The two streams lead to death because they are man's ways. The gospel leads to life because it is God's way.

The Old Testament governmental law was abolished altogether in Christ. The purpose of that form of the law was to set the Jews apart as God's distinctive chosen people and to picture the sacrifice of the coming Messiah, the Christ. When Christ came, the symbols of His sacrifice ceased to be necessary, because the completed and final sacrifice itself was fully and eternally made.

As Paul mentions in verse 14, and explains in detail in other epistles, the work of Jesus Christ does *not* alter God's moral nature or His desire for man's holiness. Rather it enables the believer to fulfill them internally as well as externally, because of His indwelling and empowering Holy Spirit (v. 16). The motive for obedience is not bondage to a governmental system of laws but is based solely on love. Even though Old Testament saints also loved God and obeyed Him because of that love, they were still obligated to the whole system of law. In Christ that obligation is removed, and only love remains. It is the love and respect for God's holiness that puts reverent fear in our hearts. That is the glorious spiritual **freedom** into which God has **called** everyone who trusts in His Son.

In Galatians 5:13b-15, Paul gives four purposes of God's call to the freedom of loving Him: to oppose the flesh, to serve others, to fulfill His moral law, and to avoid harming others.

To Oppose the Flesh

only do not turn your freedom into an opportunity for the flesh, (5:13b)

Perhaps partly as a response to the Judaizers' charges that he was a libertine, and as a warning to believers who were tempted to abuse their Christian liberty, Paul makes clear that the freedom of the gospel is not tolerance of self-indulgence. It is not a means for satisfying the desires of **the flesh** but for opposing them.

Aphormē (**opportunity**) was often used to indicate a central base from which all operations of a military campaign originated. In this context **flesh** does not refer to the physical body but to the sinful inclination of fallen mankind, the old self, whose supreme desire is to do its own will and to satisfy its sinful appetites. It is a synonym for sinful self-will. Paul's declaration is that Christian **freedom** is not a base of operations from which **the flesh** is given **opportunity** to carry on its campaigns of sin freely and without consequence.

Christ does not give **freedom** to believers so they can do what *they* want but so they can, for the first time, do what *God* wants, because of love for Him. Within the bounds of their particular situations and abilities, even the most ungodly unbelievers are already free to do what they themselves want to do. They have more than ample **opportunity** to indulge the desires of **the flesh**, and it was hardly necessary for Christ to provide *that* sort of liberty.

But Paul's point is immeasurably more important than that obvious truth. The great reality he declares here is that it is *from* sin, represented by the **flesh**, that the gospel saves believers. Whatever Christian **freedom** is, it is clearly not the right of believers to return to that from which Christ paid with His own life to save them. "Act as free men," Peter admonishes, "and do not use your freedom as a covering for evil, but use it as bondslaves of God" (1 Pet. 2:16).

Under the cloak of Christian liberty, some professed Christians claim they are free to get drunk, enjoy worldly amusements, feed their minds on smutty books, magazines, and movies, and live in almost unrestrained self-indulgence. But such a person gives strong evidence that he is not a Christian at all. Although a true believer may fall into serious sin, his renewed conscience and Christ's own indwelling Spirit will not allow him to enjoy it for long. And he surely will not continually try to justify sin as a legitimate expression of Christian freedom. The new nature hates sin and loves the righteousness of God (see Rom. 7:14-25).

Teaching Christian **freedom** as **an opportunity for the flesh** is the lure of many popular false teachers. Mimicking the world's popular philosophy of situation ethics, they claim a believer is freed by Christ to express himself in virtually any way he wants as long as it seems right to him. Though that appeals to sinners, Peter rebukes such teachers for,

> speaking out arrogant words of vanity they entice by fleshly desires, by sensuality, those who barely escape from the ones who live in error, promising them freedom while they themselves are slaves of corruption; for by what a man is overcome, by this he is enslaved. For if after they have escaped the defilements of the world by the knowledge of the Lord and Savior Jesus Christ, they are again entangled in them and are overcome, the last state

has become worse for them than the first. For it would be better for them not to have known the way of righteousness, than having known it, to turn away from the holy commandment delivered to them. (2 Pet. 2:18-21)

Jude refers to false teachers as "certain persons [who] have crept in unnoticed, those who were long beforehand marked out for this condemnation, ungodly persons who turn the grace of our God into licentiousness and deny our only Master and Lord, Jesus Christ" (Jude 4). To advocate licentiousness in the name of Christian liberty is to deny the Lord Jesus Christ, who gives freedom *from* sin, not freedom *to* sin. "Put on the Lord Jesus Christ, and make no provision for the flesh in regard to its lusts," Paul wrote to the church at Rome (Rom. 13:14). To legitimately carry the name of Christ and to make provision for **the flesh** are contradictory and mutually exclusive.

One of the most amazing characteristics of Jesus was that, though He was God incarnate, He "did not please Himself" (Rom. 15:3). Those who receive Him as Lord and Savior also receive His selfless nature, and He calls on His followers to express that nature with the same love for God that motivated Him.

To Serve Others

but through love serve one another. (5:13*c*)

Second, Christian freedom takes believers to an even higher level than simply opposing the flesh. Positively, Christ frees His followers **through love** to **serve one another.** His freedom is the paradoxical freedom of loving subservience. *Compare to marriage*

Again Jesus is our great example. When the disciples bickered among themselves "as to which one of them was regarded to be greatest," Jesus said, "The kings of the Gentiles lord it over them; and those who have authority over them are called 'Benefactors.' But not so with you, but let him who is the greatest among you become as the youngest, and the leader as the servant. For who is greater, the one who reclines at the table, or the one who serves? Is it not the one who reclines at the table? But I am among you as the one who serves" (Luke 22:24-27).

"Have this attitude in yourselves which was also in Christ Jesus," Paul said, "who, although He existed in the form of God, did not regard equality with God a thing to be grasped, but emptied Himself, taking the form of a bond-servant" (Phil. 2:5-7). When Christ incarnates Himself in believers, He endows them with the same nature of servanthood He exemplified when, as the Son of God and Son of Man, He lived on earth as the Servant of God and the Servant of man.

To Fulfill God's Moral Law

For the whole Law is fulfilled in one word, in the statement, "You shall love your neighbor as yourself." (5:14)

Third, Paul explains that Christian freedom is not license to ignore God's desire for our holiness but is rather the opportunity to fulfill it. God's nature has never changed, and neither have His standards of right and wrong. The ethical truths of the Old Testament **Law** are exactly the same as those of the New Testament gospel.

Jesus echoed the greatest Old Testament principle when He declared that "the great commandment in the Law" was, "'You shall love the Lord your God with all your heart, and with all your soul, and with all your mind.' This is the great and foremost commandment. The second is like it, 'You shall love your neighbor as yourself.' On these two commandments depend the whole Law and the Prophets" (Matt. 22:36-40; compare with Deut. 6:5; Lev. 19:18). God had always called His people to serve and obey Him because they love Him.

Paul echoes and expands on that truth in his letter to the Romans: "He who loves his neighbor has fulfilled the law. For this, 'You shall not commit adultery, You shall not murder, You shall not steal, You shall not covet,' and if there is any other commandment, it is summed up in this saying, 'You shall love your neighbor as yourself.' Love does no wrong to a neighbor; love therefore is the fulfillment of the law" (Rom. 13:8-10).

Although he is not bound under the system of law as were Old Testament saints, when a Christian genuinely loves others he fulfills all the moral elements of the Mosaic law.

The first ordinance given through Moses after the Ten Commandments is a beautiful picture of serving the Lord out of love rather than mere duty. The ordinance stipulated that if one Hebrew bought another Hebrew as a slave, the slave had to be freed after serving his master for six years. "But if the slave plainly says, 'I love my master, . . . I will not go out as a free man,' then his master shall bring him to God, then he shall bring him to the door or the doorpost. And his master shall pierce his ear with an awl; and he shall serve him permanently" (Ex. 21:2-6).

The purpose of Christian freedom is for believers to do exactly as the Hebrew slave did who permanently surrendered his freedom to the master he loved. They willingly give up the freedom to serve themselves, which is freedom to serve the sinful flesh, in order to become slaves of God. "Having been freed from sin," they willingly begin the joyous privilege of becoming "enslaved to God" (Rom. 6:22).

Even under the Old Covenant of law, God demanded heart service, not mere lip service (Deut. 11:13; Josh. 24:23; 1 Kings 8:58; cf. Isa. 29:13). The inner motive of love has always been the only acceptable motivation for serving God or others. As Paul emphasizes in the remainder of the chapter (Gal. 5:16-26), the Christian has the indwelling Holy Spirit not only to rightly motivate his service to God and others but to empower it as well.

In the preceding three principles Paul deals with Christian freedom in regard to self, others, and God. True liberty in loving produces self-control, service to others, and obedience to God. Every relationship is harmonized in Christian freedom.

To Avoid Harming Others

But if you bite and devour one another, take care lest you be consumed by one another. (5:15)

The fourth purpose of Christian freedom is the reverse side of the second. Reemphasizing the need for Christians to use their freedom to serve each other (see v. 13), Paul here stresses the negative side of that truth—in the form of a warning about what happens when believers *do not* love and serve each other. They become destructive and **bite and devour one another.** Those two words speak of wild animals engaged in the fury of a deadly struggle.

Even the world knows that personal freedom cannot be unlimited. The most libertarian societies of history have been forced to recognize that they could not survive if each individual had the right to run roughshod over others while gratifying his own whims and fulfilling his own ambitions. Anarchy is obviously destructive, and one person's rights are necessarily restricted by the rights of others.

In his letter to the Romans, Paul counsels believers who are spiritually strong to avoid such conflict and to "accept the one who is weak in faith, but not for the purpose of passing judgment on his opinions. One man has faith that he may eat all things, but he who is weak eats vegetables only. Let not him who eats regard with contempt him who does not eat, and let not him who does not eat judge him who eats, for God has accepted him" (Rom. 14:1-3). *Whom do I regard w/ contempt?*

Many early Christians, both Jewish and Gentile, were so contemptuous and fearful of idolatry that they abstained from eating any meat at all, lest they inadvertently eat some that had been offered in a pagan ceremony and then sold in the pagan priests' market. Because pork was ritually unclean under the Mosaic law, many Jewish believers could not bring themselves to eat it no matter what its market source.

More mature believers realized with Paul that "in the Lord Jesus . . . nothing is unclean in itself; but to him who thinks anything to be unclean, to him it is unclean" (Rom. 14:14). The issue is not a matter of intrinsic evil but of conscience. A believer should never go against his conscience, even if it is immature; and other believers should never encourage him to do so or criticize him for his convictions. Likewise, the immature believer should not self-righteously condemn those who feel free to eat any food they desire. In either case, "if because of food your brother is hurt, you are no longer walking according to love. Do not destroy with your food him for whom Christ died" (v. 15).

As Paul has already explained (Gal. 5:6, 13), the ruling principle of Christian freedom is always love. The believer with an unnecessarily strict conscience and the one with a freed conscience are to lovingly accept and serve one another in Christ. Otherwise, they will be just like the most ungodly, self-centered pagans who **bite and devour one another** and end up being **consumed by one another.** Lovelessness is utterly destructive.

So we are called to freedom, the freedom of love that walks the bridge over legalism and license.

COURSE CORRECTION
1 Kings 17-18

WHAT DOES IT TAKE TO BRING REVIVAL?

1. A _____ SERVANT AND _____. 1 Kings 17:1

   A. Elijah knew the _____ God.

   B. Elijah knew that he was God's _____.

   C. Elijah knew the _____ _____ of God.

2. AN AWARENESS IN THE _____ OF THE PEOPLE.
   1 Kings 18:17-46

   A. The misdirected life is _____.

   B. The misdirected life must be _____.

   C. The misdirected life when _____ brings God's
      _____.

   D. The misdirected life may only be changed with God's
      _____.

1. Legalists Made Christ's Sacrifice
   Useless

2. Legalists Demand Others to
   Keep the Whole Law
        Deut 27:26

3. Legalists Cut others off
   From Christ

Walking by the Spirit—part 1 The Command and the Conflict (5:16-18)

15

But I say, walk by the Spirit, and you will not carry out the desire of the flesh. For the flesh sets its desire against the Spirit, and the Spirit against the flesh; for these are in opposition to one another, so that you may not do the things that you please. But if you are led by the Spirit, you are not under the Law. (5:16-18)

Just as Jesus Christ is the primary Person behind justification, the Holy Spirit is the primary Person behind sanctification. A believer can no more sanctify himself than he could have saved himself in the first place. He cannot live the Christian life by his own resources any more than he could have saved himself by his own resources.

In its most profound yet simple definition, the faithful Christian life is a life lived under the direction and by the power of the Spirit. That is the theme of Galatians 5:16-26, in which Paul tells believers to "walk by the Spirit" (vv. 16, 25) and to be "led by the Spirit" (v. 18). The opening paragraph (vv. 16-18) of this section introduces the passage by setting forth the command and the conflict of the Spirit-led life.

THE COMMAND

But I say, walk by the Spirit, and you will not carry out the desire of the flesh. (5:16)

The contrasting themes of the book of Galatians are law and grace, which Paul repeatedly shows are incompatible, either as means of salvation or of sanctification. A person cannot come to God by means of law-keeping nor can he sustain living for God by keeping the law, not even the God-given law of Moses in which the Old Covenant centered. Because no man can perfectly obey it, the law has never been, and was never intended to be, a means of salvation. It was given by God to reveal God's holy standards and to make men despair of their own failing human efforts at pleasing Him, thus driving them to Jesus Christ, who alone by grace can make them acceptable to the Father. Through the law, "the Scripture has shut up all men under sin, that the promise by faith in Jesus Christ might be given to those who believe" (Gal. 3:22). The law was never meant to be a savior, but only a tutor to lead men to the Savior (v. 24).

The believer has no use for the law as a means of salvation, because through Christ he has already been saved and adopted into God's heavenly household as a son (Gal. 3:26). Nor does he need the governmental system of law to guide him *in* his new life, because he has Christ's own **Spirit** as his permanent, indwelling Guide. In fact, the more a believer attempts to force himself to live by rules and regulations, no matter how lofty they may be, the more he stifles the work of the Holy Spirit.

Although Bible study, prayer, worship, witnessing, and certain behavior standards are commanded of believers and are essential to faithful Christian living, spirituality cannot be measured by how often or how intensely we are involved in such things. To use them as measures of spirituality is to become entrapped in legalism, whose only significance is in the outward, the visible, the humanly measurable. To live solely by a set of laws is to live by the flesh in self-righteousness and hypocrisy and to suppress the **Spirit**, who alone is able inwardly to produce works of true righteousness. Holiness comes only from the Holy Spirit. Holy living does not come from *our* performance for God but from *His* performance through us by His own Spirit. Holy living is "to be strengthened with power through His Spirit in the inner man" as we are "filled with the Spirit" (Eph. 3:16; 5:18).

All a believer absolutely needs to live a holy life according to the will of God is the Holy Spirit, who is given to him the moment he believes (Rom. 8:9). Even the newest, most untaught Christian is indwelt by God's own resident Teacher and Strengthener. Although **the Spirit** uses Scripture to assist believers to grow in truth and holiness, He Himself is the supreme source of those virtues (cf. Col. 3:16).

Only pride or ignorance could lead a believer to live by an outward list of rules and commands in his own limited and sinful power when he can live by the perfect and fully sufficient inner power of the Holy Spirit. Yet that is what many believers in the Galatian churches were trying to do, and what many believers since that time have also endeavored to do.

The fact that *peripateō* (**walk**) is used here in the present tense indicates that Paul is speaking of continuous, regular action, in other words, a habitual way of life. And the fact that the verb is also in the imperative mood indicates he is not giving believers an option but a command.

Among other things, walking implies progress, going from where one is to where he ought to be. As a believer submits to the Spirit's control, he moves forward in his spiritual life. Step by step the Spirit moves him from where he is toward where God wants him to be. So while it is the Spirit who is the source of all holy living, it is the believer who is commanded to walk. This is the apparent paradox of the divine and human that is seen in salvation (John 6:35-40), in Scripture inspiration (cf. 1 John 1:1-3 with 2 Pet. 1:19-21), in eternal security (cf. Rom. 8:31-39 with Col. 1:21-23), and even in ministry (Col. 1:28-29).

In emphasizing the central work of the Holy Spirit in the believer's life, some Christians have lost the tension between the human and the divine and have taught the idea suggested in such popular expressions as "Let go and let God" and "the surrendered life." Rightly used, such expressions can be helpful. If they are understood to mean letting go of one's own resources and self-will and surrendering to God's truth and power, the idea is scriptural. But if, as is often the case, they are used to teach the idea that Christian living is little more than passive submission and yieldedness to God, they are contrary to all the militant terms and commands for great effort and commitment that pervade the New Testament (see, e.g., 1 Cor. 9:24-27; Heb. 12:1-3).

If human will and actions did not play a direct and aggressive part in the Christian life, the New Testament would contain only this one instruction for believers: **walk by the Spirit.** Every other command would be superfluous. That is essentially the theology of what is often called quietism, of which the old Quakers were the best-known advocates. The Keswick tradition, the preaching of the famous evangelist Charles Finney, and Hannah Whitall Smith's *The Christian's Secret of a Happy Life* also reflect a strong quietistic orientation. Passive surrender to God is taught to the almost total exclusion of human volition and action.

Many advocates of a moderate quietistic approach have been godly saints and greatly used by the Lord. But the unbalanced emphasis of their teaching tends to inhibit rather than enhance the work of the Spirit. It runs the danger of underplaying, if not actually contradicting, the many other New Testament commands to believers besides that of submitting to the Holy Spirit.

The *power* for Christian living is entirely from the Holy Spirit, just as the power of salvation is entirely in Jesus Christ. But both in the justifying work of Christ and in the sanctifying work of the Holy Spirit, man's will is active and commitment is called for.

The Christian is not to sit on the sidelines, as it were, and simply watch the Holy Spirit do battle for him. He is called to consider himself "to be dead to sin, but alive to God in Christ Jesus," to refuse to let "sin reign in [his] mortal body," to resist presenting "the members of [his] body to sin as instruments of unrighteousness," and rather to present them "as instruments of righteousness to God" (Rom. 6:11-13). "Let us not lose heart in doing good," Paul says later in this letter, "for in due time we shall reap if we do not grow weary. So then, while we have opportunity, let us do good to all men, and especially to those who are of the household of the faith" (Gal. 6:9-10).

The believer who is led by the Holy Spirit must be willing to go where the Spirit guides him and do what the Spirit leads him to do. To claim surrender to the Holy Spirit but not be personally involved in God's work is to call Jesus, "Lord, Lord," and not do what He says (Luke 6:46).

Though most often referring to an evil lust, the word *epithumia* can refer to a strong, compelling **desire** of any sort, good or evil. Jesus used the word to express His intent to eat the Passover meal with His disciples (Luke 22:15), and Paul used it to express his longing "to depart and be with Christ, for that is much better" (Phil. 1:23). In this verse it is employed in relation to the evil will of **the flesh** bent on damnation. In verse 17 the term is used both in relation to the evil will of the flesh and in relation to the holy will of the Spirit.

To **walk by the Spirit** and thereby **not carry out the desire of the flesh** articulates the same principle as to "put on the Lord Jesus Christ, and make no provision for the flesh in regard to its lusts" (Rom. 13:14). To **walk by the Spirit** is to "behave properly as in the day," whereas to **carry out the desire of the flesh** involves such things as "carousing, . . . drunkenness, . . . sexual promiscuity and sensuality, . . . strife and jealousy" (v. 13). The two behaviors are mutually exclusive, so that at all times in our Christian lives we are either walking by the Spirit or are functioning in fleshly desire, but never both at the same time.

The life walked by the Spirit is the Christlike life, the saturation of a believer's thoughts with the truth, love, and glory of His Lord and the desire to be like Him in every way. It is to live in continual consciousness of His presence and will, letting "the word of Christ richly dwell within you" (Col. 3:16). Life walked by the Spirit is life patterned after the teaching and example of the Lord Jesus Christ. It is a life whose constant, overriding desire is to "be found in Him, not having a righteousness of [its] own derived from the Law, but that which is through faith in Christ, the righteousness which comes from God on the basis of faith" and the desire to "know Him, and the power of His resurrection and the fellowship of His sufferings" (Phil. 3:9-10). Surely, it is no different from being "filled with the Spirit" (Eph. 5:18), a phrase referring to the controlling power exerted by the Spirit on a willing Christian. (For a more detailed study of this concept, see my commentary *Ephesians* [Chicago: Moody, 1986], pp. 245-69.)

THE CONFLICT

For the flesh sets its desire against the Spirit, and the Spirit against the flesh; for these are in opposition to one another, so that you may not do the things that you please. But if you are led by the Spirit, you are not under the Law. (5:17-18)

Along with many others in the New Testament, these two verses make it obvious that walking by the Spirit is not simply a matter of passive surrender. The Spirit-led life is a life of conflict, because it is in constant combat with the old ways of the flesh that continue to tempt and seduce the believer. **The flesh sets its desire against the Spirit, and the Spirit against the flesh.**

It should be noted that **the flesh** is the term Paul often uses to describe what remains of the "old man" after a person is saved. It refers to unredeemed humanness, the part of a believer that awaits future redemption at the time of his glorification

154

(Rom. 8:23). Until then he has a redeemed self (cf. Gal. 2:20) living in an unredeemed humanness, and that creates great conflict.

Paul himself, like every other believer, faced that constant struggle with **the flesh**, as he confesses in his letter to the Romans.

> For I know that nothing good dwells in me, that is, in my flesh; for the wishing is present in me, but the doing of the good is not. For the good that I wish, I do not do; but I practice the very evil that I do not wish. . . . I find then the principle that evil is present in me, the one who wishes to do good. For I joyfully concur with the law of God in the inner man, but I see a different law in the members of my body, waging war against the law of my mind, and making me a prisoner of the law of sin which is in my members. (Rom. 7:18-19, 21-23)

This specific usage of *sarx* (**flesh**) is set among several other usages in the New Testament. The term occasionally refers to the physical body, in particular to the muscle, skin, and other tissues that cover the skeleton, as well as to general humanness. It was in that sense that Jesus used the word when He told His disciples after His resurrection, "See My hands and My feet, that it is I Myself; touch Me and see, for a spirit does not have flesh and bones as you see that I have" (Luke 24:39) and when He said, "The flesh is weak" (Matt. 26:41).

Sarx is also used to comprehensively describe the state of the unsaved, those who are "in the flesh" and thus totally under the control of sinful passions (Rom. 7:5). As such, "flesh" is generally used in a figurative, theological sense, referring to man's fallen nature, his unredeemed self.

When speaking of "Abraham, our forefather according to the flesh" (Rom. 4:1), Paul was not referring to the racial lineage of Jews. In this context he was contrasting those people, whether Jew or Gentile, who are *spiritually* descended from Abraham—either "according to the flesh" (that is, before Abraham trusted in God) or according to his faith, by which he became "the father of all who believe" (v. 11).

In the present text and others, **flesh** also relates to the moral and spiritual weakness and helplessness of human nature still clinging to redeemed souls, such as that mentioned by Paul in Romans 7 and quoted above (cf. Rom. 6:19). The **flesh** of Christians is their propensity to sin, their fallen humanness that awaits redemption, in which the new and holy creation dwells (cf. Gal. 2:20; 2 Cor. 5:17).

The flesh is that part of a believer that functions apart from and **against the Spirit**. It stands against the work of the Spirit in the believer's new heart. The unsaved person often regrets the sinful things he does because of guilt and/or painful consequences, but he has no spiritual warfare going on within him, because he has only a fleshly nature and is devoid of the Spirit. The sinful things he does, though often disappointing and disgusting to him, are nevertheless consistent with his basic nature as an enemy of God (Rom. 5:10) and a child of His wrath (Eph. 2:3). He therefore has no real internal conflict beyond whatever conscience may remain in his sinful state.

It is only in the lives of believers that **the Spirit** can fight **against the flesh,** because it is only in believers that **the Spirit** dwells. Only a believer can truthfully say, "I joyfully concur with the law of God in the inner man, but I see a different law in the members of my body, waging war against the law of my mind" (Rom. 7:22-23). Only in believers are **the** unredeemed **flesh** and **the Spirit** living in the redeemed self **in opposition to one another, so that** believers **may not do the things that** they **please.** Believers do not always do what they wish to do. There are those moments in every Christian's experience when the wishing is present but the doing is not. The Spirit often halts what our flesh desires, and the flesh often overrides the will that comes from the Spirit. It is no surprise that this frustrating conflict led Paul to exclaim, "Wretched man that I am! Who will set me free from the body of this death?" (Rom. 7:24).

Although the Christian life is warfare, it is warfare in which victory is always possible. In His high priestly prayer Jesus spoke of the authority His Father had given Him "over all mankind" (lit., "all flesh," from *sarx;* John 17:2). Every believer has the indwelling power of God's own **Spirit** to do battle with his own weak and sinful **flesh,** in order that he **may not do the things** that **please** his flesh. In Romans 8:2, the apostle wrote: "the law of the Spirit . . . has set you free from the law of sin and of death." In other words, a third party is key to the conflict between the new creation and the **flesh**—the Holy **Spirit.** He energizes the new inner man for victory over his **flesh.**

As sons of God and servants of Jesus Christ, believers "are under obligation, not to the flesh, to live according to the flesh—for if [they] are living according to the flesh, [they] must die; but if by the Spirit [they] are putting to death the deeds of the body, [they] will live. For all who are being led by the Spirit of God, these are sons of God" (Rom. 8:12-14). "The Spirit also helps our weakness" when praying, Paul assures us; "for we do not know how to pray as we should, but the Spirit Himself intercedes for us with groanings too deep for words" (v. 26).

As already mentioned, the most effective way for a Christian to oppose the desires and deeds of **the flesh** is to starve them to death, to "make no provision for the flesh in regard to its lusts" (Rom. 13:14). The surest way to fall into a sin is to allow oneself to be in situations where there is temptation to it. On the other hand, the safest way to avoid a sin is to avoid situations that are likely to pose temptations to it. A believer should "consider the members of [his] earthly body as dead to immorality, impurity, passion, evil desire, and greed, which amount to idolatry" (Col. 3:5). When our Lord told us to pray, "Do not lead us into temptation" (Matt. 6:13), He revealed that there is a part to sinful temptation that we must avoid.

A believer who is not actively involved in resisting evil and obviously seeking to do good is not being **led by the Spirit,** no matter how much he may think he is "surrendered." The faithful believer is not an observer but "a good soldier of Christ Jesus" who is engaged in the "active service" of his Lord (2 Tim. 2:3-4).

The faithful believer is also compared to an athlete. Paul commands Christians to "run in such a way that [they] may win" and to exercise self-control. He speaks of himself as running "in such a way, as not without aim," of boxing "in such a way, as not beating the air," and of buffeting his body to make it his slave (1 Cor. 9:24-27).

A believer can accomplish nothing for the Lord in his own power, but, on the other hand, the Spirit can accomplish little through a believer apart from the believer's submission and commitment. The opposite extreme of quietism is traditionally labelled "pietism," in which a believer legalistically strives in his own power to do everything the Lord commands of him. There the emphasis is overbalanced on the side of discipline, self-effort, and personal diligence.

In his second epistle, Peter beautifully explains the true balance of the Christian life. According to "His divine power [God] has granted to us everything pertaining to life and godliness, through the true knowledge of Him who called us by His own glory and excellence. For by these He has granted to us His precious and magnificent promises, in order that by them you might become partakers of the divine nature, having escaped the corruption that is in the world by lust" (2 Pet. 1:3-4). That is God's commitment, in the power of which the believer's commitment should be to apply all diligence and in faith to supply moral excellence, knowledge, self-control, perseverance, and godliness (vv. 5-6).

It is not a matter of "All of Him and none of us," as the popular saying has it; and it is certainly not a matter of all of us and none of Him. It is the balance of our yieldedness and commitment with the Spirit's guidance and power. "Work out your salvation with fear and trembling," Paul says; "for it is God who is at work in you, both to will and to work for His good pleasure" (Phil. 2:12). The mystery of this perfect and paradoxical balance cannot be fully understood or explained, but it can be fully experienced.

As a repeated warning to believers who were being influenced by the Judaizers, Paul added, **But if you are led by the Spirit, you are not under the Law.** To live **under the Law** is to live by the flesh, even when one is not actually committing sin, because that is the only avenue available to the legalist. The flesh is powerless to fulfill **the Law**, and **the Law** is powerless to conquer the flesh. Rather, "sin, taking opportunity through the commandment, produced in me coveting of every kind; for apart from the Law sin is dead. And I was once alive apart from the Law; but when the commandment came, sin became alive, and I died; and this commandment, which was to result in life, proved to result in death for me; for sin, taking opportunity through the commandment, deceived me, and through it killed me" (Rom. 7:8-11).

In his *Pilgrim's Progress,* John Bunyan describes Interpreter's house, which Pilgrim entered during the course of his journey to the Celestial City. The parlor of the house was completely covered with dust, and when a man took a broom and started to sweep, he and the others in the room began to choke from the great clouds of dust that were stirred up. The more vigorously he swept, the more suffocating the dust became. Then Interpreter ordered a maid to sprinkle the room with water, with which the dust was quickly washed away. Interpreter explained to Pilgrim that the parlor represented the heart of an unsaved man, that the dust was original sin, the man with the broom was the law, and the maid with the water was the gospel. His point was that all the law can do with sin is to stir it up. Only the gospel of Jesus Christ can wash it away.

"The power of sin is the law," Paul declares; "but thanks be to God, who gives us the victory through our Lord Jesus Christ" (1 Cor. 15:56).

To be **led by the Spirit** is the same as walking by Him (vv. 16, 25) but carries additional emphasis on His leadership. We do not walk along with Him as an equal, but follow His leading as our sovereign, divine Guide. "For all who are being led by the Spirit of God, these are sons of God," Paul says (Rom. 8:14). The converse is also true: Those who are sons of God are led by the Spirit of God. Believers do not need to pray for the Spirit's leading, because He is already doing that. They need to seek for willingness and obedience to follow His leading.

When Christ enters a person's life, the Holy Spirit enters simultaneously (cf. Rom. 8:9). And the moment He enters He begins to lead God's newborn child in the way of freedom (Gal. 5:1), holiness (5:16), truth (John 16:13-15), fruitfulness (Gal. 5:22-23), access to God in prayer (Eph. 2:18), assurance (Rom. 8:16), witnessing (Acts 1:8), and submissive joy (Eph. 5:18-21).

No wonder Paul rejoiced that "what the Law could not do, weak as it was through the flesh, God did: sending His own Son in the likeness of sinful flesh and as an offering for sin, He condemned sin in the flesh, in order that the requirement of the Law might be fulfilled in us, who do not walk according to the flesh, but according to the Spirit" (Rom. 8:3-4).

Walking by the Spirit—part 2 The Contrast and the Conquest (5:19-25)

16

Now the deeds of the flesh are evident, which are: immorality, impurity, sensuality, idolatry, sorcery, enmities, strife, jealousy, outbursts of anger, disputes, dissensions, factions, envying, drunkenness, carousing, and things like these, of which I forewarn you just as I have forewarned you that those who practice such things shall not inherit the kingdom of God. But the fruit of the Spirit is love, joy, peace, patience, kindness, goodness, faithfulness, gentleness, self-control; against such things there is no law. Now those who belong to Christ Jesus have crucified the flesh with its passions and desires.

If we live by the Spirit, let us also walk by the Spirit. (5:19-25)

In describing the believer's walk by the Spirit, Paul first sets forth the command and the conflict (vv. 16-18) of that walk. Next he focuses on the contrast between the works of the flesh and the fruit of the Spirit (vv. 19-23) and then presents the conquest (vv. 24-25) that has been provided.

THE CONTRAST

Now the deeds of the flesh are evident, which are: immorality, impurity, sensuality, idolatry, sorcery, enmities, strife, jealousy, outbursts of anger,

disputes, dissensions, factions, envying, drunkenness, carousing, and things like these, of which I forewarn you just as I have forewarned you that those who practice such things shall not inherit the kingdom of God. But the fruit of the Spirit is love, joy, peace, patience, kindness, goodness, faithfulness, gentleness, self-control; against such things there is no law. (5:19-23)

As a motivation to godly living, Paul places the products of life lived in the flesh side by side with the products of life lived by the Spirit. The sins of the first list are the ugly and repulsive results of evil desire, whereas the virtues of the second are the beautiful and attractive results of walking by the Spirit. Neither list is exhaustive but only suggestive (see v. 21, "things like these"; and v. 23, "such things") of things that first of all were pertinent to the Galatian church and, second, are pertinent to all believers.

THE DEEDS OF THE FLESH

Now the deeds of the flesh are evident, which are: immorality, impurity, sensuality, idolatry, sorcery, enmities, strife, jealousy, outbursts of anger, disputes, dissensions, factions, envying, drunkenness, carousing, and things like these, of which I forewarn you just as I have forewarned you that those who practice such things shall not inherit the kingdom of God. (5:19-21)

The deeds of the flesh reflect the sinful desires of unredeemed humanness, which are in spiritual warfare against the desires of the Spirit (vv. 16-17; cf. 24). These **deeds** are so **evident** that Paul mentions them primarily by way of a reminder.

Jesus made clear that man's basic problem is not with what is outside of him but with what is within him. "That which proceeds out of the man, that is what defiles the man. For from within, out of the heart of men, proceed the evil thoughts, fornications, thefts, murders, adulteries, deeds of coveting and wickedness, as well as deceit, sensuality, envy, slander, pride and foolishness. All these evil things proceed from within and defile the man" (Mark 7:20-23).

Jesus' list is much like Paul's, and in both passages the point is made that these evils originate from within man himself, not from Satan or the world outside. In that brief account Jesus mentions three times that the sins come from within man himself, and Paul identifies his list of sins as **deeds of the flesh,** that is, works produced by man's own unregenerate nature.

There are only two possible views of man's nature: he is seen either as basically good or basically evil. The humanistic view is that he is born morally good, or at least morally neutral. The Bible, however, maintains the opposite, that man is inherently corrupt and depraved in every aspect of his being. Consequently, although man's environment is never perfect and often has a detrimental effect on him, that is never his worst problem. It is primarily man who pollutes the environment, not the environment that pollutes him.

That is why better housing, transportation, education, jobs, income, medical care, and all other such things—desirable as they may be—can do nothing to solve man's basic problem, which is sin inside of him. No outward benefit can improve him inwardly. Instead, better outward conditions offer better and more sophisticated opportunities to do evil and for those very benefits themselves to be corrupted by the people they are designed to help.

Though the sins that Paul lists here (cf. Rom. 1:29-31; 2 Cor. 12:20-21) are natural characteristics of unredeemed mankind, not every person manifests all of the sins or manifests them to the same degree. However, every person possesses **the flesh**, which is sinful and will therefore be manifested in sinful behavior, whatever the particular forms of it may be. These are normal and continual behaviors for unbelievers in their course of life in the flesh, but are abnormal and interruptive behavior in the lives of Christians, who live in the Spirit. A Christian can walk in the Spirit and avoid them all, or he can give in to **the flesh** and fall victim to any of them.

Paul's list of **the deeds of the flesh** encompasses three general areas: sex, religion, and human relationships.

The first group of sins relates to man's defilement in the area of sex. **Immorality** is from *porneia,* from which is derived the English *pornography.* The term has a broad meaning, referring to all illicit sexual activity—especially, but not limited to, adultery, fornication, homosexuality, bestiality, and prostitution. In 1 Corinthians 5:1, Paul uses the term to refer to a form of incest (sexual relationships of a man with his mother or stepmother) that even the pagans did not practice. In the next two chapters (6:13, 18; 7:2; cf. Eph. 5:3; 1 Thess. 4:3) he uses the same word to represent sexual sin in general.

Impurity is from *akatharsia,* which literally means "unclean" and was used medically to refer to an infected, oozing wound. It is the negative form of *katharsia,* which means "clean" and is the word from which we get *catharsis,* a cleansing. In Scripture the term is used of both moral and ceremonial uncleanness, any **impurity** that prevents a person from approaching God.

Sensuality is from *aselgeia,* which originally referred to any excess or lack of restraint but came to be associated primarily with sexual excess. It is unrestrained sexual indulgence, such as has become so common in the modern Western world. It refers to uninhibited sexual indulgence without shame and without concern for what others think or how they may be affected (or infected).

The second group of sins, specifically **idolatry** and **sorcery,** relates to man-made religion, which is as much a product of the flesh as are sexual sins. The deeds of the flesh not only defile men themselves but also their relationship to God. All human religion is based on self-effort, on man's sinful insistence that he can make himself acceptable to his humanly-conceived God by his own merits. Consequently, human religion is the implacable enemy of divine grace and therefore of the gospel.

Idolatry is the obvious sin of worshiping man-made images of whatever sort. **Sorcery** translates *pharmakeia,* from which we get *pharmacy* and *pharmaceutical.* It was originally used of medicines in general but came to be used primarily of mood- and mind-altering drugs similar to those that create so much havoc in our own day.

Many ancient religious ceremonies involved occultic practices in which drugs were used to induce supposed communication with deities, and *pharmakeia* thereby came to be closely related to witchcraft and magic. Aristotle and other ancient Greek writers used the word as a synonym for witchcraft and black magic, because drugs were so commonly used in their practice.

The third group of sins relates to human relationships, which are defiled by these specific sins as well as by many others.

Enmities is in the plural and refers to hateful attitudes, which result in **strife** among individuals, including bitter conflicts. Wrong attitudes invariably bring wrong actions.

Jealousy is a form of anger and hateful resentment caused by coveting for oneself what belongs to someone else. **Outbursts of anger** are sudden, unrestrained expressions of hostility toward others, often with little or no provocation or justification. It is the all-too-common sin of unbridled temper. Although **jealousy** does not necessarily result in **outbursts of anger** in the way that **enmities** result in **strife,** the first sin in each case refers to attitude or motive and the second to action.

Disputes, dissensions, factions, and **envyings** are more particular and ongoing expressions of the general sins that precede them in this list. They represent animosities between individuals and groups that sometimes continue to fester and grow long after the original cause of conflict has passed. From the feuds of old-time mountain clans that lasted for generations to national hostilities that last for centuries, these sins can become an established and destructive way of life.

Drunkenness and **carousing** probably had special reference to the orgies that so often characterized the pagan worship ceremonies that many of the Gentile converts of Galatia had once participated in. In a more general and universal sense, however, they refer to becoming drunk under any circumstance and to all rowdy, boisterous, and crude behavior.

As already observed, **and things like these** indicates that Paul's list of deeds of the flesh is only representative and not exhaustive. Nor were **these** sins ones that Galatian believers had only recently been tempted by or fallen into. **I forewarn you** again, Paul says, **just as I have forewarned you** about them in the past. These appear to have been sins that were dominant in the culture and by which the Galatians were still being tempted.

 The high point of the apostle's forewarning is sobering: **those who practice such things shall not inherit the kingdom of God.** Because the list of sins is so all-encompassing and the warning so severe, this passage has caused many believers to doubt their salvation. Such fears have been compounded by the unfortunate rendering of the King James Version: "they which do such things." "Who hasn't done some of those things?" people wonder. "What Christian can claim he has not committed a single one of those sins since he was saved? Who could possibly enter the kingdom of God if committing just one of those sins keeps him out?"

The key word in Paul's warning is **practice,** which translates a present active participle of *prassō,* indicating durative, ongoing action. It is the continual, habitual **practice** of **such things** that marks a person as unregenerate and therefore barred from entrance into **the kingdom of God.** Scripture always assesses a person's character on the basis of his common, habitual actions, not his occasional ones. People who habitually indulge in sin show themselves to be enemies of God, whereas those who habitually do good show themselves to be His children. The unregenerate person occasionally does humanly good things, and the regenerate person occasionally falls into sin. But the basic character of the unregenerate is to **practice** the evil deeds of the flesh and of the regenerate person to bear the good fruit of the Spirit. This is the heart of John's teaching in 1 John 3:4-10.

> Everyone who practices sin also practices lawlessness; and sin is lawlessness. And you know that He appeared in order to take away sins; and in Him there is no sin. No one who abides in Him sins; no one who sins has seen Him or knows Him. Little children, let no one deceive you; the one who practices righteousness is righteous, just as He is righteous; the one who practices sin is of the devil; for the devil has sinned from the beginning. The Son of God appeared for this purpose, that He might destroy the works of the devil. No one who is born of God practices sin, because His seed abides in him; and he cannot sin, because he is born of God. By this the children of God and the children of the devil are obvious: anyone who does not practice righteousness is not of God, nor the one who does not love his brother.

Paul makes a similar statement in 1 Corinthians 6:9-10, "Or do you not know that the unrighteous shall not inherit the kingdom of God? Do not be deceived; neither fornicators, nor idolaters, nor adulterers, nor effeminate, nor homosexuals, nor thieves, nor the covetous, nor drunkards, nor revilers, nor swindlers, shall inherit the kingdom of God." He then makes clear that such things are no longer the **practice** of believers: "And such were some of you; but you were washed, but you were sanctified, but you were justified in the name of the Lord Jesus Christ, and in the Spirit of our God" (v. 11).

Even though they are not habitually doing such evils, Paul calls on saints to walk in the Spirit so that they do not even do them occasionally.

THE FRUIT OF THE SPIRIT

But the fruit of the Spirit is love, joy, peace, patience, kindness, goodness, faithfulness, gentleness, self-control; against such things there is no law. (5:22-23)

Contrasted with the deeds of the flesh is **the fruit of the Spirit.** Deeds of the flesh are done by a person's own efforts, whether he is saved or unsaved. **The fruit of the Spirit,** on the other hand, is produced by God's own **Spirit** and only in the lives of those who belong to Him through faith in Jesus Christ.

The spiritual behavior of walking by the Spirit (v. 16) has the negative effect of causing the believer to put away the habitual, ongoing evil deeds of the flesh and positively causes him to bear the good **fruit** produced by **the Spirit.**

The first contrast between the deeds of the flesh and **the fruit of the Spirit** is that the products of the flesh are plural, whereas the product of **the Spirit** is singular. Although Paul does not mention the truth here, there is also a contrast between the degrees to which the deeds and **the fruit** are produced. A given person may habitually practice only one or two, or perhaps a half dozen, of the sins Paul mentions here. But it would be practically impossible for one person to be habitually active in all of them. **The fruit of the Spirit,** on the other hand, is always produced completely in every believer, no matter how faintly evidenced its various manifestations may be.

The Bible has much to say about fruit, which is mentioned some 106 times in the Old Testament and 70 times in the New. Even under the covenant of law, a believer produced good fruit only by God's power, not his own. "From Me comes your fruit," the Lord declared to ancient Israel (Hos. 14:8).

In the New Testament such things as praise of the Lord (Heb. 13:15), winning converts to Christ (1 Cor. 16:15), and godly work in general (Col. 1:10) are spoken of as spiritual fruit produced through believers. But such action fruit must come from attitude fruit, and that is the kind of **fruit** Paul focuses on in Galatians 5:22-23. If those attitudes are characteristic of a believer's life, the fruit of active good works will inevitably follow.

The Spirit never fails to produce some **fruit** in a believer's life, but the Lord desires "much fruit" (John 15:8). As an unredeemed person, possessing only a fallen, sinful nature will inevitably manifest that nature in "the deeds of the flesh" (v.19), so a believer, possessing a redeemed new nature will inevitably manifest that new nature in **the fruit of the Spirit.** But it is always possible for the believer to bear and manifest more fruit if he is receptive to **the Spirit.**

The Spirit's provision of **fruit** might be compared to a man standing on a ladder in an orchard, picking the fruit and dropping it into a basket held by a helper below. No matter how much fruit is picked and dropped, the helper will not receive any unless he is standing under the ladder with his basket ready.

The fruit of the Spirit is the outward indicator of salvation. A believer's sonship to God and citizenship in His kingdom (cf. v. 21) are manifested by the fruit the Spirit produces in his life. "You will know [men] by their fruits," Jesus said. "Grapes are not gathered from thorn bushes, nor figs from thistles, are they? Even so, every good tree bears good fruit; but the bad tree bears bad fruit. A good tree cannot produce bad fruit, nor can a bad tree produce good fruit" (Matt. 7:16-18).

In verses 22-23 Paul lists nine representative characteristics of the godly fruit produced by the Holy Spirit in a believer's life. Although many attempts have been made to categorize these nine virtues in various groupings, most such schemes seem artificial and irrelevant. Whether or not satisfactory classifications of them can be made, it is important to remember that these are multiple characteristics of but one fruit and are therefore inextricably related to one another. They are not produced nor can they be manifested in isolation from each other.

Rather paradoxically, all of the nine manifestations of **the fruit of the Spirit** are also *commanded* of believers in the New Testament. Also in every case, Jesus can be seen to be the supreme example and the Holy Spirit to be the source.

Love. The first characteristic of spiritual fruit is **love**, the supreme virtue of Christian living (1 Cor. 13:13). Some commentators insist that in this context **love** is a synonym for **fruit** and therefore encompasses the other characteristics in the list. In any case, **love** is clearly dominant. As Paul has just declared, "the whole Law is fulfilled in one word, in the statement, 'You shall love your neighbor as yourself'" (Gal. 5:14; cf. Rom. 13:10).

Agapē **love** is the form of love that most reflects personal choice, referring not simply to pleasant emotions or good feelings but to willing, self-giving service. "God demonstrates His own love toward us, in that while we were yet sinners, Christ died for us" (Rom. 5:8). In the same way, the most extreme sacrificial choice a loving person can make is to "lay down his life for his friends" (John 15:13). The apostle John expresses those two truths together in his first letter: "We know love by this, that He laid down His life for us; and we ought to lay down our lives for the brethren" (1 John 3:16). But **love** is tested long before it is called on to offer that supreme sacrifice. As John goes on to say, "Whoever has the world's goods, and beholds his brother in need and closes his heart against him, how does the love of God abide in him?" (v. 17). A person who thinks his love is great enough to sacrifice his life for fellow believers but who fails to help them when they have less extreme needs is simply fooling himself.

True *agapē* **love** is a sure mark of salvation. "We know that we have passed out of death into life," John says, "because we love the brethren. . . . Everyone who loves is born of God and knows God" (1 John 3:14; 4:7). By the same token, as John repeatedly makes clear throughout the same letter, having a habitually unloving spirit toward fellow Christians is reason for a person to question his salvation (see e.g., 2:9, 11; 3:15; 4:8, 20).

Jesus Christ is the supreme example of this supreme virtue. It was not only the Father's love but also His own love that led Jesus to lay down His life for us, demonstrating with His own self-sacrifice the love that gives its life for its friends. And before He made the ultimate sacrifice, He demonstrated the same self-giving **love** in many lesser ways. As Jesus saw Mary and the others weeping because of Lazarus's death, He, too, wept (John 11:33-35). He did not grieve for the fact that Lazarus had died, because He purposely delayed coming to Bethany until His dear friend was dead, in order to demonstrate His power to raise him from the grave. Jesus wept because of the great evil, destruction, and human misery caused by sin, whose final wages is always death (Rom. 6:23).

For believers, **love** is not an option but a command. "Walk in love," Paul declared, "just as Christ also loved you, and gave Himself up for us, an offering and a sacrifice to God as a fragrant aroma" (Eph. 5:2). Yet the command cannot be fulfilled apart from the Holy Spirit, the source of this and all the other manifestations of spiritual **fruit**. "The love of God has been poured out within our hearts through the Holy Spirit who was given to us," Paul explained to Roman believers (Rom. 5:5), and it was for such "love in the Spirit" that he gave thanks for the believers in Colossae (Col. 1:8).

Joy. The second manifestation of the **fruit of the Spirit** is **joy**. *Chara* (**joy**) is used some 70 times in the New Testament, always to signify a feeling of happiness that is based on spiritual realities. **Joy** is the deep-down sense of well-being that abides in the heart of the person who knows all is well between himself and the Lord. It is not an experience that comes from favorable circumstances or even a human emotion that is divinely stimulated. It is God's gift to believers. As Nehemiah declared, "The joy of the Lord is your strength" (Neh. 8:10). **Joy** is a part of God's own nature and **Spirit** that He manifests in His children.

Speaking of how we feel about the Lord Jesus Christ, Peter wrote, "Though you have not seen Him, you love Him, and though you do not see Him now, but believe in Him, you greatly rejoice with joy inexpressible and full of glory" (1 Pet. 1:8). **Joy** is the inevitable overflow of receiving Jesus Christ as Savior and of the believer's knowing His continuing presence.

Joy not only does not come from favorable human circumstances but is sometimes greatest when those circumstances are the most painful and severe. Shortly before His arrest and crucifixion, Jesus told His disciples, "Truly, truly, I say to you, that you will weep and lament, but the world will rejoice; you will be sorrowful, but your sorrow will be turned to joy" (John 16:20). To illustrate that truth Jesus compared divine **joy** to a woman in childbirth. "She has sorrow, because her hour has come; but when she gives birth to the child, she remembers the anguish no more, for joy that a child has been born into the world. Therefore you too now have sorrow; but I will see you again, and your heart will rejoice, and no one takes your joy away from you" (vv. 21-22).

God's **joy** is full, complete in every way. Nothing human or circumstantial can add to it or detract from it. But it is not fulfilled in a believer's life except through reliance on and obedience to the Lord. "Ask, and you will receive," Jesus went on to explain, "that your joy may be made full" (John 16:24). One of John's motivations in writing his first epistle was that his joy might "be made complete" (1 John 1:4).

Jesus Himself is again our supreme example. He was "a man of sorrows, and acquainted with grief" (Isa. 53:3; cf. Luke 18:31-33), but, just as He had promised for His disciples, His sorrow was turned into joy. "For the joy set before Him [He] endured the cross, despising the shame, and has sat down at the right hand of the throne of God" (Heb. 12:2). Despite the misunderstanding, the rejection, the hatred, and the pain He endured from men while incarnate among them, the Lord never lost His joy in the relationship He had with His Father. And that joy He gives to each of His followers.

Although **joy** is a gift of God through His **Spirit** to those who belong to Christ, it is also commanded of them. "Rejoice in the Lord always; again I will say, rejoice!" Paul commands (Phil. 4:4; cf. 3:1). Because **joy** comes as a gift from Him, the command obviously is not for believers to manufacture or try to imitate it. The command is to gratefully accept and revel in this great blessing they already possess. "For the kingdom of God is not eating and drinking, but righteousness and peace and joy in the Holy Spirit" (Rom. 14:17).

Peace. If joy speaks of the exhilaration of heart that comes from being right with God, then **peace** (*eirēnē*) refers to the tranquility of mind that comes from that saving relationship. The verb form has to do with binding together and is reflected in the modern expression "having it all together." Everything is in place and as it ought to be.

Like joy, **peace** has no relationship to circumstances. Christians know "that God causes all things to work together for good to those who love God, to those who are called according to His purpose" (Rom. 8:28). Because God is in control of all aspects of a believer's life, how his circumstances may appear from a human perspective makes no ultimate difference. That is why Jesus could say without qualification to those who trust in Him, "Let not your heart be troubled" (John 14:1). There is absolutely no reason for a believer to be anxious or afraid.

Jesus was the Prince of Peace, both in the sense that He was supremely peaceful Himself and in the sense that He dispenses His **peace** to those who are His. Even when He confronted Satan face-to-face in the wilderness, Jesus had perfect peace, knowing His heavenly Father was continually with Him and would supply His every need (Matt. 4:1-11). It is His own peace that He bequeaths to His disciples: "Peace I leave with you; My peace I give to you; not as the world gives, do I give to you" (John 14:27).

"The things you have learned and received and heard and seen in me, practice these things," Paul said; "and the God of peace shall be with you" (Phil. 4:9). Because they have the God of peace in their hearts, believers need "be anxious for nothing," having "the peace of God, which surpasses all comprehension, [to] guard [their] hearts and [their] minds in Christ Jesus" (v 6-7).

Patience. *Makrothumia* (**patience**) has to do with tolerance and longsuffering that endure injuries inflicted by others, the calm willingness to accept situations that are irritating or painful.

God Himself is "slow to anger" (Ps. 86:15) and expects His children to be the same. Just as believers should never "think lightly of the riches of [God's own] kindness and forbearance and patience" (Rom. 2:4), they should themselves manifest those attributes of their heavenly Father.

In the last days, arrogant unbelievers will taunt Christians by asking, "Where is the promise of [Christ's] coming? For ever since the fathers fell asleep, all continues just as it was from the beginning of creation" (2 Pet. 3:4). In their sin-darkened minds unbelievers will fail to see that, just as in the days of Noah, when God patiently delayed the Flood in order to give men more time to repent (1 Pet. 3:20), it is also because of His merciful patience that He forestalls Christ's second coming and the accompanying judgment on unbelievers, "not wishing for any to perish but for all to come to repentance" (2 Pet. 3:9).

Paul confessed that, as the foremost of sinners, he found mercy in God's sight "in order that in [him] as the foremost, Jesus Christ might demonstrate His perfect patience, as an example for those who would believe in Him for eternal life" (1 Tim. 1:15-16).

Believers are commanded to emulate their Lord's **patience.** "As those who have been chosen of God, holy and beloved," they are to "put on a heart of . . .

patience" (Col. 3:12), especially with fellow believers, "showing forbearance to one another in love" (Eph. 4:2). Like Timothy, all Christian teachers and leaders are to minister "with great patience" (2 Tim. 4:2).

Kindness. *Chrēstotēs* (**kindness**) relates to tender concern for others. It has nothing to do with weakness or lack of conviction but is the genuine desire of a believer to treat others gently, just as the Lord treats him. Paul reminded the Thessalonians that, even though he was an apostle, he "proved to be gentle among [them], as a nursing mother tenderly cares for her own children" (1 Thess. 2:6-7).

Jesus' **kindness** is the believer's example. When "some children were brought to Him so that He might lay His hands on them and pray; and the disciples rebuked them, . . . Jesus said, 'Let the children alone, and do not hinder them from coming to Me; for the kingdom of heaven belongs to such as these'" (Matt. 19:13-14). On another occasion He said, "Come to Me, all who are weary and heavy-laden, and I will give you rest. Take My yoke upon you, and learn from Me, for I am gentle and humble in heart; and you shall find rest for your souls" (Matt. 11:28-29).

Just as their Lord is kind, His servants are commanded not to "be quarrelsome, but [to] be kind to all" (2 Tim. 2:24). And just as He does with all the other manifestations of His divine **fruit,** the Holy Spirit gives God's children **kindness** (2 Cor. 6:6).

Goodness. *Agathos* (**goodness**) has to do with moral and spiritual excellence that is known by its sweetness and active kindness. Paul helped define this virtue when he observed that "one will hardly die for a righteous man; though perhaps for the good man someone would dare even to die" (Rom. 5:7). A Christian can be morally upright but still not manifest the grace of **goodness.** He may be admired and respected for his high moral standards and might even have a friend who would risk his life for him. But the upright person who also has **goodness** is much more likely to have self-sacrificing friends.

Joseph was such a righteous and good man. When he learned that Mary was pregnant but did not yet know it was by the Holy Spirit, "being a righteous man" he could not bring himself to marry her, assuming she had been unfaithful. But being also a good man, he could not bear the thought of disgracing his beloved Mary and therefore "desired to put her away secretly" (Matt. 1:19).

David had a deep understanding of God's goodness, as he repeatedly reveals in his psalms. "Surely goodness and lovingkindness will follow me all the days of my life, and I will dwell in the house of the Lord forever," he rejoiced (Ps. 23:6). He confessed that he would, in fact, "have despaired unless [he] had believed that [he] would see the goodness of the Lord in the land of the living" (Ps. 27:13).

As with every grace the Spirit provides, believers are commanded to exemplify **goodness.** Later in the letter Paul exhorts, "While we have opportunity, let us do good to all men, and especially to those who are of the household of the faith" (Gal. 6:10). "To this end also we pray for you always," he wrote to the Thessalonians, "that our God may count you worthy of your calling, and fulfill every desire for goodness and the word of faith with power" (2 Thess. 1:11).

Faithfulness. *Pistis* (**faithfulness**) is the manifestation of the fruit of the

Spirit that pertains to loyalty and trustworthiness. Jeremiah declared that "the Lord's lovingkindnesses indeed never cease, for His compassions never fail. They are new every morning; great is Thy faithfulness" (Lam. 3:22).

Because Jesus was faithful, He "emptied Himself, taking the form of a bond-servant, and being made in the likeness of men. And being found in appearance as a man, He humbled Himself by becoming obedient to the point of death, even death on a cross." And because of the Son's faithfulness, the Father "highly exalted Him, and bestowed on Him the name which is above every name" (Phil. 2:7-9).

And as He was faithful when He came to earth the first time, He will be faithful to come again "in just the same way as you have watched Him go into heaven" (Acts 1:11). "Faithful is He who calls you," Paul said, "and He also will bring it to pass" (1 Thess. 5:24). In his great vision on Patmos, John saw Christ seated on "a white horse, and He who sat upon it is called Faithful and True" (Rev. 19:11).

The "servants of Christ, and stewards of the mysteries of God" are to be like their Lord in being "found trustworthy" (1 Cor. 4:1-2). "Be faithful unto death," the Lord assures His followers, "and I will give you the crown of life" (Rev. 2:10).

Gentleness. *Prautēs* includes the idea of **gentleness,** but is usually better translated *meekness.* In his helpful volume *Synonyms of the New Testament,* R. C. Trench writes that *prautēs* does not consist in a person's "outward behaviour only; nor yet in his relations to his fellow-men; as little in his mere natural disposition. Rather it is an inwrought grace of the soul; and the exercises of it are first and chiefly towards God. It is that temper of spirit in which we accept His dealings with us as good, and therefore without disputing or resisting" (Grand Rapids: Eerdmans, 1953). It is that humble and gentle attitude that is patiently submissive in every offense, while being free of any desire for revenge or retribution.

Of the nine characteristics of the fruit of the Spirit, this one and the one following do not apply to God as God. The Old Testament never refers to God as being meek, and in the New Testament only the Son is spoken of as meek, and that only in His incarnation.

In the New Testament *prautēs* is used to describe three attitudes: submissiveness to the will of God (Col. 3:12), teachableness (James 1:21), and consideration of others (Eph. 4:2).

Although He was God, while He lived on earth as the Son of Man, Jesus was "gentle [*prautēs*] and humble in heart" (Matt. 11:29; cf. 21:5; 2 Cor. 10:1). Like their Lord, believers are to actively pursue meekness and gentleness (1 Tim. 6:11) and to wear them like a garment (Col. 3:12).

Self-control. *Enkrateia* (**self-control**) has reference to restraining passions and appetites. As with meekness, however, this grace does not apply to God, who obviously does not need to restrain Himself. "For I, the Lord, do not change," He informs us (Mal. 3:6). In His eternal being, the Lord "Jesus Christ is the same yesterday and today, yes and forever" (Heb. 13:8). Perfect holiness possesses perfect control.

But in His incarnation Christ was the epitome of self-control. He was never tempted or tricked into doing or saying anything that was not consistent with His Father's will and His own divine nature. Again like Jesus, believers should "exercise self-control in all things" (1 Cor. 9:25; cf. 7:9), "applying all diligence, in [their] faith [to] supply . . . self-control" (2 Pet. 1:5-6).

Against such things there is no law, Paul says. Even unbelievers do not make laws against **such things** as those which the fruit of the Spirit produces. The world does not make laws against such behavior, but generally prizes it. Even if some consider **such things** to be signs of weakness, they cannot escape recognizing that they are never harmful.

There is certainly **no law** of God **against such things,** because those are the very virtues He wants all men to have and that He gives to them when they put their trust in Jesus Christ as Lord and Savior. "For if these qualities are yours and are increasing," Peter explains in regard to a similar list of virtues, "they render you neither useless nor unfruitful in the true knowledge of our Lord Jesus Christ" (2 Pet. 1:8).

The believer who walks in the Spirit and manifests His fruit does not need a system of **law** to produce the right attitudes and behavior—they rise from within him.

THE CONQUEST

Now those who belong to Christ Jesus have crucified the flesh with its passions and desires.

If we live by the Spirit, let us also walk by the Spirit. (5:24-25)

All persons **who belong to Christ Jesus** by faith in Him and His perfect saving work **have crucified the flesh with its passions and desires.**

Have crucified the flesh is a strategic statement to grasp, because crucifixion was a means of execution. All but four uses of the term in the New Testament refer to the death of Jesus Christ on the cross. Three of the exceptions help in understanding the fourth, which is in the present text.

The first of the three is in the book of Romans, where Paul affirms that at the time of our justification, "our old self was crucified with [Christ]" (6:6). The other two are in Galatians, one before and one after the present text. The apostle says, "I have been crucified with Christ" (2:20), and, near the end of the epistle, asserts that "the world has been crucified to me" (6:14).

In each of those three passages, "crucified" is simply a vivid and dramatic way to say "killed," or "executed." In the first two passages Paul is teaching that at salvation his old, sinful, unregenerate self was executed and he was born a new man in Christ Jesus. In the third passage he is saying that the world has been executed and is now dead to him, so that it is no longer his master, holding him in bondage. He is therefore now free to serve the Lord.

 Obviously, in none of those passages does Paul mean to imply that the crucifixion analogy carries the idea of total death, in which all influence ceases. Sin was still a reality in his life, and so was the temptation of the world. But there was a sense in which the power of the old self and of the world was broken. Those influences no longer dominated him.

In the text of Galatians 5:24, Paul is saying that **the flesh** has been executed. But how could that be in light of what he has just said in this chapter about believers having a constant war with the ever-present **flesh?** In what sense is **the flesh** killed at conversion?

It cannot be in the actual, complete, present sense or it would contradict the reality of the continual spiritual conflict with **the flesh** indicated here and in Romans 7:14-25. And it cannot be that Paul has some future sense in mind or he would have used a future verb form, saying, "shall crucify the flesh," referring to the time of glorification.

The best understanding is to see **have crucified** as an allusion to the cross of Jesus Christ, which, as a past event, fits the aorist tense used here by Paul. It looks back to the cross, the time at which the death of **the flesh** was actually accomplished. Yet, because we are still alive on the earth and still possess our humanness, we have not yet entered into the future fullness of that past event.

Meanwhile, **the flesh with its passions** (or affections) **and desires** is dead in the sense of no longer reigning over us or of holding us in inescapable bondage. Like a chicken with its head cut off, **the flesh** has been dealt a death blow, although it continues to flop around the barnyard of earth until the last nerve is stilled.

Because **the flesh** is defeated forever, and we now live in the realm where Christ reigns over us by His Spirit, we should live according to the Spirit and not the flesh.

Because believers have new life in Jesus Christ, they should also have a new *way* of life. **If we live by the Spirit,** and we do, Paul says, **let us also walk by the Spirit,** as we must. He earnestly prayed that the Colossian Christians would "walk in a manner worthy of the Lord, to please Him in all respects, bearing fruit in every good work. . . . As you therefore have received Christ Jesus the Lord, so walk in Him, having been firmly rooted and now being built up in Him and established in your faith" (Col. 1:10; 2:6-7; cf. Eph. 4:1; 1 Thess. 2:12).

Restoring a Sinning Brother (5:26–6:6)

17

Let us not become boastful, challenging one another, envying one another.

Brethren, even if a man is caught in any trespass, you who are spiritual, restore such a one in a spirit of gentleness; each one looking to yourself, lest you too be tempted. Bear one another's burdens, and thus fulfill the law of Christ. For if anyone thinks he is something when he is nothing, he deceives himself. But let each one examine his own work, and then he will have reason for boasting in regard to himself alone, and not in regard to another. For each one shall bear his own load.

And let the one who is taught the word share all good things with him who teaches. (5:26–6:6)

Sin is a reality in every Christian's life. "If we say that we have no sin, we are deceiving ourselves, and the truth is not in us," John warns believers. In fact, he goes on to say, "If we say that we have not sinned, we make [God] a liar, and His word is not in us" (1 John 1:8, 10). "We all stumble in many ways" (James 3:2).

If Christians were not subject to sin they would not need "the full armor of God" in order to "stand firm against the schemes of the devil" and "to resist in the evil day" (Eph. 6:11, 13). Nor would they need to heed James's warning about being tempted and carried away by their own lusts or his admonition to put "aside all

173

filthiness and all that remains of wickedness" (James 1:14, 21).

As mentioned in the previous chapter under the discussion of the deeds of the flesh (Gal. 5:19-21), sin not only affects the believer himself but also God and others, including both believers and unbelievers. First of all, in regard to himself, his sin results in loss of confidence and loss of inner joy, peace, and all the other fruit of the Spirit. In expressing the opposite side of that truth, Peter says that "as long as you practice these things," referring to the list of spiritual virtues he has just given, "you will never stumble" (2 Pet. 1:10, cf. vv. 5-7).

Sin in the life of a believer also weakens his anticipation of Christ's second coming. The more a Christian sins, the less anxious he will be to meet his Lord. "And now, little children," John says, "abide in Him, so that when He appears, we may have confidence and not shrink away from Him in shame at His coming" (1 John 2:28).

Sin also defeats and sometimes destroys a believer's usefulness and inhibits the ministry of his spiritual gifts. A sinful life cannot produce good works any more than a bad tree can produce good fruit (Matt. 7:16-20; cf. John 15:2). On the other hand, "If a man cleanses himself from these things," that is, the sins previously mentioned, "he will be a vessel for honor, sanctified, useful to the Master, prepared for every good work" (2 Tim. 2:21; cf. vv. 14, 16-18).

Second, sin in a believer affects God. Paul shockingly compares an immoral believer to one who would link up a harlot to the Lord. How could such an unthinkable thing be? "Do you not know," Paul asked the fleshly Corinthian Christians, "that the one who joins himself to a harlot is one body with her? For He says, 'The two will become one flesh.' But the one who joins himself to the Lord is one spirit with Him" (1 Cor. 6:16-17). The Lord Himself is thereby brought into the sin. Later in the same letter the apostle says, "Is not the cup of blessing which we bless a sharing in the blood of Christ? Is not the bread which we break a sharing in the body of Christ? . . . You cannot drink the cup of the Lord and the cup of demons; you cannot partake of the table of the Lord and the table of demons. Or do we provoke the Lord to jealousy? We are not stronger than He, are we?" (10:16, 21-22). Because many of the Corinthian believers mocked and provoked God by persisting in gross sins, many of them were "weak and sick, and a number sleep," that is, were dead (11:30). When believers sin they "grieve the Holy Spirit of God" (Eph. 4:30).

Third, sin in a Christian affects other people, both believers and unbelievers. His sin cannot be prevented from infecting fellow believers, because they are all one as Christ's own body. "For by one Spirit we were all baptized into one body" (1 Cor. 12:13).

The greatest heartache a pastor can have is to see believers under his care willfully continue in sin and thereby lose personal blessing as well as usefulness. Still worse is the fact that they dishonor and grieve the Lord and violate the purity and unity of the church.

The most important pursuit for all Christians, individually and corporately, is holiness. The first mission of the church is to honor and glorify God, and He can be honored and glorified by His children only as they grow to be like Him in character. Although evangelism is the cutting edge of the church's ministry, holiness is the only foundation on which effective evangelism or any other ministry can be built. The supreme priority of the church is holiness, purity of inward life. God can accomplish whatever He desires through a believer or a church that is holy, but He can do little through one that is not.

Positively, holiness involves growing in Christlikeness, in knowledge of and obedience to God's Word, and in submission to His Spirit. Negatively, it involves correcting that which is impure, first in a believer's own life and then also in the lives of other believers. That negative aspect of holiness is the theme of Galatians 5:26–6:6.

Paul's admonition, **Let us not become boastful, challenging one another** [by being combative], **envying one another,** seems to fit better at the beginning of chapter 6, serving as a contrast to the kind of behavior called for in verses 1-6. The apostle admonishes believers to look at their own lives and to stop boasting, provoking arguments, and being envious of **one another.** Those sinful attitudes are marks of immature, sinful Christians who place their own interests above the interests of fellow believers (cf. Phil. 2:1-4). They are characteristics of believers who are not walking by the Spirit but who are in the flesh and are therefore disrupting the body fellowship by producing the deeds of the flesh rather than the fruit of the Spirit (see vv. 16-25). And such attitudes preclude helpful discipline of one another.

It is worth being reminded that the pursuit of holiness can be perverted into self-righteous, proud piosity. No sin does greater damage to the church or is more offensive to God than self-righteousness. Jesus' most scathing rebukes and warnings were against the scribes and Pharisees, whose very names are synonyms for hypocritical self-righteousness. Nothing undermines true righteousness so much as self-righteousness. Holiness must therefore be that true holiness that is manifest in meekness and is credited completely to the grace of God and the work of the Spirit and the Word.

But though a Christian's first concern must be for his own holiness and purity of life, God's Word makes clear that he also has a responsibility for the holiness and purity of the rest of the church. Speaking to believers about believers, Paul says, "Do not participate in the unfruitful deeds of darkness, but instead even expose them; for it is disgraceful even to speak of the things which are done by them in secret" (Eph. 5:11-12). He instructed Titus, who was then pastor of the church in Crete, to "speak and exhort and reprove with all authority" and to "reject a factious man after a first and second warning, knowing that such a man is perverted and is sinning, being self-condemned" (Titus 2:15; 3:10-11).

The unredeemed flesh naturally resists discipline, and no one enjoys being rebuked. But the spiritually sensitive Christian knows that, although "all discipline for the moment seems not to be joyful, but sorrowful; yet to those who have been trained by it, afterwards it yields the peaceful fruit of righteousness" (Heb. 12:11). He knows that God disciplines for the same reason that a loving parent disciplines: for the good of His child. He therefore does "not regard lightly the discipline of the Lord, nor faint when [he is] reproved by Him," because he realizes that "those whom the Lord loves He disciplines, and He scourges every son whom He receives" (vv. 5-6).

Paul repeatedly warned the Corinthian church about the need to cleanse itself of persistently sinning members. Speaking specifically about a man who had committed incest with his mother or stepmother, he wrote, "I have decided to deliver such a one to Satan for the destruction of his flesh, that his spirit may be saved in the day of the Lord Jesus" (1 Cor. 5:5). As the next verse makes clear, his rebuke was of the entire church, not simply of the man who had committed a despicable sin that even the pagans did not practice (see v. 1). Apparently the rest of the congregation winked at the sin or even tried to justify it on the basis of a false type of Christian liberty. "Your boasting is not good," Paul says. "Do you not know that a little leaven leavens the whole lump of dough? Clean out the old leaven, that you may be a new lump, just as you are in fact unleavened. For Christ our Passover also has been sacrificed. . . . I wrote to you not to associate with any so-called brother if he should be an immoral person, or covetous, or an idolater, or a reviler, or a drunkard, or a swindler—not even to eat with such a one. . . . Remove the wicked man from among yourselves" (vv. 6-7, 11, 13). To the Thessalonians he wrote, "Now we command you, brethren, in the name of our Lord Jesus Christ, that you keep aloof from every brother who leads an unruly life" (2 Thess. 3:6; cf. v. 14).

It is not about the sins of unbelievers that Christians should have the greatest concern. When the unsaved commit sin, they are simply expressing their unredeemed natures. Paul states plainly that his call for separation was not from sinning unbelievers but sinning believers. When "I wrote you in my letter not to associate with immoral people," he explained, "I did not at all mean with the immoral people of this world, . . . for then you would have to go out of the world" (1 Cor. 5:9-10). "It is time for judgment to begin with the household of God," Peter declared (1 Pet. 4:17).

Leaders of the church are not exempted from discipline. They are, in fact, even more accountable for what they say and do. Although a church should "not receive an accusation against an elder except on the basis of two or three witnesses," if that criterion is met, elders "who continue to sin" are to be rebuked "in the presence of all, so that the rest also may be fearful of sinning" (1 Tim. 5:19-20).

Jesus precisely established the pattern for discipline of an erring church member. "If your brother sins, go and reprove him in private; if he listens to you, you have won your brother. But if he does not listen to you, take one or two more with you, so that by the mouth of two or three witnesses every fact may be confirmed. And if he refuses to listen to them, tell it to the church; and if he refuses to listen even to the church, let him be to you as a Gentile and a tax-gatherer" (Matt. 18:15-17).

Every kind of sin, from disorderly conduct to immorality to false teaching, is to be disciplined. And all Christians, from the newest believer to the most experienced leader, are subject to that discipline. To be spiritually healthy and effective in its ministry the church must deal with sin within its own ranks. To trifle with sin, to ignore it under the guise of love, or to fail for any other reason to cleanse the church of it is disastrous. To preach against sin but not enforce that preaching by confronting sin in the lives of individuals in the fellowship is to disconnect preaching from life and to turn it into an unproductive exercise in oratory.

As is often the case, however, there is also an opposite danger. Just as the flesh makes it easy to ignore sin within the church it also makes it easy to discipline in the wrong way and with the wrong spirit. There is always temptation to deal with sinning members out of a self-righteous, judgmental attitude rather than from a genuinely humble and righteous concern for the purity of the Lord's Body.

Addressing that danger, Paul admonishes the Galatian church to take special care to discipline in the right way. Rather than being **boastful, challenging one another**, and **envying one another**, church members must be loving, gracious, and helpful to **one another**, even to those who sin and offend. In 6:1-6, the apostle declares that when a sinning brother is disciplined, the spiritual members of the church should pick him up, hold him up, and build him up.

Pick Him Up

Brethren, even if a man is caught in any trespass, you who are spiritual, restore such a one in a spirit of gentleness; each one looking to yourself, lest you too be tempted. (6:1)

The first responsibility of a spiritual believer who seeks to restore a fallen brother is to help pick him up. When a person stumbles, his first need is to get up, and often he needs assistance in doing it. An integral part of church discipline, therefore, is helping a fallen brother get back on his feet spiritually and morally.

Even if a man is caught in any trespass, he deserves help and encouragement as well as rebuke. **Caught** may imply that the person was actually seen committing the **trespass**, indicating there was no doubt about his guilt. But the Greek verb (*prolambanō*) also allows for the idea of the man's being **caught** by the **trespass** itself, as it were. That is the sense of the King James rendering, "overtaken in a fault," and seems appropriate in this context.

That interpretation is also supported by Paul's use of *paraptōma* (**trespass**), which has the basic idea of stumbling or falling. The **man** does not commit the sin with premeditation but rather fails to be on his guard or perhaps flirts with a temptation he thinks he can withstand. Or he simply tries to live his life in his own power and fails, producing a deed of the flesh instead of the fruit of the Spirit.

Responsibility for the discipline of those who stumble, as well as for those who commit more serious sins, rests on the shoulders of church members **who are spiritual. Spiritual** believers are those walking in the Spirit, filled with the Spirit, and manifesting the fruit of the Spirit, who, by virtue of their spiritual strength, are responsible for those who are fleshly.

It should be noted that, whereas maturity is relative, depending on one's progression and growth, spirituality is an absolute reality that is unrelated to growth. At any point in the life of a Christian, from the moment of his salvation to his glorification, he is either **spiritual**, walking in the Spirit, or fleshly, walking in the deeds of the flesh. Maturity is the cumulative effect of the times of spirituality. But any believer, at any point in his growth toward Christlikeness, can be a **spiritual** believer who helps a sinful believer who has fallen to the flesh.

The spiritually and morally strong have a responsibility for the spiritually and morally weak. "We who are strong," Paul says, "ought to bear the weaknesses of those without strength and not just please ourselves" (Rom. 15:1). **Spiritual** believers are to "admonish the unruly, encourage the fainthearted, help the weak, be patient with all men" (1 Thess. 5:14).

It is not that **spiritual** believers are to be suspicious and inquisitive. Those are hardly qualities of spirituality. But they will be sensitive to sin whenever and wherever it may appear within the Body and should be prepared to deal with it in the way God's Word prescribes.

When the scribes and Pharisees brought to Jesus the woman caught in the act of adultery, they reminded Him that the law of Moses required that she be stoned to death. Instead of replying, Jesus bent down and began writing in the sand—perhaps listing sins of which those in the crowd were guilty. "When they persisted in asking Him, He straightened up, and said to them, 'He who is without sin among you, let him be the first to throw a stone at her.' And again He stooped down, and wrote on the ground. And when they heard it, they began to go out one by one, beginning with the older ones." When Jesus then asked her if any of her accusers had stayed to condemn her, she replied, "'No one, Lord.' And Jesus said, 'Neither do I condemn you; go your way. From now on sin no more'" (John 8:3-11).

Jesus was not interested in destroying the woman but in helping her, and that should be the attitude of His followers toward other people, especially toward fellow believers.

Jesus' command "Do not judge lest you be judged" (Matt. 7:1) is often used by Christians to oppose discipline in the church and is sometimes quoted by outsiders in opposing the church's taking strong stands against certain evils. As the context makes clear, however (see vv. 3-5), Jesus was talking about a self-righteous, condemning person who acts as judge, passing sentence on others, since he sees only the best in himself and the worst in everyone else. If such a person confesses and is cleansed of his own sin, the Lord went on to say, he then *is* qualified to confront his brother with the purpose not to condemn but "to take the speck out of [his] brother's eye" (v. 5). He is then **spiritual** and has the right and even obligation to help his brother overcome a **trespass.**

James's similar warning about judging others is also often used to oppose discipline. But again the context makes clear that in his saying, "Who are you who judge your neighbor?" James was not talking about helping a brother out of a sin but about judgmentally speaking condemnation "against a brother" (James 4:11-12). A Christian who "speaks against a brother" is proud, self-righteous, and cruel. He seeks only to exalt himself by pushing down others. A **spiritual** believer who humbly seeks to **restore** a sinning brother, however, is not speaking against him but serving him in the best possible way.

A pastor once commented, "I have often thought that if I ever fall into a *paraptōma* [**trespass**], I will pray that I don't fall into the hands of those censorious, critical judges in the church. Let me fall into the hands of barkeepers, streetwalkers, or dope peddlers, because such church people would tear me apart with their long, wagging, gossipy tongues, cutting me to shreds."

Only **spiritual** believers have the wisdom or the right to discipline fellow believers, just as only spiritual believers have the right to leadership in the church (1 Tim. 3:1-13; Titus 1:5-9). Before God, in fact, they do not have the right *not* to discipline. They are commanded **to restore such a one.** When a church is committed to restoring fallen members, it is on its way to being pure and usable.

Katartizō (to **restore**) literally means to mend or repair and was sometimes used metaphorically of restoring harmony among quarreling factions in a dispute. It was also used of setting a broken bone or putting a dislocated limb back in place. That is the figure used by the writer of Hebrews in calling on believers to "strengthen the hands that are weak and the knees that are feeble, and make straight paths for your feet, so that the limb which is lame may not be put out of joint, but rather be healed" (Heb. 12:12-13).

Spiritual believers **restore** a fallen believer first of all by helping him recognize his **trespass** as a **trespass.** Until a person admits his sin, he cannot be helped out of it. Once he has done that, he must be encouraged to confess his sin before God and turn away from it in repentance, sincerely seeking God's forgiveness.

Restoration of fallen brothers and sisters is always to be done **in a spirit of gentleness,** which is characteristic of those who walk by the Spirit (Gal. 5:23). A Christian who is critical and judgmental as he attempts to help a fallen brother does not show the grace of Christ or help his brother, but instead stumbles himself.

After a church has exercised proper discipline, the members should "forgive and comfort" the one who has been disciplined, "lest somehow such a one be overwhelmed by excessive sorrow" (2 Cor. 2:7). He should not be regarded "as an enemy, but [admonished] as a brother" (2 Thess. 3:15).

From the caution **each one looking to yourself, lest you too be tempted,** it is clear that even **spiritual** believers can stumble. They are made of the same stuff as those who have fallen. Because the exhortation **looking to yourself** is so vital, Paul uses a strong word (*skopeō*, to observe or consider) in the present tense, which emphasized a continual, diligent attentiveness to their own purity. They, **too,** could **be tempted** and even fall into the same sin for which they disciplined a brother.

The attitude of every Christian should always be the attitude of Jesus. And when a believer needs to help discipline a fallen brother, he should ask for a special portion of Christ's love and gentleness. If the Father does not want even one of His own to be devastated (Matt. 18:14), and if "the Son of Man did not come to destroy men's lives, but to save them" (Luke 9:56), how much less do His followers have the right to be destructive rather than helpful?

HOLD HIM UP

Bear one another's burdens, and thus fulfill the law of Christ. For if anyone thinks he is something when he is nothing, he deceives himself. But let each

one examine his own work, and then he will have reason for boasting in regard to himself alone, and not in regard to another. For each one shall bear his own load. (6:2-5)

The second responsibility of a spiritual believer who seeks to restore a fallen brother is to help hold him up once he is back on his feet. It is not enough simply to help him turn from his sin and then leave him alone. It is immediately after a spiritual victory that Satan often makes his severest attacks on God's children.

Christians are continually (present tense) to **bear one another's burdens. Bear** has the thought of carrying with endurance, and **burdens** is from *baros,* which refers to heavy loads that are difficult to lift and carry. Used metaphorically, as here, it represents any difficulty or problem a person has trouble coping with. In this context the reference suggests **burdens** that tempt a sinning believer to fall back into the trespass from which he has just been delivered. A persistent, oppressing temptation is one of the heaviest burdens a Christian can have.

To be freed from a sin is not always to be freed from its temptation. The spiritual believer who truly loves his brother and sincerely wants to restore him to a walk by the Spirit will continue to spend time with him and make himself available for counsel and encouragement. Prayer is the most powerful weapon believers have in conquering sin and opposing Satan, and nothing helps a brother carry his **burdens** as much as prayer for him and with him.

The brother who has been delivered from a trespass has an obligation to let his spiritual friends help him carry his **burdens.** It is not spirituality but pride that makes a person want to "go it alone." James tells believers to "confess [their] sins to one another, and pray for one another, so that [they] may be healed" (James 5:16). God Himself is the believer's ultimate source of strength, and on Him we are called to cast our burdens (Ps. 5:22) and our cares (1 Pet. 5:7). But He often uses fellow believers as His agents to help carry the **burdens** of His children.

Strong as he was in the Lord, Paul himself was not free from temptation or discouragement. He confessed that "when we came into Macedonia our flesh had no rest, but we were afflicted on every side: conflicts without, fears within. But God, who comforts the depressed, comforted us by the coming of Titus; and not only by his coming, but also by the comfort with which he was comforted in you, as he reported to us your longing, your mourning, your zeal for me; so that I rejoiced even more" (2 Cor. 7:5-7).

When believers **bear one another's burdens,** they **fulfill the law of Christ.** Jesus said, "A new commandment I give to you, that you love one another, even as I have loved you" (John 13:34). **The law of Christ** is the law of love, which fulfills all the rest of God's law (Gal. 5:14; Rom. 13:8, 10).

It is a misguided and unscriptural philosophy that causes some pastors to think they should not get too close to members of their congregation. Obviously they should never show favoritism, and there is danger in becoming too involved in superficial social relationships. But a pastor who does not intimately attend to the people under his care cannot possibly minister to them effectively.

For if anyone thinks he is something when he is nothing, Paul continues, **he deceives himself.** At first glance that statement seems somewhat out of place. But in light of the call for spiritual believers to restore sinning brothers "in a spirit of gentleness" (v. 1), the need for such a warning becomes apparent.

One of the chief reasons many Christians do not bother to help fellow Christians is that they feel superior to sinners and wrongly consider themselves to be spiritually **something** when the truth is they are really **nothing.** Like the Pharisees, their concern is not for the true righteousness that God gives and that comes only through humility (see Matt. 5:3-8) but for their own self-righteousness, which has no part in God's kingdom or its work (v. 20). Their desire is not to help a stumbling brother but to judge and condemn him. At best, they leave him to "stew in his own juice," thinking, if not saying, "He got himself into this mess; let him get himself out."

Conceit can coexist with outward morality, but it cannot coexist with spirituality. In fact, conceit is the ultimate sin, first on the list of things God hates (Prov. 6:16-17). The Christian who **thinks he is something when he is nothing** needs help in facing his own sin before he can be qualified to help anyone else out of a sin. He needs first to "take the log out of [his] own eye" (Matt. 7:5). If he refuses to see his own spiritual need, **he deceives himself** and is useless in serving God or in helping fellow believers. The Greek verb behind **deceives** means "to lead one's mind astray" and relates to subjective fantasies that are self-deceptive.

Therefore every Christian should **examine his own work, and then he will have reason for boasting in regard to himself alone, and not in regard to another.** A believer's first responsibility is to **examine** (from *dokimazō,* to approve after testing) himself, to be sure his own attitudes and life are right in the eyes of the Lord before he attempts to give spiritual help to others. **Then,** and only then, will he **have reason for boasting** in a proper way. If anything remains for boasting after honest self-examination, it will be that which induces boasting in the Lord (cf. 2 Cor. 10:12-18).

God does not grade on the curve but by His own absolutes. He does not compare believers to each other but to His divine, perfect standards of righteousness. And if the Lord does not judge a believer by comparing him with other believers, how much less should a believer judge himself in that way? (cf. 2 Cor. 10:12).

If there is **reason for** a believer's **boasting,** or rejoicing, **in regard to himself,** that is, in regard to what God has done in and through him, it is on the basis of his faithfulness and obedience, not on the basis of what he may have accomplished **in regard to,** or compared to, **another.** If he is truly more faithful and useful than some of his fellow believers, that is God's doing, not his own.

Paul's command **for each one** to **bear his own load** seems to contradict what he has just said about bearing one another's burdens (v. 2). But he uses a different term here. *Phortion* (**load**) refers to anything that is carried, and has no connotation of difficulty. It was often used of the general obligations of life that a person is responsible to **bear on his own.**

For a Christian, **load** can refer to "his deeds in the body, according to what he has done, whether good or bad," for which he will give account "before the judgment seat of Christ" (2 Cor. 5:10; 1 Cor. 3:12-15). His **load** can also refer to fulfilling his personal calling and ministry for the Lord. Jesus assures His followers that the "load" [*phortion*] of service He gives them "is light" (Matt. 11:30). In either case, every believer is accountable to **bear his own load,** even the light one Christ gives him, and to answer for his faithfulness in so doing when he faces Him.

Build Him Up

And let the one who is taught the word share all good things with him who teaches. (6:6)

The third responsibility of a spiritual believer who seeks to restore a fallen brother is to help build him up.

Like verse 3, this verse at first glance does not seem to fit into what Paul is focusing on in the passage. The seemingly obvious interpretation, and the one that is most common, is that Paul is exhorting congregations to pay their pastors fairly. But although that principle is taught in the New Testament (see, e.g., Luke 10:7; 1 Cor. 9:7-14), it does not seem to be what Paul is teaching here. He has just been talking about restoring sinning brothers, and in verses 7-8 he talks about sowing and reaping in the flesh or by the Spirit. Not only that, but no mention is made of financial support or necessarily of any kind of material support. **Good things** could include material goods, but that does not seem to be the sense here.

The Greek can be translated, "Let him who receives instruction share with him who gives instruction in all good things," and such a rendering seems appropriate.

Share is from *koinōneō*, which has the basic idea of sharing equally. It is the verb form of the noun commonly translated "fellowship." Paul is talking about mutuality, not of one party serving or providing for the other but of both parties sharing together. **The one who is taught the word** and the one **who teaches** have a common fellowship and should **share all good things** together.

The most common term for material things that are favorable, or good, is *kalos*. But **good things** translates the plural of *agathos,* which is used in the New Testament primarily of spiritual and moral excellence. Paul uses this word in describing the gospel itself, the "glad tidings of good things" (Rom. 10:15). The writer of Hebrews uses it in the same way, of "the good things to come" of which "Christ appeared as a high priest" (Heb. 9:11) and of which the law was "only a shadow" (10:1).

Under this interpretation, the sharing of **all good things** is the third step in the restoration of a fallen believer. The spiritual Christian who has picked up and held up his fallen brother also builds him up in **the word**, in whose **good things** they fellowship together.

Sowing and Reaping
(6:7-10)

18

Do not be deceived, God is not mocked; for whatever a man sows, this he will also reap. For the one who sows to his own flesh shall from the flesh reap corruption, but the one who sows to the Spirit shall from the Spirit reap eternal life. And let us not lose heart in doing good, for in due time we shall reap if we do not grow weary. So then, while we have opportunity, let us do good to all men, and especially to those who are of the household of the faith. (6:7-10)

The universe is under the control of inviolable laws, as scientists and other learned men throughout history have recognized. The physical sciences are, in essence, the study of those physical laws. Apart from the consistent operation of absolute laws, science as we know it could not exist.

One evidence of the Bible's divine authorship is that, insofar as it touches on science, it is always accurate—although it was written several millennia before most of the scientific truths it touches on were humanly discovered. Only the Being who made the universe could have given information to the human writers of Scripture that was unerringly consistent with every proven law and fact of science.

The eminent geologist James Dwight Dale told a graduating class at Yale University, "As you face scientific problems, remember that . . . there is nothing truer in the universe than scientific statements in the Word of God."

The sacred writings of Hindus, Buddhists, and other pagan religions reflect and even teach the most bizarre ideas about the nature and operation of the universe. Science could never have originated out of such religions because they have no concept of divine design, order, and operation. Without exception, their cosmologies are built on blind chance or the capricious whims of manlike deities. The idea of a divinely ordered universe regulated by absolute laws is completely foreign to their most basic beliefs.

The Bible, on the other hand, not only is accurate when it relates physical facts but clearly teaches that the universe is orderly and dependable, and not by accident or chance but by the sovereign design and power of God, its Creator. God "stretches out the north over empty space, and hangs the earth on nothing," Job declared. "He wraps up the waters in His clouds; and the cloud does not burst under them. . . . He has inscribed a circle on the surface of the waters, at the boundary of light and darkness" (Job 26:7-8, 10). Long before the voyages of Columbus and other adventurers proved the earth was round, Isaiah wrote, "It is He who sits above the vault of the earth" (Isa. 40:22). The Hebrew *hûg* ("vault"), which literally refers to a circle and is so translatéd in many versions, can also mean sphere. Yet the idea of the earth's being round, much less spherical and suspended in space, was unknown to the ancient world.

It is grossly inconsistent for philosophers to argue that there are no moral absolutes, when everything physical that can be observed and measured is clearly and undeniably regulated by absolute and inviolable laws—apart from which even the smallest organism or subsystem in our vast and intricate universe could not operate.

Even the ancient Greeks recognized that there was a standard of right and wrong, a basic kind of moral sowing and reaping. According to their mythology, the goddess Nemesis sought out and punished every person who became inordinately proud and arrogant. No matter how much they might seek to evade her, she always found her victims and executed her sentence.

The Bible elucidates absolute moral law very clearly and frequently. For example, God had "granted sovereignty, grandeur, glory, and majesty to Nebuchad-nezzar," but because of the king's arrogant pride, the Lord deposed him from the throne and made him become like a wild animal that ate grass. "Yet you, his son," Daniel declared before Belshazzar during the great banquet in Babylon, "have not humbled your heart, even though you knew all this, but you have exalted yourself against the Lord of heaven; and they have brought the vessels of His house before you, and you and your nobles, your wives and your concubines have been drinking wine from them; and you have praised the gods of silver and gold, of bronze, iron, wood and stone, which do not see, hear or understand. But the God in whose hand are your life-breath and your ways, you have not glorified." That is why "the hand was sent from Him, and this inscription was written out," the prophet went on to explain, an inscription whose interpretation was: "God has numbered your kingdom and put an end to it. . . . you have been weighed on the scales and found deficient. . . . your kingdom has been divided and given over to the Medes and Persians" (Dan. 5:18-28).

The modern world has its own Belshazzars. Ernest Hemingway became famous for snubbing his nose at morality and at God, declaring that his own life proved a person could do anything he wanted without paying the consequences. Like many others before and after him, he considered the ideas of the Bible to be antiquated and outdated, completely useless to modern man and a hindrance to his pleasure and self-fulfillment. Moral laws were to him a religious superstition that had no relevance. In a mocking parody of the Lord's Prayer he wrote, "Our nada [Spanish for "nothing"] who art in nada." But instead of proving the impunity of infidelity, the end of Hemingway's life proved the folly of mocking God. His debauched life led him into such complete despair and hopelessness that he put a bullet in his head.

Other famous authors, such as Sinclair Lewis and Oscar Wilde, who openly attacked the divine moral standard and thumbed their noses at God, mocking His Word and His law, were nonetheless subject to that law. Lewis died a pathetic alcoholic in a third-rate clinic in Italy, and Wilde ended up an imprisoned homosexual, in shame and disgrace. Near the end of his life he wrote, "I forgot somewhere along the line that what you are in secret you will some day cry aloud from the housetop."

Until the last days there will continue to be "mockers, following after their own ungodly lusts" (Jude 18). But their "end is destruction, whose god is their appetite, and whose glory is in their shame" (Phil. 3:19).

In every dimension, including the moral and spiritual, the universe is structured on inexorable laws. In Galatians 6:7-10, Paul uses a well-known law of botany—that a given seed can reproduce only its own kind—to illustrate God's parallel and equally inviolable laws in the moral and spiritual realms.

Paul has completed the presentation of his main thesis, that legalism, in particular the legalism of the Judaizers, has no part either in receiving or in living the Christian life. After giving instruction for spiritual believers to restore their sinning brothers who have fallen to the flesh, he now admonishes any of the fallen brethren who might presume upon God's grace and resent being rebuked and offered help.

Do not be deceived, he warns them, **God is not mocked. Deceived** is from *planaō,* which has the primary meaning of leading astray. In part, the apostle was calling on the misguided Galatians to stop being **deceived** by others, because many of them had been led astray, or "bewitched" (3:1), by the Judaizers into thinking that obedience to the Mosaic law, represented especially by circumcision, was necessary for receiving and living the Christian life (2:15-21; 3:2-3; 4:8-11).

The great danger of false teachers is not only in the evil of the teachings themselves but in their being taught as God's truth. A person who teaches heresy in the name of Satan, or simply on the basis of his own authority, seldom has much influence, especially in the church. It has always been and will continue to be false teachers who claim to teach in God's name who are the most destructive. "Evil men and impostors will proceed from bad to worse, deceiving and being deceived" (2 Tim. 3:13). During the last days, Jesus said, such deceptive teachers will multiply greatly in both numbers and influence. "For false Christs and false prophets will arise and will show great signs and wonders, so as to mislead, if possible, even the elect" (Matt. 24:24).

It is for that reason that careful and consistent teaching of the full counsel of

God's Word is so important, not only for building up the church in the Lord but also for protecting it against being weakened and destroyed. An untaught believer is a weak believer and therefore a vulnerable believer. Scripture not only is the believer's food but also his armor (Eph. 6:10-17).

The supreme deceiver, of course, is Satan, who, "whenever he speaks a lie, . . . speaks from his own nature; for he is a liar, and the father of lies" (John 8:44). The Lord assures His children that Satan's conquest is certain, that "the serpent of old who is called the devil and Satan, who deceives the whole world [will be] thrown down to the earth, and his angels . . . thrown down with him" (Rev. 12:9). But in the meanwhile he is the great adversary, whose chief purpose is to deceive and destroy.

But the strongest implication of Paul's warning in Galatians 6:7 seems to be that misled believers were deceiving themselves. As Jeremiah warns, "The heart is more deceitful than all else and is desperately sick" (Jer. 17:9; cf. Obad. 3). "Therefore, just because you are saved," Paul was essentially saying, "don't think you can sin with impunity. You are terribly **deceived** if you think that God does not deal severely with sin in the lives of His children—including the sin of legalism, which substitutes man's work for God's."

John specifically warns believers that, "if we say that we have no sin, we are deceiving ourselves, and the truth is not in us" (1 John 1:8). James gives a similar warning to those who think it is enough simply to know God's Word without obeying it: "Prove yourselves doers of the word," he says, "and not merely hearers who delude themselves" (James 1:22).

When believers fail to acknowledge the reality or seriousness of sin in their lives, their hearts are **deceived** and **God is . . . mocked.** The second consequence is by far the worse, because it amounts to treating the Lord with contempt. **Mocked** is from *muktērizō*, which literally means to turn up one's nose, and therefore to scorn or sneer. In the passage cited above from his first letter, John declares that for a Christian to deny his sin is to make God a liar (1 John 1:10) and to mock His absolute holiness.

For a believer to sin willingly in any way and to any degree is to deny his Lord. But to sin while thinking he is somehow immune from God's standard of holiness is to mock the Lord and to mimic the world.

In Galatians 6:7b-10, Paul drives home the point that even believers can become guilty of mocking God and that being saved does not exempt them from the inexorable consequences of His law of sowing and reaping. After stating and explaining this divine law, he then shows how it is spiritually fulfilled and applied.

THE DIVINE LAW STATED

for whatever a man sows, this he will also reap. (6:7b)

In its literal, physical sense, that rudimentary law of agriculture is self-evident. It is absolutely universal, applying equally to every farmer and gardener in every time and place—to the young and the old, the experienced and the inexperienced, the wise and the foolish, and the saved and the unsaved. It is as impartial, predictable, and immutable as the law of gravity. There are no exceptions, and the person who plants the seed makes no difference at all in the law's operation. **Whatever** he **sows, this he will also reap.**

On arriving home after vacation, our family discovered a large, strange plant thriving in the garden. It proved to be a giant sunflower, which, as it was later discovered, had been planted there by a friend as a practical joke. Despite our perplexity, however, the idea never entered our minds that the plant could somehow have sprung up from a carrot, cucumber, or squash seed. Before we had any idea as to how the plant came to be in the garden, we knew it had grown from a sunflower seed and no other kind. In the natural world men never question the law of sowing and reaping.

But the principle is just as true in the moral and spiritual realms, although men's sin and self-deception often prevent them from seeing or acknowledging it. God's Word is clear. "Those who plow iniquity and those who sow trouble harvest it" (Job 4:8). Those who spurn God's way "shall eat of the fruit of their own way, and be satiated with their own devices. For the waywardness of the naive shall kill them, and the complacency of fools shall destroy them. But he who listens to [God's wisdom] shall live securely, and shall be at ease from the dread of evil" (Prov. 1:31-33; cf. 11:18). The wicked "sow the wind, and they reap the whirlwind," whereas those who "sow with a view to righteousness, reap in accordance with kindness" (Hos. 8:7; 10:12).

To a great extent, a person's character is the product of seeds planted in his early life. A child brought up to have his own way will grow into an adult who wants his own way. One English writer observed, "What strikes me more and more each day is the permanence of one's early life, the identity between youth and manhood. Every habit, good and bad, of those early years seems to have permanently affected my whole life. The battle is largely won or lost before it seems to begin."

That observation does not surprise the person who knows Scripture. "Train up a child in the way he should go," it teaches, and "even when he is old he will not depart from it" (Prov. 22:6).

The law of sowing and reaping is just as valid in the spiritual as in the physical and moral realms. The frustration and hopelessness of humanistic psychology, psychiatry, and counseling can be traced, among other things, to their refusal to consider the immutable spiritual law of sowing and reaping. A person's character cannot change until his nature is changed, and that can happen only through the new creation that comes from trust in Jesus Christ.

"Be sure your sin will find you out," God warned ancient Israel (Num. 32:23). "Thou hast placed our iniquities before Thee, our secret sins in the light of Thy presence" (Ps. 90:8), the psalmist confessed. In the spiritual world a person sows what he reaps. "There will be tribulation and distress for every soul of man who does evil, . . . but glory and honor and peace to every man who does good" (Rom. 2:9-10).

The law of sowing and reaping is not contradicted by the gospel of grace. The law of salvation in Jesus Christ is, in fact, the ultimate demonstration of that law. Jesus Christ sowed perfect righteousness and reaped eternal life, which He gives to those who trust in His finished work. The believer reaps eternal life because, in faith, he is united with Christ and with what He has sown and reaped on man's behalf.

But the believer is not thereby exempt from all the consequences of his own sowing. He will never reap the ultimate consequences of sin, which are death and judgment, because his Lord already reaped those consequences for him. But he continues to reap the earthly heartaches, wounds, shame, and pain of his sins and foolishness. God's law of cause and effect still operates in the lives of His children.

A genuine feeling of guilt reaped from sin is a believer's ally and friend. It is God's warning that something is wrong. When heeded, true guilt is purifying, because it prevents a person from committing a sin or, after he has committed it, will lead him to repentance—in light of which the Lord "is faithful and righteous to forgive [his] sins and to cleanse [him] from all unrighteousness" (1 John 1:9).

THE DIVINE LAW EXPLAINED

For the one who sows to his own flesh shall from the flesh reap corruption, but the one who sows to the Spirit shall from the Spirit reap eternal life. (6:8)

The Christian has only two "fields" in which he can sow, that of **his own flesh** and that of **the Spirit.** As has been stated, the **flesh** refers to the believer's uncleansed humanness, which awaits the day of glorification (Rom. 8:23). But in the meanwhile it can produce all manner of selfish, fleshly desires that are contrary to God's will and standards and are expressed in everything from blatant immorality to cold indifference to the things of the Lord. The **flesh** is the residence of sin that still remains in a believer's life (Rom. 7:18). The person who **sows to his own flesh** panders to its evil desires instead of letting the Spirit subdue it. He submits to its passions instead of overcoming it.

The particular sin that Paul addresses so strongly throughout this letter is the sin of legalism, particularly that of the heretical Judaizers, who undermined the gospel of grace by placing human works between Christ's sacrifice and man's salvation. Because that sin was so centered in **the flesh,** it led to countless other sins. It turned believers back to their own resources and power, in which they could do nothing but stumble from one trespass to another, producing only the deeds of **the flesh** (see 5:19-21; 6:1).

Corruption is from *phthora,* which refers to degeneration, going from better to worse. It was sometimes used of decaying food, which turns from that which is beneficial to that which is harmful. The deeds of **the flesh** are always corruptive and can only make a person progressively worse. The ultimate **corruption** is eternal death, the wages of sin (Rom. 6:23).

Although his trust in Christ saves him from spiritual death, a sinning believer can nevertheless **reap corruption,** suffering physical death and many other tragic earthly consequences, as did some of the unrepentant Corinthians (1 Cor. 11:30).

The British evangelical leader John R. W. Stott has written, "Every time we allow our mind to harbor a grudge, nurse a grievance, entertain an impure fancy, wallow in self-pity, we are sowing to the flesh. Every time we linger in bad company whose insidious influence we know we cannot resist, every time we lie in bed when we ought to be up and praying, every time we read pornographic literature, every time we take a risk that strains our self-control we are sowing, sowing, sowing, to the flesh" (*The Message of Galatians* [London: Inter-Varsity, 1968], p. 170).

On the other hand, the believer **who sows to the Spirit shall from the Spirit reap eternal life.** The Christian who is preoccupied with the things of God rather than the fleshly things of the world will produce the fruit of the Spirit (5:22-23). To sow **to the Spirit** is the same as to walk by the Spirit (5:16), to be led by the Spirit (5:18), and to be filled with the Spirit (Eph. 5:18). It is the same as abiding in Christ and in His Word and having His words abide in us (John 8:31; 15:7). It is the same as walking in Christ (Col. 2:6) and setting one's "mind on the things above, not on the things that are on earth" (3:2). It is the same as giving one's body as "a living and holy sacrifice, acceptable to God," and not being "conformed to this world, but [being] transformed by the renewing of your mind, that you may prove what the will of God is, that which is good and acceptable and perfect" (Rom. 12:1-2).

The product of sowing **to the Spirit** is **eternal life.** It is not that only Spirit-filled believers go to heaven. Every believer goes to heaven because every believer is forever a child of God and a citizen of God's kingdom.

Throughout Scripture, **eternal life** refers primarily to quality, not duration. The believer begins participating in **eternal life** the moment he trusts in Jesus Christ as Lord and Savior. But just as his life does not always perfectly reflect the righteousness he has before God in Christ, neither does it always perfectly reflect the **eternal** quality of **life** he has in Him.

Because it is **external,** no sin in a believer's life can separate him from **eternal life,** but *any* sin in his life corrupts his reflection and enjoyment of that **eternal life.** That is why some Christians are among the most miserable, unhappy, and wretched of people. A persistently sinning believer can sometimes be more miserable than an unbeliever, simply because his sin is in constant conflict with and warring against his new nature in Christ. The sinning Christian has a battle raging within him that an unbeliever never experiences. The believer **who sows to his own flesh** does not lose **the Spirit,** but he loses the fruit of the Spirit, among which are love, joy, peace, and patience (5:22). David did not pray, "Restore my salvation to me," but, "Restore to me the joy of Thy salvation" (Ps. 51:12).

That fruit represents all the blessings of a life sown **to the Spirit,** life that, in faithfulness and obedience, fully enjoys "every spiritual blessing in the heavenly places in Christ" and "the riches of the glory of His inheritance in the saints" (Eph. 1:3, 18).

THE DIVINE LAW FULFILLED

And let us not lose heart in doing good, for in due time we shall reap if we do not grow weary. (6:9)

For those who walk and sow in the Spirit, the fruit of patience (see 5:22) often seems among the most elusive. After years of faithful, unselfish service to the Lord, a believer may have experienced little obvious evidence of the Lord's blessing. Like Paul, he may have more problems, frustrations, and persecution at the end of his life than he had when he was a new believer.

The Puritan saint John Brown wrote, "Many Christians are like children; they would sow and reap the same day." It is easy to become tired of sowing and be anxious for the harvest.

Lose heart is from *enkakeō* and **grow weary** is from *ekluō*. Both terms carry the ideas of becoming exhausted and giving up. They are the opposite of being "steadfast, immovable, always abounding in the work of the Lord, knowing that your toil is not in vain in the Lord" (1 Cor. 15:58). It was to counter the temptation to **lose heart** and **grow weary** that the writer of Hebrews said,

> Therefore, since we have so great a cloud of witnesses surrounding us, let us also lay aside every encumbrance, and the sin which so easily entangles us, and let us run with endurance the race that is set before us, fixing our eyes on Jesus, the author and perfecter of faith, who for the joy set before Him endured the cross, despising the shame, and has sat down at the right hand of the throne of God. For consider Him who has endured such hostility by sinners against Himself, so that you may not grow weary and lose heart. (Heb. 12:1-3)

Sometimes, of course, the problem is not spiritual weariness but spiritual laziness, becoming weary from doing nothing rather than from **doing good**. Sometimes the problem is spiritual hypocrisy, hearing and talking about serving the Lord but doing little of it (cf. James 1:22).

But when a believer is genuinely and persistently faithful in **doing good**, he has God's assurance that **in due time** he **shall reap**. As in regard to reaping eternal life (v. 8), Paul is not talking here about salvation but about blessing, and ultimately eternal reward. He is saying that it is possible to serve God for a long time and then to give up and lose blessing here and reward in glory. The apostle John warned, "Watch yourselves, that you might not lose what we have accomplished, but that you may receive a full reward" (2 John 8).

Paul knew what it was not to **lose heart** and **grow weary** in the Lord's work. On the shore near Miletus, he declared to the elders from Ephesus, "I do not consider my life of any account as dear to myself, in order that I may finish my course, and the ministry which I received from the Lord Jesus, to testify solemnly of the gospel of the grace of God" (Acts 20:24). To the Corinthian church he said,

> Since we have this ministry, as we received mercy, we do not lose heart, but we have renounced the things hidden because of shame, not walking in craftiness or adulterating the word of God, but by the manifestation of truth

commending ourselves to every man's conscience in the sight of God. . . . We are afflicted in every way, but not crushed; perplexed, but not despairing; persecuted, but not forsaken; struck down, but not destroyed; always carrying about in the body the dying of Jesus, that the life of Jesus also may be manifested in our body, . . . knowing that He who raised the Lord Jesus will raise us also with Jesus and will present us with you. (2 Cor. 4:1-2, 8-10, 14)

Paul reaped blessing in this life because he never gave up. He called the Thessalonian believers his "joy or crown of salvation" (1 Thess. 2:19). At the end of his life he could say, "I have fought the good fight, I have finished the course, I have kept the faith; in the future there is laid up for me the crown of righteousness, which the Lord, the righteous judge, will award to me on that day; and not only to me, but also to all who have loved His appearing" (2 Tim. 4:7-8). The reaping is both in this life and in the life to come.

THE DIVINE LAW APPLIED

So then, while we have opportunity, let us do good to all men, and especially to those who are of the household of the faith. (6:10)

Here is a final, practical injunction that goes with the principle of sowing and reaping, given as a guide to believers in their walk in the Spirit.

Opportunity translates *kairos,* which literally refers to a fixed and distinct period of time. The phrase **while we have** does not refer to occasional opportunities that may arise in a believer's life but to the total **opportunity** of his present earthly existence. The idea is, **while we have opportunity** during our life on earth. In other words, a believer's entire life is his unique but limited **opportunity** to serve others in the Lord's name. The idea is also implied of seeking for and even making particular opportunities within the broader opportunity of our time on earth. The reflexive exhortation, **let us do** is from *ergazomai,* which means to be active, to work effectively and diligently, and is here a self-call to great effort in taking every opportunity to sow for God's glory.

Good is from *agathos* and has a definite article in front of it in the Greek. In other words, Paul is speaking of a particular **good,** *the* **good.** It is the *agathos* goodness of moral and spiritual excellence that is a fruit of the Spirit (5:22), not simply *kalos* goodness that is limited to physical and temporal things. It is the internal goodness produced by the Spirit in the hearts of obedient believers, which then finds expression in external goodness spoken by his mouth and performed by his hands.

It is also **good** that is unqualified and unrestricted, to be shown **all men,** including unbelievers. "For such is the will of God," Peter said, "that by doing right you may silence the ignorance of foolish men" (1 Pet. 2:15). One of the best ways to thwart criticism of Christianity is for Christians to do good to unbelievers. Loving concern will do more to win a person to Christ than the most carefully articulated argument.

The heart of every Christian testimony should be kindness. "In all things show yourself to be an example of good deeds," Paul admonished Titus, "with purity in doctrine, dignified, sound in speech which is beyond reproach, in order that the opponent may be put to shame, having nothing bad to say about us" (Titus 2:7-8). Later in the same letter Paul says, "Concerning these things I want you to speak confidently, so that those who have believed God may be careful to engage in good deeds. These things are good and profitable for men" (3:8).

As important as doing **good** to unbelievers is, however, it is **especially** to be demonstrated **to those who are of the household of the faith.** The first test of our love for God is our love for His other children, our brothers and sisters in Christ. "We know that we have passed out of death into life," John says, "because we love the brethren" (1 John 3:14). "If someone says, 'I love God,' and hates his brother, he is a liar; for the one who does not love his brother whom he has seen, cannot love God whom he has not seen. And this commandment we have from Him, that the one who loves god should love his brother also" (4:20-21).

Such sowing makes for joyful reaping, and it is also dynamic testimony to those outside salvation. How we treat each other is our greatest attraction to a world seeking love, kindness, and compassion.

Glorying in the
Flesh (6:11-13)

19

See with what large letters I am writing to you with my own hand. Those who desire to make a good showing in the flesh try to compel you to be circumcised, simply that they may not be persecuted for the cross of Christ. For those who are circumcised do not even keep the Law themselves, but they desire to have you circumcised, that they may boast in your flesh. (6:11-13)

The end of Paul's letter to the Galatian churches carries the same weight of seriousness, urgency, and indignation as the rest of it. At both the beginning and end (1:3; 6:18) he commends his readers to God's grace, and his deep concern for the spiritual welfare of those to whom he writes is evident throughout the epistle. But he takes no time for the personal amenities found in most of his other writings. It is almost as if the courier were standing at the door, waiting for Paul to finish writing so he could rush the letter on its way.

Except for the closing benediction (v. 18), verses 11 to the end are largely a parting salvo against the Judaizers, whose heretical activities prompted the letter in the first place. They were teaching the spurious, man-made gospel (which was no gospel at all, 1:6-7) of salvation by works and of living under the government of law, in complete contradiction to the divine gospel of salvation by grace and living by the Spirit that Paul had preached when he ministered in Galatia.

Those two approaches to salvation are the only two that exist, the only two forms of religion that man has ever known. There is grace/faith/Spirit religion, known as Christianity, and there is law/works/flesh religion, which identifies all the rest. God's way is the way of grace, working through man's faith in the redemptive work of Jesus Christ and the sustaining power of the Holy Spirit. All other ways, no matter how seemingly different, are an attempt at salvation by fleshly works of the law. It is as if, on the market shelf of world religions, there are hundreds of attractive packages, with a great range of shapes, sizes, labels, claims, and prices. But inside all of them is the same tasteless, nutritionless sawdust of works righteousness. Standing alone, unattractive and repulsive to the natural man, is the gospel, which alone contains real food.

God's way is the way of divine accomplishment; all other ways rely on human achievement. Those who follow the religion of divine accomplishment say, "I cannot accomplish anything in my own power or goodness, and I throw myself on the mercy of God, trusting in the sufficient sacrifice of His Son on my behalf." Those who follow the way of human achievement, no matter what its packaging might be, say, "On my own merit and in my own power I can make myself acceptable to God and worthy of a place in heaven."

Before exposing the ungodly motives of the Judaizers in preaching the false gospel of Jewish legalistic achievements, Paul first gives insight into his own godly motives in preaching the true gospel of divine grace.

Because Paul does not explain his meaning, the comment **See with what large letters I am writing to you with my own hand** cannot be interpreted dogmatically. As always, however, responsible interpretation places great stress on the context.

Whatever Paul specifically meant by referring to his writing in **large letters** with his **own hand**, it is reasonable to assume his point was closely related to what he was talking about in the surrounding verses. One would expect the verse to relate closely to his preceding admonition for Christians to do good (vv. 9-10), to his following warning about the Judaizers (vv. 12-15), or to both topics, as a transition between the two.

Thus Paul's writing **with . . . large letters** may have been due to a combination of reasons. The first possibility is that he used **large letters** because of poor eyesight, an affliction suggested in this letter. Shortly after speaking of having come to Galatia with "a bodily illness" (4:13), the apostle expresses his gratitude to believers there for their willingness to "have plucked out [their] eyes and given them to [him]" (v. 15). If Paul's "thorn in the flesh" (2 Cor. 12:7) did involve an eye disease, he understandably wrote in **large letters** in order to see what he was **writing**.

Some scholars suggest that **large letters** refers to Greek uncials, a type of large, unconnected block letters, which, because they were easily seen, were used for public notices. A professional scribe, however, more often wrote in cursive, not only because it was more attractive but because it was more economical and writing materials were quite expensive. In fact, documents were often erased and their writing surfaces used again.

It is therefore possible that Paul wrote the entire letter with his own hand and called attention to the **large** uncial **letters** as a means of emphasizing content rather than form. Perhaps by the unattractive uncials, Paul was expressing a picture that served purposely to contrast his priorities with those of the Judaizers, who, like the scribes and Pharisees they emulated, were primarily concerned for appearances, for making "a good showing in the flesh" (v. 12).

Reflecting the sum of the possibilities just discussed, Paul may have used the somewhat unsightly lettering as a statement, saying, in effect, "Because of my poor eyesight, you know how hard it is for me to write by my own hand, but what I have to say is so important and urgent that I want you to have this letter in your hands as soon as possible, with as bold lettering as possible. Unlike the Judaizers, I have never tried to impress you with my scholarship, personal skills, or superficial formalities. When I first came to you, you accepted my message with gladness, although my bodily presence was unattractive. This epistle is not written attractively, either, but I hope you will receive its message with the same urgency with which it is sent."

Whatever else it may indicate, **with my own hand** shows that Paul normally dictated his letters to a scribe, or amanuensis, who did the actual writing. It was his custom, however, to write a short salutation in his own handwriting (see 1 Cor. 16:21; Col. 4:18; 2 Thess. 3:17) in order to prove the genuineness of the letter. During the time of the early church, many forged documents were circulated in the name of the apostles in order to gain credibility. Paul referred to that practice of deception when he cautioned the Thessalonian believers not to "be quickly shaken from [their] composure or be disturbed either by a spirit or a message or a letter as if from [him], to the effect that the day of the Lord [had] come" (2 Thess. 2:2).

If the Judaizers falsely claimed to speak for the Jerusalem apostles, as they likely did (see Acts 15:1-5), they would not have hesitated to claim to speak for Paul, if doing so would serve their purpose. Paul was therefore concerned not only that the Galatian believers clearly understand what he was writing but that they clearly understand that he was indeed the one who was writing it.

As already mentioned, it is likely that Paul wrote the entire letter. In all other places in the New Testament where it appears, the Greek aorist active indicative of *graphō* (**I am writing**) refers to something already written, not to something yet to be written. It is therefore possible to translate the phrase as, "I have written," in which case it could refer to the letter as a whole, rather than to some final letters he was about to add on the end.

Perhaps Paul was anxious to get his message to the Galatians but had no scribe available at the time. Or, as already suggested, because of the severity of the message itself, he may have wanted to make the letter more personal by writing it all, even with his limitations, in his **own hand.**

Most of the letter is spent condemning the false teachings of the Judaizers. Now Paul also condemns their motives for teaching their legalistic perversion of the gospel.

He declares that they were motivated by religious pride, by cowardice, and by hypocrisy.

RELIGIOUS PRIDE

Those who desire to make a good showing in the flesh try to compel you to be circumcised, (6:12a)

First of all the Judaizers were motivated by religious pride, a **desire to make a good showing in the flesh.** Here **the flesh** has reference to the works of their humanness and self-effort apart from the Spirit. They were not concerned about pleasing God by inward righteousness but about impressing other men by outward legalism.

It was in regard to such demonstrations of religious pride that Jesus gave repeated warnings in the Sermon on the Mount. Concerning religious life in general, He said, "Beware of practicing your righteousness before men to be noticed by them; otherwise you have no reward with your Father who is in heaven" (Matt. 6:1). About giving He said, "When therefore you give alms, do not sound a trumpet before you, as the hypocrites do in the synagogues and in the streets, that they may be honored by men. Truly I say to you, they have their reward in full" (v. 2). Concerning prayer He warned, "And when you pray, you are not to be as the hypocrites; for they love to stand and pray in the synagogues and on the street corners, in order to be seen by men. Truly I say to you, they have their reward in full" (v. 5). About fasting He said, "Whenever you fast, do not put on a gloomy face as the hypocrites do, for they neglect their appearance in order to be seen fasting by men" (v. 16). To the greedy, scoffing Pharisees He gave the specific warning, "You are those who justify yourselves in the sight of men, but God knows your hearts; for that which is highly esteemed among men is detestable in the sight of God" (Luke 16:14-15).

On another occasion Jesus told a parable designed especially for "certain ones who trusted in themselves that they were righteous, and viewed others with contempt." He told of a Pharisee who stood up proudly in the Temple and thanked God for his own goodness and of a tax-gatherer who stood some distance away and was too ashamed of his sin even to look toward heaven, as in the customary praying posture. Instead, he beat his breast and pleaded with God for mercy. The despised tax-gatherer "went down to his house justified," Jesus declared, whereas the highly respected Pharisees did not (Luke 18:9-14).

It was against proud and arrogant religious leaders that Paul warned, "See to it that no one takes you captive through philosophy and empty deception, according to the tradition of men, according to the elementary principles of the world, rather than according to Christ" (Col. 2:8; cf. v. 20). The "tradition of men" and "elementary principles of the world" referred not only to the outmoded ceremonial laws and rituals of the Old Covenant but to any external religious activity that is not "according to Christ," that is, that originates in and exalts the flesh, rather than originates in the Spirit and exalts God. "These are matters which have, to be sure, the appearance of wisdom in self-made religion and self-abasement and severe treatment of the body," Paul goes on to say, but they "are of no value against fleshly indulgence" (v. 23).

Liturgies, rituals, and other prescribed religious acts and observances not only have no value in opposing the flesh but are most often produced by the flesh in order to please the flesh. They give the flesh great satisfaction in making displays of religious devotion that require no heart righteousness or reliance on the Holy Spirit. Because they are strictly superficial, the most fleshly and ungodly person can learn to practice them with skill and feigned sincerity.

No matter how much it may claim to be Christian, no religion that relies on the flesh and promotes religious conceit has any part in Christ. Christ accomplished the perfect and completed work of salvation, and only that work can be of any spiritual benefit to a person. No act, no ritual, no ceremony, no deprivation of the body, no self-inflicted sacrifice can add the smallest value to what Christ has done. Instead, every such flesh-motivated and flesh-oriented activity is an offense to God and brings His condemnation rather than His approval.

To reinforce their own legalistic religiosity, the Judaizers also tried **to compel** others in the churches **to be circumcised** as a necessary element in obtaining salvation. But, like the scribes and Pharisees, they would "travel about on sea and land to make one proselyte," and when they succeeded they would make him "twice as much a son of hell as" themselves (Matt. 23:15).

COWARDICE

simply that they may not be persecuted for the cross of Christ. (6:12b)

The Judaizers not only were proud but cowardly. They advocated legalism to protect their lives and material welfare as well as to feed their fleshly egos. **Simply that they may not be persecuted** expresses their motive. They were not willing to pay the price of persecution in order to be identified with Jesus Christ. They would use His name and attend His church only if there was no offense to those around them. Most of such offense could be avoided if they denied the meaning of Christ's death.

From the first century, **the cross** has been the recognized insignia of Christianity. During the Roman persecutions, the fish became a common sign, but only among Christians themselves as a secret means of identifying one another. The only sign that has continuously and universally represented the Christian faith is **the cross.** Even secular Roman historians, including Tacitus in the first century and Suetonius in the second century, commonly referred to Christians as the followers of a criminal crucified under Pontius Pilate.

Crucifixion did not originate with the Romans, but it was refined by them and was perhaps the most cruel and agonizing means of execution ever devised. It was designed not merely to kill, which could be done more easily in many other ways, but to degrade and humiliate. It was generally reserved for special enemies of the state who were publicly executed as a deterrent to sedition, rebellion, and other serious offenses. Because of its unusual and prolonged pain and cruelty, no Roman citizen could be executed by that means.

Yet that symbol of a horrible means of death became for Christians the most cherished symbol of life, because **Christ** had suffered and died on a **cross** as the full and final sacrifice to save them from sin and death. God transformed the most fearful expression of man's hatred into the most beautiful expression of His divine love.

The book of Galatians has been called "The Crucifixion Epistle," not only because it directly mentions the cross or crucifixion some seven times (2:20; 3:1; 5:11, 24; 6:12, 14 [twice]) but because God's redemptive grace, the theme of the epistle, became effective for men only through **the cross of Christ**. The sign of **the cross** points to grace.

For that reason, **the cross of Christ** has always been an offense to the religions of works, "to Jews a stumbling block, and to Gentiles foolishness" (1 Cor. 1:23). Even before Jesus was crucified, the idea of His sacrificial death was repugnant to many Jews who had shown superficial interest in His teaching. In the synagogue at Capernaum, He declared, "My flesh is true food, and My blood is true drink. He who eats My flesh and drinks My blood abides in Me, and I in him. As the living Father sent Me, and I live because of the Father, so he who eats Me, he also shall live because of Me. This is the bread which came down out of heaven; not as the fathers ate, and died, he who eats this bread shall live forever" (John 6:55-58). In response to that "difficult statement, . . . many of His disciples withdrew, and were not walking with Him anymore" (vv. 60, 66).

Paul refers to the "enemies of the cross of Christ" as those "whose end is destruction, whose god is their appetite, and whose glory is in their shame, who set their minds on earthly things" (Phil. 3:18-19). Any person, whether religious or irreligious, nominally Christian or pagan, who denies or rejects the sufficiency of Christ's sacrifice for the salvation of men is an enemy of the cross.

The Judaizers identified themselves with the church but not with **the cross** and therefore not truly with **Christ**. They recognized Jesus as the Messiah and proclaimed allegiance to Him, but they had no part in Him because they refused to receive His finished work on **the cross** on their behalf. Their trust was in their own human works, represented by circumcision, rather than in God's provision of salvation by grace through the power of **the cross of Christ**. They wanted a Messiah to deliver them from their oppressors, but not a Savior to deliver them from their sins. They could handle that by themselves, they thought.

When used in a soteriological (salvation) context, as here, **the cross** does not refer to the pieces of wood on which Jesus was hung but to the entire work of divine redemption that His death on **the cross** accomplished. It is not the fact that Jesus was crucified like a common criminal that is the offense of **the cross**, but the truth of the substitutionary atonement, which allows no place for human pride, status, or achievement.

Because, even as professed Christians, they continued to trust in themselves, the Judaizers had no allegiance to **the cross of Christ**. Their concern was for their safety, not their salvation, and they hoped that adherence to outward forms such as circumcision would minimize the offense to other Jews and to Gentiles and would thereby give them protection from **persecution**. By teaching obedience to the Mosaic law and the rite of circumcision they hoped to blunt criticism, alienation, and rejection by fellow Jews. A Jew who became a Christian was often subject to social ostracism and financial ruin. He was put out of the synagogue and often out of his own household. Fellow Jews refused to do business with him, and he often found it difficult to buy food and clothing even if he had money to pay for them.

The Judaizers also hoped that identifying themselves with the law of Moses would help them keep the protected status Jews then enjoyed in the Roman Empire. Because their leader had been crucified under Roman law, Christians were frequently under suspicion by Roman officials and often experienced harassment that Jews did not.

Because the redemptive work of **the cross** undercuts every human religious system of works righteousness, it is always a cause for offense and **persecution**. When Peter and the other apostles boldly preached the cross in Jerusalem, the Jewish leaders were "cut to the quick and were intending to slay them" (Acts 5:29-33). Throughout the book of Acts, Christians suffered the most severe opposition and persecution when they proclaimed the power of **the cross**. The Judaizers wanted no part of such suffering, indicating they had no genuine love for Christ and no desire to take up their own crosses and follow Him (see Matt. 10:38). They were like the seed in our Lord's parable that was sown in the rocky soil and which represents those who abandon the truth when persecution comes (Matt. 13:20-21).

HYPOCRISY

For those who are circumcised do not even keep the Law themselves, but they desire to have you circumcised, that they may boast in your flesh. (6:13)

The third reason the Judaizers gloried in the flesh was their hypocrisy. Hypocrisy is inseparable from cowardice, because if a person were not afraid of what other people might say or do, he would have no reason for pretending to be something he is not.

The Judaizers who were **circumcised** did **not even** sincerely try to live by the standards of the Mosaic **Law,** much less by the power of the Holy Spirit. They were not even honest Jews, much less genuine Christians, Paul implies. Their religion was pure pretense, a sham display put on for the benefit of others. They performed the easy, outward surgery on each other, but never lived out the rest of God's law.

They were greatly concerned about making proselytes to their perverted form of the gospel, which was symbolized not by baptism but circumcision. **They desire to have you circumcised,** Paul told the Galatians, in order **that they may boast in**

your flesh. Although they themselves never kept it, the Judaizers zealously worked to win converts to **the Law,** so they could brag about their effectiveness in gaining proselytes.

Since the time when Cain offered his unacceptable offering to the Lord, man has used religion as a cover for his sin. As the Judaizers demonstrate, it is possible to be extremely active in the church and yet be morally and spiritually corrupt. Nowhere is hypocrisy easier or more dangerous than in God's work. And nowhere does it arouse His wrath more than where it is practiced in His name.

Of the "scribes and Pharisees" who had "seated themselves in the chair of Moses," Jesus said: "Therefore all that they tell you, do and observe, but do not do according to their deeds; for they say things, and do not do them. And they tie up heavy loads, and lay them on men's shoulders; but they themselves are unwilling to move them with so much as a finger" (Matt. 23:2-4).

The greatest burden the scribes and Pharisees put on men's shoulders was the unbearable burden of salvation by works. Because of their hypocrisy, it was no great burden to those religious leaders, but to the conscientious Jew it was unimaginably frustrating and hopeless. He found himself under the relentless demands of law upon law, tradition upon tradition, ceremony upon ceremony—so many of them that he could not even know about them all, much less keep them all.

"They do all their deeds to be noticed by men," Jesus continued; "for they broaden their phylacteries, and lengthen the tassels of their garments. And they love the place of honor at banquets, and the chief seats in the synagogues, and respectful greetings in the market places, and being called by men, Rabbi" (vv. 5-7). They did everything possible to call attention to themselves, glorying in the recognition and praise they received because of their positions, titles, and converts.

They honored and pleased themselves, but they dishonored and displeased God, who hates pride and loves humility. Therefore "do not be called Rabbi," Jesus told His disciples; "for One is your Teacher, and you are all brothers. And do not call anyone on earth your father; for One is your Father, He who is in heaven. And do not be called leaders; for One is your Leader, that is, Christ" (vv. 8-10). The greatest among the followers of Jesus Christ are those who, as servants (v. 11), help others carry their burdens.

Throughout the rest of that chapter in Matthew, Jesus continues to excoriate the scribes and Pharisees for their hypocrisy. He condemns them for exalting themselves, for shutting men out of the kingdom by their legalism, for making pretentious but insincere prayers, for making loopholes to escape the keeping of vows, for being meticulous about tithing herbs but neglecting justice and mercy and faithfulness, for being careful to appear clean on the outside of their lives but of having no concern for inward holiness, and for building tombs to the prophets they had murdered (vv. 13-31). All of those religious ideas and activities were designed to build pride and cover sin, to **boast in** the **flesh.**

As the end times draw nearer, religious hypocrisy, like every other sin, will increase. "Realize this," Paul warned Timothy, "that in the last days difficult times will come. For men will be lovers of self, lovers of money, boastful, arrogant, revilers, disobedient to parents, ungrateful, unholy, unloving, irreconcilable, malicious gossips, without self-control, brutal, haters of good, treacherous, reckless, conceited, lovers of pleasure rather than lovers of God; holding to a form of godliness, although they have denied its power" (2 Tim. 3:1-5).

Every person is faced with the choice between the damning religions of human achievement and the saving truth of divine accomplishment in Jesus Christ.

Glorying in the Cross (6:14-18)

20

But may it never be that I should boast, except in the cross of our Lord Jesus Christ, through which the world has been crucified to me, and I to the world. For neither is circumcision anything, nor uncircumcision, but a new creation. And those who will walk by this rule, peace and mercy be upon them and upon the Israel of God.

From now on let no one cause trouble for me, for I bear on my body the brand-marks of Jesus.

The grace of our Lord Jesus Christ be with your spirit, brethren. Amen. (6:14-18)

As mentioned in the previous chapter, the only two basic religions in the world are that of divine accomplishment and that of human achievement. The religion of divine accomplishment is the gospel of Jesus Christ, who, by God's sovereign grace, provided for man's redemption through the sacrifice of Himself on the cross. The religion of human achievement encompasses all the other religions of the world, which share the common basis of works righteousness, of seeking to please God by various forms and methods of human merit and effort.

The religion of works righteousness was begun with Satan's rebellion against God. As Lucifer, the highest of the angels, he attempted to usurp God's throne and glory by his own creaturely efforts (see Isa. 14:12-15; Luke 10:18). It was with the lure of self-effort that he tempted Eve, and indirectly Adam, to eat the forbidden fruit, deceiving them into thinking that by self-willed disobedience they could wrest divinity for themselves (Gen. 3:1-7). It was the same lure of self-willed effort that prompted Cain to offer his own kind of sacrifice to the Lord and to offer it in presumption rather than faith (4:3-7). In each case God rejected and condemned the self-willed efforts of His creatures. He cast Satan out of heaven, cast Adam and Eve out of the Garden, and refused to accept the faithless sacrifice of Cain.

If one carefully studies the various religions and cults of the world, he will soon discover that, without exception, they are founded on some form of human effort and works righteousness. And without exception, all religions and cults that deal with the supernatural trace their origins to angels, extraterrestrial creatures, or other spirit beings. For example, the angel Moroni is said to have presented the Book of Mormon on golden plates to Joseph Smith; the angel Gabriel supposedly dictated the Koran to Muhammad; and it was on supposed angelic revelations to Mrs. Herbert Armstrong that Armstrongism (the Worldwide Church of God) was founded. In addition to that, every human religion and cult denies the Trinity, denies the sole divinity of Jesus among men, and denies His unique and complete sacrificial atonement for man's sin.

Paul speaks of "false apostles, deceitful workers, disguising themselves as apostles of Christ. And no wonder," he goes on to say, "for even Satan disguises himself as an angel of light. Therefore it is not surprising if his servants also disguise themselves as servants of righteousness; whose end shall be according to their deeds" (2 Cor. 11:13-15).

Only grace-centered, biblical Christianity is from God. Every other form of religion is from Satan, inspired by his demon spirits, promoted by his lying human agents (1 Tim. 4:1-2), and centered in works righteousness. Those who trust in Jesus Christ and His finished work of redemption are saved, whereas those who trust in any other means of salvation remain lost. They "do not know God and . . . and do not obey the gospel of our Lord Jesus." Consequently, "these will pay the penalty of eternal destruction, away from the presence of the Lord and from the glory of His power" (2 Thess. 1:8-9).

Before the Messiah came to earth, Old Testament Judaism was the most perfect expression of belief in God, because it was founded on His revealed Word and pointed to the need for a Savior. But after the saving Messiah (Christ) came, Judaism was no longer valid in God's sight, and a Jew who rejected Christ was spiritually as pagan as any Gentile worshiper of Astarte or Zeus. In the same way, professed Christians who in the name of Jewish legalism sought to add human effort to the finished work of Christ were also ungodly enemies of God. Such were the Judaizers of Galatia, who boasted in their flesh (Gal. 6:13).

May it never be translates *mē genoito,* a strong negative that carries the idea of virtual impossibility. Paul uses the same phrase numerous times in the book of Romans to firmly reject various false interpretations of the gospel (see 3:4, 6, 31; 6:2, 15). He uses it here to tell the Galatians that it was inconceivable for him even to think of boasting in anything but **the cross of our Lord Jesus Christ.**

Although *kauchaomai* (to **boast**) often refers to evil boasting (see, e.g., 1 Cor. 1:29; 3:21; Eph. 2:9), it here carries the idea of good glorying or rejoicing, as it does in Romans 5:2, 3, 11 ("exult") and Philippians 3:3 ("glory"). By definition, the English word *boasting* is an expression of pride, which was the furthest thing from Paul's intent. The Greek term carries the basic meaning of praise, and whether it represents a sin or a virtue depends on whether self or God is being praised. The praise of the Judaizers was of themselves for their work in subverting some of the Galatians back into Jewish legalism (Gal. 6:13). Paul's praise, on the other hand, was **in the cross of our Lord Jesus Christ.** Wherever he went, Paul "determined to know nothing . . . except Jesus Christ, and Him crucified" (1 Cor. 2:2).

Paul gloried in **the cross** because it was the sacrifice of the **Lord Jesus Christ** on the cross that was the source of his and every believer's righteousness and acceptance before God and brought the end of his hopeless frustration in pursuing God through works. God "made Him who knew no sin to be sin on our behalf that we might become the righteousness of God in Him" (2 Cor. 5:21). Christians honor and praise **the cross** because Christ's sacrifice there provided redemption and eternal life, and that is why it is the supreme symbol of the gospel, the religion of divine accomplishment.

No matter how relatively good a person manages to be in his own power, he falls far short of the absolute moral and spiritual perfection that God requires. Jesus said that the divine requirement for men is to be perfect as God is perfect (Matt. 5:48), and it is only through **the cross** that divine perfection is graciously made available to those who believe and are given the perfect righteousness of Christ. "God demonstrates His own love toward us, in that while we were yet sinners, Christ died for us. Much more then, having now been justified by His blood, we shall be saved from the wrath of God through Him" (Rom. 5:8-9).

The liberal who believes in man's innate goodness or in his ability to save himself has great difficulty in showing the cross as a demonstration of God's love. If men were inherently good or if they were able to achieve their own salvation, then Christ's death on the cross was a wasteful travesty on the part of God. To send a man, not to mention His own divine Son, to die such a horrible death to save those who do not need to be saved would hardly have been an act of love. The cross would then have been a cruel and meaningless piece of pageantry.

If a man were sitting safely on a pier and someone jumped into the water and drowned in a supposed effort to rescue him, the act would be considered pointless and mad, not loving.

"In this is love," John explained, "not that we loved God, but that He loved us and sent His Son to be the propitiation for our sins" (1 John 4:10). Jesus' crucifixion was necessary because mankind is not sitting safely on the pier of life but is lost in sin and doomed to death (Rom. 6:23). The crucifixion was necessary because there was no other way for man to be saved. It is the power of **the cross** that purifies man from his sin and makes him presentable to God. "He Himself bore our sins in His body on the cross, that we might die to sin and live to righteousness; for by His wounds you were healed" (1 Pet. 2:24).

When men identify themselves with Christ's death on **the cross,** God the Father identifies them with the perfect righteousness of His Son, whose blood was shed there. "Now in Christ Jesus you who formerly were far off have been brought near by the blood of Christ" (Eph. 2:13). Believers are "justified as a gift by His grace through the redemption which is in Christ Jesus; whom God displayed publicly as a propitiation in His blood through faith" (Rom. 3:24-25; cf. 4:25; 6:10; 1 Cor. 15:3). Believers will never face God's judgment and condemnation for their sin because Jesus was judged and condemned on their behalf. "There is therefore now no condemnation for those who are in Christ Jesus. For the law of the Spirit of life in Christ Jesus has set you free from the law of sin and of death. For what the Law could not do, weak as it was through the flesh, God did: sending His own Son in the likeness of sinful flesh and as an offering for sin, He condemned sin in the flesh" (Rom. 8:1-3).

It was not that Paul had nothing to glory in from the human point of view. He had considerably more to **boast** about than the Judaizers (see Gal. 6:13). "If anyone else has a mind to put confidence in the flesh," he said, "I far more: circumcised the eighth day, of the nation of Israel, of the tribe of Benjamin, a Hebrew of Hebrews; as to the Law, a Pharisee; as to zeal, a persecutor of the church; as to the righteousness which is in the Law, found blameless." But realizing the worthlessness of those things, he continued,

> Whatever things were gain to me, those things I have counted as loss for the sake of Christ. More than that, I count all things to be loss in view of the surpassing value of knowing Christ Jesus my Lord, for whom I have suffered the loss of all things, and count them but rubbish in order that I may gain Christ, and may be found in Him, not having a righteousness of my own derived from the Law, but that which is through faith in Christ, the righteousness which comes from God on the basis of faith, that I may know Him, and the power of His resurrection. (Phil. 3:4-10)

In Galatians 6:14-16 Paul gives three reasons for glorying only in the cross of Jesus Christ: the cross has the power to free men from the world's bondage, it has the power to do what the flesh cannot do, and it has the power to bring salvation.

THE POWER TO FREE MEN FROM THE WORLD'S BONDAGE

through which the world has been crucified to me, and I to the world. (6:14b)

The first reason Paul gives for his glorying in the cross is its power to free him from bondage to **the world** system of evil. **The world** translates *kosmos* (the opposite of *kaos,* from which we get the English *chaos*) and speaks of an ordered system. Our word *cosmetic* (derived from *kosmos*) has the basic meaning of covering up disorder with something that brings order. In the New Testament, *kosmos* refers to the order of the evil world system ruled by Satan and his agents (see John 12:31; 14:30; 1 Cor. 2:6,

8; Eph. 2:2). The life of a person apart from Jesus Christ is the life of a victim of that system. It is a meaningless life, a life with no hopeful plan, purpose, or reason for being. It is also a life ruled by the flesh, which naturally and inevitably follows the system of evil promoted by **the world,** whether in gross immorality or simply in day-to-day self-gratification.

The person without Christ is often haunted by the past. He cannot free himself from the guilt of things he has done and failed to do. Yet he has no way of relieving his guilt or his anxiety. He is often enthralled with the future, continually expecting tomorrow to bring better things and more meaning; but it never does, and life becomes a pile of frustrated dreams. Or he may decide hedonistically to live just for the day, taking all he can while he can. Because physical life is all he can see or cares about, he declares with ancient Greeks who denied the resurrection, "Let us eat and drink, for tomorrow we die" (1 Cor. 15:32). In one way or another, every unbeliever is in bondage to the futilities and frustrations of **the world.**

The person who belongs to Jesus Christ, however, is freed from the world's evil and hopelessness. He knows that his past, present, and future sins are forgiven through Christ's death, that his present life is in the Holy Spirit's care and strength, and that his future life is as secure in heaven as if he were already there. Everything a believer ultimately treasures is in heaven. His heavenly Father is there, his Savior is there, his eternal home is there, and his reward is there. His greatest hopes are there and, although they are yet to be realized, they are assured and secured by the Lord. "He who began a good work in you will perfect it until the day of Christ Jesus," Paul declares (Phil. 1:6).

But a believer's blessings are not all in the future. In this present life he has the awareness of God's presence and love and peace, the consciousness that God is alive and that he himself is alive because of what Christ accomplished on the cross on his behalf. He knows that he has been blessed "with every spiritual blessing in the heavenly places in Christ," chosen "in Him before the foundation of the world, [to] be holy and blameless before Him," in love "predestined . . . to adoption as [a son] through Jesus Christ to Himself, according to the kind intention of His will," and that he has "redemption through His blood, the forgiveness of [his] trespasses, according to the riches of His grace" (Eph. 1:3-8).

In light of the immeasurable blessings of the cross, Paul therefore says, **the world has been crucified to me, and I to the world.** As noted earlier, *kosmos* (**world**) here refers to Satan's spiritual system under which humanity is now in bondage because of sin. In a more specific aspect it refers to Satan's vast system of false religions, all of which are grounded in human merit and works righteousness. "The whole world lies in the power of the evil one," John declares (1 John 5:19). Whether a person is religious or atheistic or agnostic, if he does not know Christ he is captive to the satanic system of **the world.** Reminding them of their pre-Christian lives, Paul told the Ephesians, "You were dead in your trespasses and sins, in which you formerly walked according to the course of this world, according to the prince of the power of the air, of the spirit that is now working in the sons of disobedience. Among them we too all formerly lived in the lusts of our flesh, indulging the desires of the flesh and of the mind, and were by nature children of wrath, even as the rest" (Eph. 2:1-3).

The world is corrupt (2 Pet. 1:4) and is going to be judged (1 Cor. 11:32), and everyone who is identified with that system is corrupt and will be judged with it. But the Christian is freed from the world's corruption and judgment. The idea of the world and the believer being **crucified** to each other means they are dead to each other. As in the case of the flesh being crucified (5:24), it does not mean the world has no more influence over the believer, but that its dominion is broken and he is no longer in total bondage to it. The death blow has been dealt to **the world** system, so that soon it will not exist at all. It is still in the throes of dying, and it can still touch the believer with its corruption. In the meanwhile, the Christian's citizenship is no longer in the evil **world** system but "in heaven, from which also we eagerly wait for a Savior, the Lord Jesus Christ; who will transform the body of our humble state into conformity with the body of His glory, by the exertion of the power that He has even to subject all things to Himself" (Phil. 3:20-21).

"I manifested Thy name to the men whom Thou gavest Me out of the world," Jesus prayed to His Father. "Thine they were, and Thou gavest them to Me, and they have kept Thy word. . . . And I am no more in the world; and yet they themselves are in the world, and I come to Thee. Holy Father, keep them in Thy name, the name which Thou hast given Me, that they may be one, even as We are. . . . I do not ask Thee to take them out of the world, but to keep them from the evil one. They are not of the world, even as I am not of the world" (John 17:6, 11, 15-16).

The phrase **the world has been crucified to me** also relates to the believer's spiritual position before God, to the historical fact of his trusting in Christ for salvation and his spiritual union with Christ through His death on the cross. "For whatever is born of God overcomes the world," John tells us, "and this is the victory that has overcome the world—our faith. And who is the one who overcomes the world, but he who believes that Jesus is the Son of God?" (1 John 5:4-5). When a person receives Jesus Christ as Lord and Savior, sin becomes a dead issue, the law becomes a dead issue, and **the world** becomes a dead issue.

In light of the specific danger of the Judaizers, Paul was saying, in effect, "That part of the world system called Judaism is crucified to me and I to Judaism. It is dead to me and I am dead to it. We no longer have any part in each other." Whatever the particular manifestation of **the world** system a person is trapped in, his only escape is through the cross of the Lord Jesus Christ, through which he becomes dead to his old life and his old life becomes dead to him. "Our old self was crucified with Him, that our body of sin might be done away with, that we should no longer be slaves to sin; for he who has died is freed from sin" (Rom. 6:6-7).

The phrase **and I to the world** relates to the Christian's practical living before God. The faithful believer has no more compelling interest in the things of **the world**, though he still falls prey to its lusts. Just as they have become dead to him, he becomes dead to them. Obviously it makes no sense to associate with a corpse, which is the reason Paul asked the Colossians, "If you have died with Christ to the elementary principles of the world, why, as if you were living in the world, do you submit yourself to decrees, such as, 'Do not handle, do not taste, do not touch!' (which all refer to things destined to perish with the using)—in accordance with the commandments and teachings of men? . . . If then you have been raised up with Christ, keep seeking the things above, where Christ is, seated at the right hand of God. Set your mind on the things above, not on the things that are on earth. For you have died and your life is hidden with Christ in God" (Col. 2:20-22; 3:1-3).

THE POWER TO DO WHAT THE FLESH CANNOT DO

For neither is circumcision anything, nor uncircumcision, but a new creation. (6:15)

Second, Paul gloried in the cross because of its power to do what the flesh, weakened and corrupted by sin, cannot do. As a Jew, he had done everything he could in his own power to please God; but he discovered that, instead of pleasing God, he was actually persecuting God's own Son (Acts 9:5).

For a Jew **circumcision** is not **anything** significant, meaningful, or valuable, Paul says, and for a Gentile **uncircumcision** does not mean anything. **Circumcision** and **uncircumcision** together represent the world systems of religion, which is constituted by legalistic Judaism and all the countless forms of cults and paganism. All of those systems rely on the flesh, and consequently none of them is of any value for salvation.

But the power of the cross makes the believer **a new creation** in Jesus Christ. Jesus told the highly religious and moral Nicodemus, "Truly, truly, I say to you, unless one is born again, he cannot see the kingdom of God" (John 3:3). The old life cannot be remodeled, even by God, because there is nothing good in the flesh (Rom. 7:18) on which to build. Man needs an entirely new life, a new birth, **a new creation.** "Therefore if any man is in Christ, he is a new creature" (2 Cor. 5:17), fit for fellowship with his heavenly Father and for citizenship in his heavenly home.

THE POWER TO BRING SALVATION

And those who will walk by this rule, peace and mercy be upon them, and upon the Israel of God. (6:16)

Third, Paul gloried in the cross because it has the power to bring salvation to all of **those will walk by this rule.** Paul here seems to imply an invitation to the Judaizers and to any others who do not know Jesus Christ as Savior. They did not have to remain lost and alienated from God. Through faith in Christ, they, too, could **walk by this rule** of the gospel.

"God so loved the world," Jesus declared, "that He gave His only begotten Son, that whoever believes in Him should not perish, but have eternal life. For God did not send the Son into the world to judge the world, but that the world should be saved through Him. He who believes in Him is not judged; he who does not believe has been judged already, because he has not believed in the name of the only begotten Son of God" (John 3:16-18). The condition for salvation is belief in God's Son, and it is a condition that every person can meet if he will, for God has made salvation available to all, without exception, "not wishing for any to perish but for all to come to repentance" (2 Pet. 3:9). There are no limits to the power of the cross, because Christ "died for all, that they who live should no longer live for themselves, but for Him who died and rose again on their behalf" (2 Cor. 5:15; cf. 1 Tim. 2:6; 4:10).

Men cannot change the terms of salvation, but they can refuse the terms. And when they knowingly refuse God's offer of salvation, their judgment is greater than if they had never heard the gospel at all. "How much severer punishment do you think he will deserve who has trampled under foot the Son of God, and has regarded as unclean the blood of the covenant by which he was sanctified, and has insulted the Spirit of grace?" (Heb. 10:29).

Kanōn (**rule**) has the basic idea of measurement and was often used in the sense of a principle or standard. To **walk by this rule** is to accept the gospel of divine accomplishment through Christ's sacrifice on the cross and to walk by faith in the power of His Spirit, rather than by sight in the power of the flesh (cf. 5:16-17; 2 Cor. 5:7).

Peace and mercy represent salvation, **peace** referring to the believer's new relationship to God and **mercy** referring to the divine removal of his sins. **Peace** is the positive side of salvation, the establishing of a new and right relationship to God. **Mercy** is the negative side, the forgiving of all a believer's sins, and the setting aside of his judgment.

No matter what their religious convictions or accomplishments, those who are apart from Christ are "hostile toward God" (Rom. 8:7; cf. 5:10) and are "sons of disobedience" (Eph. 2:2). Every unbeliever is at war with God and will find **peace** only in the cross of Jesus Christ.

The Israel of God refers to Jewish believers in Jesus Christ, to those who are spiritual as well as physical descendants of Abraham (Gal. 3:7) and are heirs of promise rather than of law (v. 18). They are the real Jews, the true Israel of faith, like those referred to in Romans 2:28-29 and 9:6-7.

In a final warning, Paul says, **From now on let no one cause trouble for me, for I bear on my body the brand-marks of Jesus.** It is possible he was speaking to some Christians in Galatia who, though genuine believers, were nevertheless being influenced by the perverted gospel of the Judaizers. They not only were helping corrupt the churches but were causing Paul great **trouble** and heartache.

No doubt many believers in Galatia had witnessed Paul's receiving some of **the brand-marks** he bore on his **body.** At Lystra he was stoned, dragged out of the city, and left for dead (Acts 14:19). "Because you know how much my faithfulness to the gospel has cost me," Paul asked, **"let no one cause trouble for me."**

It is also possible Paul was speaking to unbelievers, specifically the Judaizers. Legalistic Jews liked to make pretense of great personal sacrifice and devotion, as by wearing long, gloomy faces when they fasted (Matt. 6:16). "If you are impressed with bodily afflictions for the Lord's sake," Paul would have been saying to them, "look at **the brand-marks of Jesus** I carry with me."

Every blow that Paul received was really a blow against **Jesus**, his Master and Savior. "The sufferings of Christ are ours in abundance," he told the Corinthians (2 Cor. 1:5). The apostle was "always carrying about in the body the dying of Jesus, that the life of Jesus also [might] be manifested in [his] body" (4:10). To the Colossian church he wrote, "Now I rejoice in my sufferings for your sake, and in my flesh I do my share on behalf of His body (which is the church) in filling up that which is lacking in Christ's afflictions" (Col. 1:24).

Whenever a Christian is persecuted for his faith, it is really Christ who is being persecuted through him. When Paul was on the way to Damascus to arrest and imprison Christians there, the Lord said to him, "Saul, Saul, why are you persecuting Me?" (Acts 9:4). Because Satan and his world system can no longer afflict Christ directly, they afflict Him indirectly by persecuting the church, His Body.

In his closing benediction Paul makes a final declaration of grace over law, faith over works, the internal over the external: **The grace of our Lord Jesus Christ be with your spirit, brethren. Amen.**

In *The Holy War,* John Bunyan provides a dramatic closing scene between Emmanuel (Christ) and residents of the town of Mansoul (you and me). Emmanuel has helped them beat off the Diabolonians (Satan's army), and now he stands in the town square telling them how to stay free from Satan's clutches. Emmanuel says:

"I have loved you, Mansoul. I bought you for a price; a price not of corruptible things, as of silver and gold, but a price of blood, my own blood, which I spilled freely to make you mine, and to reconcile you to my father.

"And I stood by you in your backsliding, when you were unfaithful, though you did not know I was there. It was I who made your way dark and bitter. It was I who put Mr. Godly-Fear to work. It was I who stirred up Conscience and Understanding and Will. It was I who made you seek me, and in finding me, find your own health and happiness.

"Nothing can hurt you but sin; nothing can grieve me but sin; nothing can make you fall before your foes but sin; beware of sin, my Mansoul.

"I have taught you to watch, to fight, to pray, and to make war against your foes; so now I command you to believe that my love is *constant* to you.

"O my Mansoul, how I have set my heart, my love upon you!

"Show me your love—and hold fast—until I take you to my father's kingdom where there is no more sorrow, no grief, no pain. . . . where you shall never be afraid again. . . ."

As Emmanuel rides away in his chariot, Conscience, Understanding, and Will discuss the future and how they will have to be alert to keep the Diabolonians at bay. Unless they depend completely on King Shaddai (the Father), Emmanuel (the Son), and the Lord High Secretary (the Holy Spirit) they will fail and fall into enemy hands.

"Is this way better than the freedom you had before?" asks Understanding, referring back to days before Emmanuel had come into their lives.

"The freedom we had before was like—" Will struggled for words, "like birds flying through broken windows in-and-out of a deserted house—flying aimlessly, going nowhere."

"Do you love him because you have to?" Understanding's probing was gentle; their talk was to reiterate their faith, and in their talking they strengthened each other.

"I do not have to love him," said Will. "I am free. He has always left me free to do as I please."

"Then?"

"I love him because I want to," Will said simply. "And I can never love him enough."*

That is essentially the message of Paul's epistle to the Galatian believers and to believers of every age—the message that, because we have trusted in Him, Christ has set us free.

---

*Adapted from Ethel Barrett's *The Great Conflict* [Glendale, Calif.: Regal Books, 1969], in which the author has rewritten John Bunyan's *The Holy War* in contemporary language.

Bibliography

Burton, Ernest de Witt. *A Critical and Exegetical Commentary on the Epistle to the Galatians*. Edinburgh: T & T Clark, 1971.

Cole, R. A. *The Epistle of Paul to the Galatians*. Grand Rapids: Eerdmans, 1971.

Criswell, W. A. *Expository Sermons on Galatians*. Grand Rapids: Zondervan, 1973.

Hendriksen, William. *New Testament Commentary: Exposition of Galatians*. Grand Rapids: Baker, 1971.

Lightfoot, J. B. *The Epistle of St. Paul to the Galatians*. Grand Rapids: Zondervan, 1962.

Ridderbos, Herman N. *The Epistle of Paul to the Churches of Galatia*. Grand Rapids: Eerdmans, 1953.

Stott, John R. W. *The Message of Galatians*. London: Inter-Varsity, 1968.

Tenney, Merrill C. *Galatians: The Charter of Christian Liberty*. Grand Rapids: Eerdmans, 1950.

Vos, Howard F. *Galatians: A Call to Christian Liberty*. Chicago: Moody, 1971.

Wiersbe, Warren. W. *Be Free: An Expository Study of Galatians*. Wheaton, Ill.: Victor, 1975.

Indexes

Index of Greek Words
(* Not used in the New Testament)

215

Index of Hebrew Words

Index of Scripture

Index of Subjects